Getting Published

Fourth Edition

by Sheree Bykofsky and Jennifer Basye Sander

ALPHA

A member of Penguin Group (USA) Inc.

ALPHA BOOKS

Published by the Penguin Group

Penguin Group (USA) Inc., 375 Hudson Street, New York, New York 10014, U.S.A.

Penguin Group (Canada), 10 Alcorn Avenue, Toronto, Ontario, Canada M4V 3B2 (a division of Pearson Penguin Canada Inc.)

Penguin Books Ltd, 80 Strand, London WC2R 0RL, England

Penguin Ireland, 25 St Stephen's Green, Dublin 2, Ireland (a division of Penguin Books Ltd)

Penguin Group (Australia), 250 Camberwell Road, Camberwell, Victoria 3124, Australia (a division of Pearson Australia Group Pty Ltd)

Penguin Books India Pvt Ltd, 11 Community Centre, Panchsheel Park, New Delhi—10 017, India

Penguin Group (NZ), cnr Airborne and Rosedale Roads, Albany, Auckland 1310, New Zealand (a division of Pearson New Zealand Ltd)

Penguin Books (South Africa) (Pty) Ltd, 24 Sturdee Avenue, Rosebank, Johannesburg 2196, South Africa

Penguin Books Ltd, Registered Offices: 80 Strand, London WC2R 0RL, England

International Standard Book Number: 1-59257-518-8
Library of Congress Catalog Card Number: 2006922331

08   07   8   7   6   5   4

Interpretation of the printing code: The rightmost number of the first series of numbers is the year of the book's printing; the rightmost number of the second series of numbers is the number of the book's printing. For example, a printing code of 06-1 shows that the first printing occurred in 2006.

Printed in the United States of America

Note: This publication contains the opinions and ideas of its authors. It is intended to provide helpful and informative material on the subject matter covered. It is sold with the understanding that the authors and publisher are not engaged in rendering professional services in the book. If the reader requires personal assistance or advice, a competent professional should be consulted.

The authors and publisher specifically disclaim any responsibility for any liability, loss, or risk, personal or otherwise, which is incurred as a consequence, directly or indirectly, of the use and application of any of the contents of this book.

Most Alpha books are available at special quantity discounts for bulk purchases for sales promotions, premiums, fund-raising, or educational use. Special books, or book excerpts, can also be created to fit specific needs.

For details, write: Special Markets, Alpha Books, 375 Hudson Street, New York, NY 10014.

Publisher: *Marie Butler-Knight*
Editorial Director: *Mike Sanders*
Managing Editor: *Billy Fields*
Senior Acquisitions Editor: *Paul Dinas*
Development Editor: *Christy Wagner*
Senior Production Editor: *Janette Lynn*
Production Editor: *Kayla Dugger*

Copy Editor: *Amy Borrelli*
Cartoonist: *Richard King*
Book Designers: *Trina Wurst/Kurt Owens*
Cover Designer: *Bill Thomas*
Indexer: *Tonya Heard*
Layout: *Brian Massey*
Proofreader: *Aaron Black*

Contents at a Glance

Contents

Introduction

Books, wonderful books. It seems like such a dream that you might someday see your very own name on the cover of a book sitting proudly on a bookstore shelf. Well, dream no longer. It's high time you turned that dream into reality—*your* reality! Together, we've been in the book business for 50 plus years, and we've seen it all (or nearly all). We've been interns, editors, authors, agents, and packagers, and we've learned what works and what doesn't.

As interns, well ... we won't tell you what we did as interns, but as editors, we've evaluated thousands of projects. As authors, we've struggled to come up with ideas for books that would catch an editor's eye. As agents, we've sorted through thousands of query letters in search of potential authors, and as packagers, we've tried to craft marketable books. Now we'd like to share all our hard-won knowledge with you. In the pages that follow, we explain the whole book publishing process and guide you through it as smoothly as possible. You'll find yourself going from first-time writer straight through to publishing know-it-all in the time it takes to read this book.

Every writer has a reason for wanting to be published. Some of us want a forum for our ideas, some want fame, and some just flat out want fortune. No matter what your reason, to get published you'll need to convince many other folks along the way to believe in you and your writing. There's an art to doing that, and we explain it to you step by step in this book.

The book publishing business can be tough, and it can be crazy at times, but it's an exciting industry that's pretty darn fun just to be around. Although you may well experience some frustration and a disappointment or two on your way to becoming a published author, you can look forward to the satisfaction you'll feel: the pure pleasure of knowing that your ideas and your vision are being shared with the world.

How to Use This Book

The book publishing process is really a rather easy one to understand when you break it down into its five major steps:

Part 1, "Great Expectations: In Which You Begin to Write," explores the many reasons writers write (what's yours?) and helps you determine what the market's like for the book you want to write. What are the hot and not-so-hot topics and genres today, and how can you stay in the know?

Part 2, "Gone with the Wind: Submitting to Publishers," is where you find the different, sometimes bewildering methods of submitting your proposal. Here you find everything from how to avoid looking like an amateur on the page to the reasons why so many manuscripts are rejected.

Part 3, "Romancing the Stone: How to Get a Book Contract," tackles the age-old problem that all prospective authors face: just how do you get an editor and a publisher to fall in love with your proposal and offer you a contract? Do you need an agent, and if so, how do you get a good one? How do you find editors and win them over all by yourself, if that's the route you want to take? What can you do at a writers' conference? Here's where you find out what you need to know about how publishers decide to publish. Here's also where you find out what to ask for—and what to avoid like the plague—in book contracts.

Part 4, "War and Peace: Working with a Publisher," walks you through the actual process of being published. Now that you have a book publishing contract, a deadline, and an editor to work with, what's going to happen? Here's where you'll see the entire production process.

Part 5, "My Brilliant Career: Continuing Your Career as an Author," helps you develop a life that extends beyond just one book. From building yourself a career as a speaker or consultant, to learning how to supercharge the number of book projects you create, this is where you'll find out about the many ways to make money from your writing skills, including exploring a career as a travel writer.

But wait, there's more. At the back of the book you'll find several handy appendixes full of resources to further you along the path to getting published. And to be sure you don't get lost in publishing lingo, there's a glossary that contains all the words and terms you'll need to hold your own in conversations with agents, editors, publicists, and other book people.

New in This Edition: A CD!

Want to see what a sample book contract looks like? Say no more! You'll find one on the new-to-this-edition CD. Click around on the CD and you'll also find a sample author/agent agreement, sample book proposals, sample press releases, and a collaboration agreement.

We've also given you a sample template for a book proposal. After you've carefully studied the winning proposals included on the CD and followed the instructions on what info to put where, you'll have a book proposal in hand in no time at all!

When you have your proposal done, browse through the CD's lists of agents and writers' conferences to plan your next few steps.

Extras

Look for these little asides and comments sprinkled throughout the chapters, extra bits of inside info we just can't resist whispering into your ear as you read:

Hot Off the Press

We've got many tales to tell about the publishing world. Some will make you wiser, and some are just for chuckles.

def•i•ni•tion

Publishing terms are clearly defined here. Never again will you feel out to sea when the book talk turns technical.

Slush Pile

These are dire warnings, things to be avoided at all costs. They're the worst mistakes, the biggest pitfalls, and the most dangerous missteps to which writers can fall prey.

Experts Say

Here's where our friends and colleagues share their expertise, too. This is real advice from those involved in the book world.

Acknowledgments

Jennifer would like to thank the person from whom she has learned the most about the book business: Ben Dominitz, who founded Prima Publishing in 1984 and sold it to Random House almost 20 years later. He was always willing to take a chance on my ideas. And how can I write a book without thanking my family? My husband, Peter, and my sons, Julian and Jonathan, were all amazingly cheerful about the amount of time I was unavailable—thanks, guys. And to the fabulous Paula Munier—without her assistance, the chapters on fiction would be blank.

Sheree thanks her associate Janet Rosen, who has been so very helpful with her agency, and her esteemed associate Caroline Woods for serving as editorial assistant on this book. Thanks to all the authors whom I represent—you are the reason I love my work. I'm grateful to all my agent and editor friends and colleagues for all their guidance, support, knowledge, and all the laughs.

We'd both like to thank all the knowledgeable publishing folks who took our repeated phone calls and shared their expertise as we researched and wrote this book—and, indeed, throughout our careers. We'd also like to thank the folks at Shaw Guides for sharing their list of writers' conferences with us. Thanks also to Development Editor Christy Wagner for superhuman development editing. Finally, thanks to Paul Dinas and his colleagues at Alpha Books for giving us this opportunity to share our knowledge with you.

Trademarks

All terms mentioned in this book that are known to be or are suspected of being trademarks or service marks have been appropriately capitalized. Alpha Books and Penguin Group (USA) Inc. cannot attest to the accuracy of this information. Use of a term in this book should not be regarded as affecting the validity of any trademark or service mark.

Part 1

Great Expectations: In Which You Begin to Write

You think you'd like to write—actually, you know you'd like to write. So just how do you get started? In Part 1, we take a look at the major reasons why people write. The more you know about why you want to write, the greater your chances for doing it successfully.

We also give you an inside look at how book professionals come up with ideas for books that sell and sell. When you've mastered this end of the business, you get a close-up look at the markets for different types of books. From fiction to how-to, from health to travel, you learn what's hot and what's not.

Chapter 1

So Why Write?

In This Chapter

- The best reasons to write
- The future of books
- The big business of book business
- Getting published can be like getting on a game show
- One in 100,000

Congratulations, you've taken a big, big step. You've gone out and bought yourself a book on getting published. And that's exactly what you'll learn in the following pages: how to get published.

Just imagine the glory and hosannas that await you as a published *author:* fat royalty checks, impressive literary awards, newspaper articles, speaking engagements, applause, and public recognition. Ah, life will be grand!

Well, life *might* be grand—or there's a very good chance getting published won't change your life at all. In many ways this book hopes to serve as both a cheerleader (you *can* do it!) and a reality check (that's *reality,* not

def•i•ni•tion

An **author** is one who writes a book or books. The word usually implies a published writer. The **royalty** is the percentage of book sales the publisher pays the author for each copy of a book sold.

royalty check). Take it from a couple of women who know: writing is very hard work. Getting published is very hard work. Selling books is very hard work.

But before we usher you onto the path toward a career as an author, let's step back to ask a critical question: just why do *you* want to write a book? Writing an entire book is a whole lot of work and effort. What's in it for you?

What's Your Reason?

There are as many reasons to write as there are books on a library shelf. Is yours on the list?

 ◆ I'm compelled to write.

 ◆ I want the personal satisfaction of being published.

 ◆ I hope to advance my cause.

 ◆ I want to share my knowledge.

 ◆ I'd like to further my career.

 ◆ I'd like to achieve fame.

 ◆ I'd like to earn a fortune.

 ◆ All of the above.

I'm Compelled to Write

Some folks sit down and write because they are consumed with an inner need to write. These people must write—they can't not do it. They wake up in the middle of the night with the urge to jot down a few lines or even write entire pages. For these folks, writing comes naturally; it just feels right.

Have you ever heard a novelist say that "the characters are writing the book, and I'm just holding the pen" or "I've got to get these ideas on paper!" If either sounds like you, then you're someone who's *compelled* to write. Getting published may very well be your primary goal; making money would be nice, but it could be of secondary importance.

I Want the Personal Satisfaction of Being Published

Putting pen to paper (or fingers to keyboard) can be very fulfilling. And when your writing project is finished, you will have accomplished something very real. Instead of talking endlessly about how you plan to write a book someday, you will have done it!

Not only is the process of writing satisfying, but there are also psychological rewards to be gained from being published. The pride and satisfaction that can come from writing a book are unsurpassed. Imagine the day when you can stand in a bookstore aisle and see your name on a book. Or better yet, imagine the first time someone asks for your autograph!

I'd Like to Advance My Cause

Do you have a message you want to share with the world (or at least with anyone smart enough to buy your book)? You want to share your beliefs—political, philosophical, religious, or whatever—to advance a cause. A great example of this is John Robbins, who turned his back on his family's ice cream fortune (you've heard of Baskin-Robbins, haven't you?) to write and lecture about the dangers of the typical American diet. His book *The New American Diet* is now a classic and was his way of advancing his cause.

I Want to Share My Knowledge

You might know how to build a better mousetrap, and you think the world needs to know, too. This is not quite the same thing as writing to advance a cause, but it's a mission to help people do something—or do something better. Perhaps you've spent 20 years lying underneath cars and believe you can tell car owners a better way to care for and maintain their automobiles.

The market for how-to information seems endless, and writers with useful knowledge to share can sometimes hit the big time. "Find a need and fill it" is an old business axiom that still holds true in today's book market.

I Hope to Further My Career

Publishing a book in your field can be a very powerful way to supercharge your career. Why languish in obscurity when you can gain recognition as an expert in your field? Who knows, you could build a second career as a consultant or a speaker.

As the CEO of Veuve Clicquot, Mireille Guiliano heads a French champagne company in a very crowded and competitive field. All other champagne producers were left in the dust, though, when she wrote her *best-seller, Frenchwomen Don't Get Fat: The Secret of Eating for Pleasure.* Not only did the company and its champagne get enormous publicity, Guiliano now has an active sideline as a popular speaker. Cheers!

def•i•ni•tion

The term **best-seller** is used loosely in the publishing business. Strictly speaking, it refers to a book that has appeared on a best-seller list somewhere. In reality, publishers and their publicity staffs attach the term to almost any book they haven't lost their shirts on!

There are almost as many marketing consultants in the nation as there are stockbrokers, but only one of those marketing consultants has written a book about marketing to the group with the biggest purchasing power—moms. Maria Bailey wrote the book *Marketing to Moms: Getting Your Share of the Trillion Dollar Market* and used it as a handy springboard to increase her professional reputation. Maria is now regularly quoted in the pages of *The New York Times* and *The Wall Street Journal* and is the acknowledged "go to" expert in this field. She built a million-dollar consulting business on one book.

Don't get the idea that only businesspeople can advance their careers with a book. Doctors see a huge boost in patients when the medical books they've written become popular. It worked for Drs. Andrew Weil, Pamela Peeke, Christiane Northrup, and Nicholas Perricone. Almost any other type of career can be built up this way, including careers as motivational speakers, beauticians, massage therapists, and child-care providers. Could writing a book be your ticket to the top?

I'd Like to Achieve Fame

Similar to writers who hope to advance their careers, some writers hope getting published will make them famous, if only in their own neighborhoods, towns, states, or among their colleagues. The world is a celebrity-conscious place, and who wouldn't want the things that come with fame: the best table in a restaurant, a complimentary bottle of wine, your picture in *People* magazine, admiring fans, and maybe a spot on the couch with Matt Lauer on the *Today* show some morning.

Do you long to be recognized as you walk down the street? A published book might get you that. Fame is not always linked directly to fortune, however. And getting your book published may make its title but not your face (and sometimes not even your name) familiar to many. Quick, who wrote *Robert's Rules of Order?**

*Major Henry M. Robert compiled the Rules *in 1876.*

Hot Off the Press

A major best-seller—and a major controversy—was created when infomercial expert Kevin Trudeau self-published *Natural Cures "They" Don't Want You to Know About.* Despite being lambasted in the press for his research, his infomercials drove readers into the bookstores in huge numbers to snap up his book.

Even enormously successful writers don't have the same profile as a B actor. Would you recognize mega-best-selling author Dan Brown of *The Da Vinci Code* if he was at the table next to yours in a restaurant? Probably not.

I'd Like to Earn a Fortune

It's by no means guaranteed, but writing a book (or writing several books) is a possible route to fortune. Rick Warren of *The Purpose-Driven Life* didn't set out to earn a fortune with his book; he was happily preaching to his big church. His book has gone on to be one of the biggest sellers in publishing history, making him "fortunate" indeed.

Making big bucks by writing books is a big goal that, quite frankly, not many achieve. But if this is what drives you, then give it all you've got. Begin by making sure your book idea has mass appeal. The smaller and more specialized the potential audience for your book, the dimmer the chances you'll make lots of money from it.

Fame doesn't always follow fortune. You might have recognized Dan Brown and Rick Warren's names, but there are many authors whose names you'd never recognize who have, nevertheless, earned lots of money writing books. The unsung authors of popular textbooks and other homely books that sell year after year without ever showing up on best-seller lists might be unrecognized on the street, but they are very well known at the bank.

All of the Above

Few writers have one single reason for writing. Most of us combine an emotional need to write with a secret desire for fame and a not-so-secret desire for fortune.

Why should you stop to examine the reasons you write? Because if you understand why you want to write, you can do a much better job of planning how to get published.

Is a need for inner satisfaction the only thing driving you? If so, you might be happy seeing your work published in a small literary journal. Do you have grand plans to advance your career and raise your professional profile? That calls for a specific plan of attack. Is making a fortune your primary goal? Then you'd better skip ahead to Chapter 3 to scope out the kinds of books that are selling well. To avoid disappointment, be sure your ultimate goal and your book's sales potential match.

> **Experts Say**
>
> According to a survey by the Jenkins Group, fully 81 percent of Americans "feel they have a book in them." Many of those same folks have acted on that feeling: the Jenkins survey went on to estimate that 6 million Americans have written actual manuscripts.

As you embark on your publishing journey, understand that this is most often a long and slow process. If you want to write because you want to see your work available *right now*, look into some of the many other ways to be read. If you feel compelled to advance a cause or share your knowledge ASAP, blogs, e-books, e-zines, newsletters, or podcasts can help get you there faster.

Do People Still Buy Books?

"Writing a book will take me the next few years. By the time I finish, all bookstores might have disappeared!" It seems like every newspaper and magazine has carried a story with dire predictions: Americans don't read anymore; the book publishing industry is dead; books as we know them will soon cease to exist. Oh, and another thing—the Internet is making all other forms of media extinct. So why bother writing a book?

Our well-informed and professionally stated response to those naysayers is "Not!"

Mergers and Chains

Ever since Gutenberg invented his printing press, the publishing industry has been evolving. Many working in publishing today like to reminisce about the bygone days of yore in which literary editors and their beloved authors could while away the afternoon with a pitcher of martinis and a discussion of the finer points of writing. Large publishing companies are seldom run by men with martini pitchers in their offices these days, but rather are headed by business folks with a strong sense of the bottom line.

Even the number of large publishing houses is shrinking—these companies are being bought up and combined into "super houses" with 10 or 20 different imprints. One editor at a major New York house likes to joke that although she's had only two different jobs, as a result of mergers, she's actually worked for seven different companies.

But small and medium-sized publishers all over the country are willing to take risks with topics and authors other houses might avoid. They might also have the time to linger over a glass in the afternoon, too ....

And while publishing companies are merging, more bookstores are opening across the country. The decision-making power has quickly

Hot Off the Press

Publishing businesses are still anachronistically known as "publishing houses" after the days when most companies operated out of brownstones or townhouses that were formerly single-family dwellings.

become concentrated in the hands of two or three large retail chains, and this, too, has affected the publishing business—as has the rise in book sales in nontraditional, non-book outlets such as Target and Wal-Mart. The brunt of this change has been borne by locally owned bookstores; sadly, many small, *independent booksellers* are disappearing, most recently the famed store Kepler's in Palo Alto, California. That sudden closing caused such a local stir that a number of well-heeled patrons banded together to re-open it quickly. Not many independent bookstores have that kind of a happy ending.

def•i•ni•tion

An **independent bookseller** is a locally owned bookstore. Before the rise of national chains such as Borders and Barnes & Noble, most towns were served by independents. Sadly, many of these stores have been unable to compete and have closed their doors. Fans of independent booksellers believe the staffs there were more knowledgeable and better able to promote little-known and local authors.

But the good news for writers is, no matter where they buy, Americans are still buying books, and that is what keeps the industry going.

Online Book Sales

As further proof of the health and vibrancy of the ancient art of publishing, we need only point to the amazing explosion of book sales online. A remarkable thing about the last decade is that one of the most frequently purchased items online is also one of the most old-fashioned—books. Amazon.com continues to be far and above one of the highest-profile e-commerce companies. And beyond book sales, there's a continuing interest (at least on the part of the media) in electronic publishing, or e-books. Actual sales for e-books are estimated at just $\frac{1}{10}$ of 1 percent of the total book market, but right now let's just add it to the plus column for the future of books.

Hot Off the Press

One big topic of concern for publishers is not the fluctuations of monthly book sales in the United States, but rather the steady decline in newspaper book reviews. Newspapers depend on advertising dollars for revenue, and as their fortunes decline, they have cut back on editorial pages. Articles about books and authors still appear on a regular basis, but the traditional book review section of a newspaper is disappearing nationwide.

Leaner and Meaner

The days when publishing was a genteel pursuit for the wealthy are gone. The book business is catching up to the rest of the world and is streamlining its processes. After a few rocky years of high book returns (unsold books are 100 percent returnable to the publisher), book publishing as an industry has emerged stronger and healthier, and is competently competing in the fast-paced entertainment-driven world we now occupy. So should you put a part of your life on hold and devote yourself to writing that book you dream of? We say, "Go for it!"

Open for Business

Now that we've convinced you that the book business is a healthy one, here's your first insider's tip for success. If you learn only one thing from this book, let it be the following: *the book business is a business*. Seems simple, doesn't it? But so few authors who want to be published approach it as a business.

Product Is King

Let's forget about writing books for a moment and pretend you have an idea for a coffee company you've long dreamed of opening. What would your first step be? You'd plunge headfirst into learning everything you could about how the coffee world operates, wouldn't you? You'd spend hours sitting in Starbucks trying to figure out where their success comes from, sipping cup after cup to develop a better sense of what kind of roasted beans seem to be the most popular. You might even do a bit of travel and visit coffee plantations to see how that part of the business operates. And when you've learned everything possible, then and only then you would start to draw up the plans for your own coffee company.

Now, if you decide to write a book, do you take all those same steps to achieve success? Sadly, far too few authors do. But they should!

The book publishing industry is a business just like the coffee industry, the breakfast cereal industry, or the auto industry. Product is king, and you need to learn how to approach the industry with your product. The more businesslike you are, the greater your chances for success.

Many Happy Returns—Not!

One major facet of the book business all authors need to understand is that unlike other retail businesses, books are 100 percent returnable merchandise. If a dress shop buys a dress from a manufacturer and can't sell it, they mark it down until it moves. If a bookseller can't sell a book, they box it up and ship it back to the publisher for full credit.

This method is a leftover from the Depression era, when publishers were desperate to get more of their product into the marketplace and booksellers were tight on cash. Ever since then, publishers have tried to get this industry policy changed, but as you can imagine, booksellers like it just the way it is.

Research, Research, Research!

Start right now to learn everything you can about the book business. Become a permanent fixture in your local bookstore. Take the manager out to lunch and ask about the business. Read the trade magazine *Publishers Weekly*. Find out what the proper etiquette is when trying to get published. Learn the lingo. (Far from an admission of idiocy, buying this book was a master stroke of genius; you're on your way to learning the ropes!) Your goal is getting published, so be serious about it.

Experts Say

Trade publications in any industry are never cheap, and the publishing business is no exception. *Publishers Weekly*, the weekly magazine dedicated to the publishing industry, runs around $150 a year and is well worth subscribing to. You might be able to read it for free in your library (ask the reference librarian if they subscribe) or split the cost with a fellow writer and share a subscription. Visit www.publishersweekly.com for current prices.

Once again the Internet can be a tremendous help. Websites geared toward writers abound. One of the best is run by the *Writer's Digest* folks—check out www.writersdigest.com. To keep abreast of publishing news, take a look at www.writenews.com, or visit www.publishersmarketplace.com to read about what kinds of books are being sold and who is buying them. The Publishers Marketplace folks also put out Publishers Lunch, a free daily e-zine read by some 15,000 industry pros. It's filled with great info and also links to any major book-related news stories that occurred that day. You can sign up to receive it at their website.

But I Don't Live in New York!

Although it sometimes seems that way, not all writers live in New York City. One of the great things about becoming a writer is that you can live anywhere in the country— anywhere in the world, even—and still pursue a career writing books. As long as the UPS driver can find your house (or you've got a phone, fax, and modem), you can deal with agents, editors, and publishers.

Co-author Sheree does live in New York City and wouldn't dream of living anywhere else, but co-author Jennifer has managed to build a book publishing career without ever having moved away from her hometown of Sacramento, California—not exactly a well-known publishing metropolis. Within a few miles' range of Jennifer lives fantasy writer Peter Beagle of *The Last Unicorn*, legal thriller writer Steve Martini, and Karen Kijewski of the *Kat Kolorado* series.

Checking out other obscure (meaning not New York!) parts of the country, you'll find Deborah Donnelly writing her popular wedding planner mystery series from her home in Boise, Idaho, not far from Anthony Doerr. His first book, *The Shell Collector*, won the Barnes & Noble Discover Prize for Fiction for first-time authors and shared the New York Public Library's 2003 Young Lions award.

Don't feel left out geographically. If you're determined and professional, and if you keep at it, you can get published no matter where you live.

Think of Yourself as a Contestant

Sheree likes to encourage unpublished writers by telling them the story of how she got on the television game show *Wheel of Fortune*. She believes that for many types of books, both publishing and game shows require similar paths to success.

"I decided that I wanted to be on *Wheel of Fortune*, and so I studied everything about the show," explains Sheree. "I learned how to dress like the contestants I'd seen every night on the show, how to talk the way the contestants talked ('Hi, my name is Sheree, and I'm a literary agent'), and in general, how to act like a contestant. So when I walked into the room filled with hundreds of other folks who wanted to be on the show, I stood out as someone who looked, sounded, and acted like a contestant. And it worked! The producers chose me." And as Jennifer was a successful contestant on *The Weakest Link*, there might be something to this theory!

Literary agents, publishers, and editors (especially those involved in popular trade books) are like the producers of a game show. They know just what they're looking for to suit their needs. And it's up to you to show them that you're a contestant.

So you want to be a published author? Then learn how to walk, talk, and think like a published author. Go out of your way to meet other writers and learn what you can from them. Join writers' groups, go on writers' retreats, and buy books on writing and writers. Keep track of what authors are coming to your town to give talks and sit front and center in the audience, soaking up what they have to say. Seek out other writers online. Ask published writers to tell you how they made it. And don't be surprised when they tell you! Everyone likes to talk about his or her own success (and maybe even about some of the disappointments). You just have to ask.

100,000 Chances to Win!

When newspapers and magazines aren't trumpeting the approaching downfall of the book publishing industry, they are warning readers against the avalanche of the 100,000 or so books published each year. As writers, it's all too easy to look at that figure and be discouraged. But we say, what a great business this is! With 100,000 books published every year, that's 100,000 chances to win! Why shouldn't yours be among the chosen? Although many (if not most) manuscripts meet with rejection, the odds that one of those books will be yours are much better than the likelihood of hitting the Powerball.

Writers Wanted!

Don't ever lose sight of the fact that the book business needs writers so it can keep publishing books. Agents need authors, publishers need authors, and editors need authors—no matter what they tell you. Don't be intimidated or discouraged by your encounters with these folks, because they need you to stay in business. As best-selling author Robert G. Allen of *The One Minute Millionaire* likes to say, "It's a tough business if you don't know what you're doing. But it can be extremely lucrative and very rewarding when you learn the ropes."

If your first efforts meet with rejection, use that as an opportunity to rework and refine your ideas. Perhaps a different approach might work. In the next few chapters, you'll learn more about how to successfully develop an idea for a book and put together a proposal that will help catch an agent's (or editor's) eye.

So *why* write? Because you could get published!

The Least You Need to Know

♦ Writing can be a very rewarding experience emotionally or financially—or both!

♦ Perfectly ordinary folks have become published writers. There's no reason to be intimidated by the idea.

♦ Book publishing is a business, and you need to approach it in a businesslike manner.

♦ Americans are reading more and buying more books, and the market for books is strong and healthy.

Chapter 2

Write What?

In This Chapter

- The importance of identifying your category
- Books the world *doesn't* need
- Major book categories defined
- Good-selling categories identified

So there you are at your big family Thanksgiving dinner, seated next to your brother-in-law. "What's new with you?" he asks. "I'm writing a book," you answer proudly, anxious to trump the announcement he just made about his big promotion. "Oh yeah, what kind of book are you writing?" Silence descends as you search for a way to describe your book. All eyes turn toward you as you sit there at the festive holiday table, dumbstruck by such a basic question.

What kind of a book are you writing? It's a simple question but one that too few first-time authors can answer with ease. What's your book about? If you can't clearly define it, you're headed for trouble every step of the way.

Start at the beginning. What book category does it fall into? Envision yourself for a moment in your local bookstore. Notice how carefully the categories are divided. Shelves are dedicated to cook books, health books,

Experts Say _____

You need to know your category. Publishing pros can spot a neophyte the minute you say, "What kind of a book am I writing? Well, I'm not really sure. I don't want to define myself and my writing in a box." Pick a box. Pick a box *now*.

Westerns, new fiction, romance, and inspiration—row after row of books on all different topics. Where do you picture your book?

"What kind of a book am I writing?" you respond. "Well, it's kind of difficult to say, sort of a cross between a health book and an inspirational book, with a tiny bit of romance thrown in."

Sorry, but that won't cut it. If you can't clearly define your book, neither can an agent or a publisher—or, worse yet, a bookseller. So pick a category, the closest category that fits your book. Then stick with it.

What the World *Doesn't* Need

Books of all kinds exist, but some topics are overpublished and some categories have too many books in them. We checked with booksellers to find out what topics they felt are currently overpublished. Here are their top picks:

- ◆ Political bashing books
- ◆ Anything to do with eBay
- ◆ Celebrity tell-alls
- ◆ Low-carb anything

So are these the areas we think you should steer clear of? Not necessarily—stay clear of most of these topics unless you have some really new way of looking at them. Co-author Jennifer's long-time publishing mentor, Ben Dominitz, believes there are two good reasons to publish a book: "One, because no one has published a book on that topic, and two, because everyone has published a book on that topic."

But Enough About You

What the world hardly ever needs, however, is a book about your life story. This is harsh news to deliver so early in a book on getting published, but we want you to have an honest idea of how personal memoirs (accounts of the events in a person's life) are viewed in the world of book publishing. Somebody's got to tell you, and it might as well be us.

Personal memoirs are a tough sell. If the story of your life is rejected, don't take it personally. This is hardly a sign that your life's worthless. It only means there aren't

10,000 or more people interested in buying a book about it! From a strict business standpoint, there is no market for your story. Remember your first big lesson in Chapter 1—the book business is a business.

When is there a market for your life story or personal memoir? When it's compelling and well written. When there's a core message or theme that will appeal to large numbers of people. Why would large numbers of readers pick up a book called *Tuesdays with Morrie?* Not because we really cared about the author and his friend, but because so many of us are now confronting the issues of death and mortality.

Hot Off the Press

Don't worry that if you decide to write in one category, you'll be stuck there forever. After writing several romance novels, Janet Evanovich says she "... ran out of sexual positions and decided to move into the mystery genre." And it looks like it worked out for her!

And the Categories Are ...

Before we tell you which are the biggies, we've got to ask you one question: are you writing *fiction* or *nonfiction?*

Fiction

Long works of fiction are called novels. Short stories are just that—shorter pieces of fiction. If your writing is fiction, you're creating your own situations and characters. Or you're taking real people, places, and/or events and weaving them into your own story— or substantially embellishing them with your own creations.

def•i•ni•tion

Works of **fiction** are the products of imagination, creativity, and invention. Fiction does not claim to be true. A **nonfiction** work is one that relates actual events, facts, and information. It includes books of all types other than fiction.

Fiction comes in two major classifications: literary fiction and commercial fiction. Literary fiction has a smaller, more intellectually inclined audience. These are the kinds of books you had to read in English class—Virginia Woolf, William Faulkner—you know the type. Commercial fiction can be broken down into more classifications, such as hardcover mainstream, and then many subcategories, or genres. These include mystery, romance, science fiction, Western, and fantasy.

Nonfiction

Nonfiction is a very broad category that runs the gamut from personal finance to travel books to car manuals and everything in between.

Fiction Categories

Let's take a stroll through an imaginary bookstore and see what's on the shelf. First, we'll take a look at the major categories, or *genres*, of fiction:

- Mainstream fiction
- Westerns
- Romances
- Chick lit
- Erotica/adult books
- Mysteries
- Science fiction
- Fantasies
- Thrillers
- Religious fiction
- Horror books
- Young adult books
- Children's fiction
- Graphic novels/manga

Mainstream Fiction

Mainstream fiction is pretty much everything that isn't defined in another category! Usually published first in hardcover, mainstream fiction is suited for a large, general audience. John Updike, Michael Chabon, Toni Morrison, and Philip Roth all write in this category.

Westerns

Usually published in paperback, Westerns range from classics like Zane Grey's novels to the works of Larry McMurty or Pete Dexter's witty book *Deadwood*. Westerns are set in the Old West and are filled with tough guys on horses, bumbling sheriffs, and saloon girls with hearts of gold.

Romances

Girl meets guy; girl hates guy; guy slowly wins over girl. The romance category is a large one, ranging from historical romances to very contemporary stories that deal with modern themes. More than half of all popular paperback fiction sales are due to this evergreen category.

Chick Lit

A fairly new genre, one that emerged onto the scene with *Bridget Jones's Diary* in 1998 and has continued to grow and morph and fuel all sorts of sex-and-the-single-girl kinds of books. Jennifer Weiner is a beloved chick lit writer, as is Lauren Weisberger. Weisberger invented a variation—the single woman at work in a glamorous industry—with her best-selling title *The Devil Wears Prada*.

def·i·ni·tion

Genre fiction, usually published in paperback, refers to a particular type of fiction. This could be Western, romance, sci-fi, horror, fantasy, or the like.

Erotica/Adult Books

Yes, someone has to write those books (Anne Rice did for a while), and we'll bet you even know where this part of the bookstore is, don't you? Off in a hidden, yet well-visited corner. There's a definite formula to this kind of writing, and our shyness prevents us from describing it to you here. Suffice it to say, these paperback books are, uh, action-oriented.

Mysteries

Who dunnit, and how? Mystery novels center around a murder (or murders) and sift slowly through all the possible suspects and motives. The prolific Alexander McCall Smith, and his *No. 1 Ladies Detective Agency* series, has had great success recently in this genre. Mysteries can be published in either hardcover or paperback. Paperback mysteries are often published as a series, with at least one recurring character with unusual sleuthing ability.

Science Fiction

Sci-fi novels take place far in the future, in imaginary worlds and on imaginary planets. Kurt Vonnegut recently took umbrage at being classified as a sci-fi author, claiming in a radio interview that he "didn't write for pimply faced boys." Once again, this is primarily a paperback category.

Fantasies

Also set in imaginary realms, fantasy novels are populated with elves, maidens, and animals that talk. One famous fantasy novel is J. R. R. Tolkien's *The Hobbit*. It's usually published in paperback (unless it's a hardcover gift edition). The success of the movies based on this series has given rise to a new generation of fantasy fans. Many of the young readers now devouring the *Harry Potter* books are expected to migrate to this category when they mature.

Thrillers

Thrillers are several steps above mystery novels in terms of gore and violence. Serial killers with twisted motives and determined FBI specialists on their tail might fill the plots of this genre. James Patterson has built a franchise around his Alex Cross character. Many thriller writers publish first in hardcover.

Religious Fiction

Although there have long been novels written and published to appeal to a Christian audience, this category has exploded into the mainstream in the last few years due to the *Left Behind* series of books by Tim LeHaye and Jerry Jenkins. They both now write on their own as well. LeHaye recently published *The Europa Conspiracy*, and Jenkins released *Shadowed*.

Horror Books

Stephen King. Dean Koontz. Anne Rice. Any more questions? Horror books are an extremely popular genre. The pages drip with blood, ghouls, vampires, and other unworldly creatures that will keep you lying awake at night.

Young Adult Books

Novels written for young teens are called young adult novels, or YA, for short. For those of you dreaming of emulating J. K. Rowling's success, this is what you want to write. YA novels can fit into almost every category, including horror, romance, mystery, and others. A new player is young (early 20s) Christopher Paolini's *Inheritance Trilogy*.

Children's Fiction

Much of what we think of as children's books are fiction, although that seems like such an adult word to use. Winnie the Pooh wasn't real now, was he? Although we touch on the topic of children's books throughout the book, we do recommend reading our sister book, *The Complete Idiot's Guide to Publishing Children's Books*, now in its second edition.

Graphic Novels/Manga

Some folks think these are really just comic books by another name, but what they are is very, very popular. Graphic novels are one of the fastest-growing segments in publishing—sales were more than $200 million in 2005. Even romance publishers are looking to graphic novels and manga as a way to expand their readership.

That's it in a nutshell for fiction. Just about everything else in the bookstore is a further breakdown of the huge nonfiction category.

Nonfiction Categories

Nonfiction means you didn't make it up, so don't. The major types of nonfiction books fall into these categories:

- Biographies
- Travel books
- Self-help books
- Computer books
- Cookbooks
- Health books
- Business books
- Humor books
- Children's books
- Political controversy/current events
- History
- Inspirational books
- True crime books
- Poetry and belles-lettres
- Science books
- Puzzle books

Biographies

A biography is a nonfiction study of a real person, living or dead. The most successful biographies are well researched and lively accounts of someone with a bona fide place in history. When a real person writes his own story, it's an autobiography. *Whittaker Chambers*, by Sam Tanenhaus, is a biography. *Witness*, by Whittaker Chambers himself, is an autobiography.

Travel Books

Travel books can be broken down into destination guides, travel accounts, and travel guides. *Destination guides* are meant to provide information about traveling in a specific geographic location. They offer details on hotels, restaurants, and interesting sights in a particular place and have lots of phone numbers, addresses, and maps. The Frommer's and Fodor's lines are destination guides. The sales of guides are vulnerable to the ebb and flow of circumstance—bombings in London and Madrid affected travel to those areas and, hence, book sales. Sadly, New Orleans guidebooks had no market after Hurricane Katrina.

Travel accounts, on the other hand, are more lyrical descriptions of a place. A travel account may contain hotels, restaurants, and interesting sights, as does a travel guide, but instead of providing short descriptive listings of such places, a travel account might devote an entire chapter to describing a good meal the author ate and the breathtaking ramble she took in the nearby countryside afterward. *Honeymoon with My Brother* by Franz Wisner is a great example.

Travel guides are nondestination travel books about how to travel. A good example is *All Aboard*, a book about how to travel by train in North America.

Self-Help Books

The self-help category is another extremely large nonfiction category. Self-help includes books about improving relationships, being a good parent, managing stress, and almost anything in what's called the field of pop psychology. Self-help books are designed to help readers try to solve problems in their personal lives, like the bestseller *He's Just Not That Into You*.

Computer Books

This how-to category came into prominence in the early days of the computer age when none of us could turn on the computer without checking the manual first. The sales have faded somewhat, but high-end programming manuals and other specialized books still have an audience.

Cookbooks

Everybody knows what these are—books filled with recipes. For many years, the cookbook field has been dominated by celebrity chefs with television shows like Emeril Lagasse, Nigella Lawson, and Rachel Ray. The cookbook category also includes quirky food titles such as *Candy Freak* by Steve Almond about his obsession with, um, candy.

Health Books

Health books provide helpful information about our bodies. From books by medical doctors about specific ailments to alternative health titles, the health book category has grown significantly in the past 15 years. Diet books are also included in this category—everything from *French Women Don't Get Fat* to Jennifer's own book *The Martini Diet*. Healthy, indeed!

Business Books

The business books category lumps together everything from books on management techniques to books on selling real estate, from exposés of high-finance shenanigans to personal finance guides. Two very different best-selling books, *The Tipping Point* and *Rich Dad, Poor Dad*, are both, strictly speaking, business books.

Humor Books

Cartoon books, joke books, parodies, and books with humorous observations are all classified as humor. This category ranges from *Dilbert* and *Garfield* to Dave Barry. It also includes *French Cats Don't Get Fat* by Henry Beard. Maybe he'll also spoof *The Martini Diet?*

Children's Books

Nonfiction books for children abound. Some books explain science, some are biographies of important figures, and some are activity books for rainy days. An extremely popular area is that of bodily functions. A book called *Grossology* started the trend. You can imagine how delighted young children are to read all about snot!

Political Controversy/Current Events

Although some booksellers wish they'd see the end of these books (as they frequently run counter to the bookseller's own politics), they still sell. From *Here's Where I Stand* by Jesse Helms, to *Using Terri* about the Terri Schiavo case, these books come from both politicians and political observers.

History

History books for the general audience (as opposed to textbooks) have always existed but were brought into new popularity by the works of the late Stephen Ambrose and television programs such as Ken Burns's *Civil War* on PBS, which sent readers to the bookstore. David McCullough now dominates this category, with his books *1776*, *John Adams*, and *Truman*.

Inspirational Books

These books first appeared in the 1960s and for a time were referred to as "New Age." Well, the new age is here and is more often now referred to as "body, mind, and spirit." The inspirational category is a big one, from the body, mind, and spirit stuff to feel-good books like the *Chicken Soup for the Soul* juggernaut. Bernie Siegel of *Love, Medicine, and Miracles* fame continues to publish in this category with *101 Exercises for the Soul*.

True Crime Books

Ever heard of Ann Rule? This author of the Ted Bundy book *The Stranger Beside Me* and others, including *Every Breath You Take*, is the queen of true crime books. True crime books deliver the heart-pounding story behind the dry newspaper headlines. Murders, terrorists, gangs of bank robbers—all real-life events are fodder for a true crime book. For several months in 2004 and 2005, books on Scott Peterson clogged the best-seller list, but with this fickle category, look for new titles on whatever chilling crime has just been committed.

Poetry and Belles-Lettres

Poetry is getting harder and harder to define. Long gone are the days when poetry was prose that rhymed. (If you're a poet, you just know it.) And belles-lettres? That's a very fancy term that refers to literary studies and writing. Extremely high-end literary works fall under this category. Interest in poetry has risen recently due to the poetry slams that take place around the country, and the recent bequest of $100 million to *Poetry* magazine might also give this part of the industry a shot in the arm.

Hot Off the Press

Publishing poetry has never been a way to get rich; more often, it is a way to stay poor. Copper Canyon Press's Sam Hammill recently joked that after publishing poetry for decades he'd only recently entered the middle class. Copper Canyon is in Port Townsend, Washington, and one of their books recently won the National Book Award for poetry.

Science

Well-researched and well-written books on scientific topics do a steady business, and sometimes books like *Galileo's Daughter* can break out and become best-sellers. Science books are not something that can be tossed off in a matter of months, so this category demands both original thought and solid credentials.

Puzzle Books

Long a stalwart category (and the publishing foundation of at least one company, Simon & Schuster, which got its start with crossword puzzle books), puzzle books continue to sell. Every so often a new craze hits; right now it's Sudoku. If you're a dedicated and creative puzzle person, this might be a category for you.

Although most would-be writers daydream about becoming wealthy novelists, in fact the book that holds the record for the longest time spent on *The New York Times* best-seller list was a nonfiction book. *Midnight in the Garden of Good and Evil* spent a stunning 216 weeks on the hardcover list. John Berendt's second book, *The City of Falling Angels*, sold 35,000 copies the first week and debuted at the number-one spot. So maybe a career in one of these aforementioned nonfiction categories can pay off.

So what did we leave out? Gardening books, sports books, reference books—there are far more than just the nonfiction book categories we listed here. But we're not writing *The Complete Idiot's Guide to Book Categories* (which, FYI, would be categorized as a reference book). Instead of writing another 20 pages on this, we've got a better idea for you: walk out the door of your imaginary bookstore and through the door of a real one. Spend as much time as you can there. Wander the aisles. Familiarize yourself with the ways bookstores divide their sections and subsections. You might even get a job in a bookstore, if only during the holiday season, as a way to learn more about the different types of books.

Slush Pile

Don't describe your book as "a little bit of this and a little bit of that." To succeed in today's book market, you need to be very clear about the category that best describes your book. (Read more about the individual markets in Chapter 5.)

Here's another great way to learn more: pick a book off the shelf and turn it over. On the back cover of most paperback books—and some hardcovers, too—on the very top line, you will see a category printed. In the book trade, this is often called the shelf reference. This is how the publisher defines the book (and this is where the publisher hopes the bookseller will shelve it). Become familiar with these categories and then choose which category best defines your book.

Life in the Fast Lane

Although book sales are strong overall right now, it is possible to identify some categories that are moving faster than others. Here's a quick look at two of them: poker and gaming books, and the chick lit fiction arena.

Poker and Gaming

"Poker used to be dull to watch," Sheree says, "until the invention of the 'lipstick camera.' Now that you can see what cards the players are holding, it is a big spectator sport." Sheree is herself an expert tournament player, and has been pleased to see how hot this category has become. Turn on any TV, and you'll be able to find a televised celebrity poker game. Because of that, hordes of folks are taking up poker and need the books to teach them how. Sheree shares her own knowledge in *Secrets the Pros Won't Tell You About Winning Hold'em Poker*, with Lou Krieger.

The Sudoku puzzle books are also flying off the shelf. Booksellers are seeing big sales here, but how long the craze will last is anyone's guess.

Chick Lit

When will chick lit be over as a fiction trend? Not too soon, many publishers, writers, and agents hope! Almost any novel targeted toward women can fall into the chick lit category, that's how broad the genre has grown. Include a snarky girl with attitude, a few possible suitors, a troubling challenge to overcome, and a constant battle with chocolate, and you've got yourself chick lit. Check out the books on the "new in trade paperback" fiction section of the bookstore to acquaint yourself with this still-hot genre.

From Category to Specific Topic

Now that you have a better understanding of where the book category lines are drawn, is there a market for what you want to write? In the next few chapters, you'll discover professional tips on how to create a best-selling book idea, if you don't already have one. We also give you a solid sense of the kinds of books publishers, both big and small, are seeking—and how to find the right publishing house for your book.

The Least You Need to Know

- You are either writing fiction or nonfiction, not both.

- Countless categories and subcategories of fiction exist, from mainstream novels to mystery, from romance to science fiction, and many in between.

- Nonfiction is an even larger category, with cookbooks, travel books, self-help books, how-to books, and so on. This category covers any book that contains true information.

- The best way to learn all the different categories and distinctions is to spend time in bookstores, looking, looking, looking ….

- Do careful research to be sure you're not trying to enter an already overpublished area or write a book about a trend that has already passed.

If You Need an Idea, Stalk the Best-Seller List

In This Chapter

- ◆ Develop a high-concept approach
- ◆ Find a subject need and fill it
- ◆ To write well, read
- ◆ Eavesdrop your way to the top
- ◆ Hang out in bookstores

Most writers start with an idea and move on from there. Chances are, you bought this book because you already have an idea, and you think it's a good one. So why do you have to wade through all the information in this chapter about how to come up with a good book idea? You've already got one of those.

That's great, but we want you to know how the professionals do it. We want you to have a solid understanding of how the book business works and how to succeed in that world, no matter what your main reason is for wanting to get published. Even if you don't expect to make lots of money from your book, you do want people to buy it and read it, don't you? To share your knowledge and to advance your cause, you need readers.

Despite the relative health of the book business today, publishers are taking fewer chances on books than before. If getting published is your goal, it's more important than ever that the book you're writing will work in the marketplace. The methods you'll learn about in this chapter have been used by professional writers to develop marketable ideas that sold—and sold well.

The High-Concept Approach

Have you heard the term "high concept" before? It's a movie business expression. The screenwriter pitches his idea to the producer like this: "Baby, you'll love this one! It's a cross between *Top Gun* and *The Sting*. A group of Air Force pilots pull a fast one on some Libyan terrorists." In two sentences, the screenwriter paints a picture the producer can quickly understand and get a sense of its market potential. That's high concept.

To the chagrin of many traditionalists, the book business has gradually become more like the movie business. That means if you want your book to sell well, you've got to start thinking like the movie guys. Because sometimes the movie guys end up in the book business.

 Hot Off the Press

A recent *New York Times* article about a newly launched imprint geared toward younger readers contained a quote from an editor about what was truly important: "It's not about the book, it's about the money you can make from the book." Shocked? You shouldn't be. Publishing is a business, and making money is what business is all about.

It's a fact—best-selling books become movies. Of course *The Da Vinci Code* went to film. Of course the *Harry Potter* movies continue to appear. Writers everywhere were pleased by the movie *Capote*, not only a book based on a book (*In Cold Blood*), but a movie about a writer! Even better.

Having your book turned into a film or television project sounds glamorous, a certain way to pocket riches. The truth is a bit disappointing, though. Many projects that are *optioned* never get developed. Jennifer's *Christmas Miracles* book has been optioned twice and never made it beyond that stage. If you get the call from Hollywood after your book comes out, don't quit your day job. Film scouts are always on the lookout for projects with potential and are continually reading the publishing trade press for early glimpses of projects, so the chances that someone will see a mention of your book are actually pretty good. Whether they pick up the phone and call your publisher for a review copy or make an offer beyond that really aren't.

def•i•ni•tion

If a movie producer sees potential in your project you might be offered an **option,** a contract that gives them the right to develop your work. Options are usually for a defined period of time, say 12 or 24 months. If the project isn't developed within that time frame, the option expires.

Find a Need and Fill It

Granted, not all books and all reasons for publishing are conceived to appeal to a mass market—is it possible to sit down and consciously create a best-selling book? It has happened before, but there are no sure things in life. Many a high-stakes publishing gamble that looked like a shoo-in was a huge flop.

You can set out to uncover a large potential audience and deliver a book they will buy. Let's take a look at what can make it happen.

Finding the Success Factor

So many of us are attracted to the romantic idea of the life of the writer: long mornings spent with a steaming cup of tea and a blank pad of paper, setting the scene for the muse to come gliding in to inspire and guide us. That may be one way to write. But if you want to write and publish successful books, here is a better way: sit down with your cup of tea and a copy of *The New York Times* best-seller list. Try to analyze why each book is on that list.

Hot Off the Press

Sometimes publishing success is as random as choosing a seat on the subway—literally. That's what happened to author/illustrator Daniel Peddle. He saw a woman reading a young adult novel on the subway and chose the seat next to her. Striking up a conversation, it turned out that—surprise!—she was a children's book editor. She gave him her card, he followed up, and the result was a two-book contract.

Was it the Oprah factor? That worked in a big way for James Frey's *A Million Little Pieces*. His book was the first book Oprah chose when she went back to new books from the classics (after many big writers begged her to change her mind about not promoting new books). Oprah can sell anything (even cars!), but being chosen for her book club is a one-in-a-million chance.

Of course, it can also halt sales! Frey's book started a free fall after he admitted to taking liberties with his life story and Oprah took him to the woodshed in front of millions of viewers.

Other network television shows such as *Live with Regis and Kelly* have formed book clubs that have also contributed to hefty sales—is that the reason a book has appeared on the list? Could be. Is it because the author already has widespread name recognition or a huge following, like Rush Limbaugh or Dr. Laura Schlessinger or Bill O'Reilly? Millions of people tune in or turn on some of the people whose names are regularly found on the best-seller list. Was it an infomercial? As we've mentioned before, Kevin Trudeau and his book *Natural Cures "They" Don't Want You to Know About* created a big best-seller (and a big controversy). His infomercial drove folks into the bookstores looking for his self-published book, resulting in hundreds of thousands of copies sold.

Or is it because a huge potential audience is interested in this kind of information? Is it a novel with a theme that will appeal to large numbers of readers? Autism and Asperger's Syndrome are both much-talked about now, and a novel with an autistic hero, *The Curious Incident of the Dog in the Nighttime*, was a best-seller. It gave readers a fictional glimpse in to the mind of a young boy and clearly struck a chord with many people wondering how these syndromes affect the mind.

Wide Appeal = Good Sales

Unless you work for Oprah or already have your own radio or TV show, if you have your sights on selling in big numbers, you're most likely to score by choosing a subject with wide appeal.

Hot Off the Press _____

Best-seller Robert G. Allen shares this three-step formula for creating a hot book: (1) Identify a core human desire or need. (2) Find new technology for solving this. (3) Find a new way to market to this core desire/need. That's how he wrote his best-selling no-money-down real estate books.

Audience Appeal

A big *audience?* How big? If fame and fortune are your primary goals, you need to write a book that will sell big, which means it will sell to everyone. Robert Kiyosaki did this when he wrote a book called *Rich Dad, Poor Dad.* Who *wouldn't* want to do what the subtitle promised—learn what rich people teach their children that poor people don't know! What about *The Purpose-Driven Life?* It clearly struck a chord with millions of readers feeling a lack of some kind and seeking more meaning and a deeper spirituality in their lives. Who *wouldn't* want to have more purpose in their life?

def•i•ni•tion

A book's **audience** is that portion of the population that will be interested enough in the book's topic to buy a copy.

You must be clear-eyed about how large the potential audience is for your book. Just because your mother raves about your idea doesn't guarantee it a mass audience. Even if your mother *and* your neighbor like the idea, that still isn't enough. If you're hoping for big sales, you need to uncover big topics with big appeal.

Look Around You

How do you come up with an idea for a book with a big audience? The most important trait to practice is observation. Always keep a keen eye trained on what's going on around you. What topics are in the news? On television? In magazine articles? What are your friends talking about? What kinds of concerns keep you awake at night?

To get published, you've got to work on your writing skills. But you've also got to develop your ability to create book ideas. Try the following exercise to get started.

What's Making the News?

Every day, sit down with a copy of *USA Today.* It might not be the most sophisticated newspaper in the country, but it gives lots of coverage to topics of interest to middle America. Read the newspaper from cover to cover, and think of one book idea based on the articles you've read.

Perhaps there's a large article in the food section about organic farms and people who gave up their corporate careers to pursue a life of growing good produce. Or maybe you find a chart showing how many parents are home-schooling their young children instead of sending them to a troubled public school. Could you use these articles to come up with an idea for a nonfiction book or a novel that involves themes and characters that would appeal to the special interests of large audiences?

Timing can be everything in this business, and if your proposal lands on an editor's desk the same day she just read an article on the topic, it just might do the trick.

A recent example is a front-page story in *USA Today* with the headline "Boomer Brain Meltdown: Generation Faces More Frequent Memory Lapses." Big topic, big audience. Have there been books on memory before? Yes. Will there continue to be interest in this topic in the years to come? Yes.

Try, Try Again

Let's be realistic: most of the ideas you come up with using this method will be throwaways. But the more you do it, and the more you begin to think like this, the better the odds are that you'll eventually come up with a best-selling book idea. Not to mention it's a fun way to spend the morning!

What's That You Said?

Eavesdropping is also a critical skill for writers. Yep, we want you to listen in when other people talk. Let's call this skill "heightened observation." Not only can you get a great idea for a book, but you might also come up with a great idea for the title!

def•i•ni•tion

Writers' conferences are organized events during which beginning writers can meet industry folk such as agents and editors. Famously discovered at the Squaw Valley Writers' Conference was a woman who wrote business brochures for a living. You'd recognize her name now—Amy Tan.

At a *writers' conference*, Jennifer was seated in the back of a large room, so far back that she couldn't clearly hear the speakers. At one point she thought she heard an inspirational writer use the phrase "romancing the soul." Wow, she thought, if that isn't a book title it should be! It wasn't … but it is now that Jennifer packaged it. It also turns out that the writer actually said something quite different. So if you can't pay attention when others talk, at least let your mind wander around the edges of what they're saying.

Jennifer's travel guide *The Air Courier's Handbook* was also a product of eavesdropping. She overheard two guys in a restaurant talking about cheap courier travel—something she herself was interested in. She leaned over and introduced herself and got the phone number for a courier firm. She then went on to travel as a courier and later wrote a book about it. That's called listening for fun and profit.

Recently she even eavesdropped on herself (yes, it's possible!). While talking to her cell phone–grasping 6-year-old about yet another thing he wanted, she threw up her hands and said loudly, "If you give a kid a cell phone …!" Immediately a tiny bell went off in her head. Hmmm … that sounds like *If You Give a Mouse a Cookie*, a best-selling tale of a greedy mouse who wants one thing and then another and another—quite similar to what children want when it comes to high-tech toys and electronic gear. Knowing it would strike a familiar chord for parents everywhere, she sat down and wrote a proposal for a spoof book, *If You Give a Kid a Cell Phone*.

> **Experts Say** _____
>
> "If you want to write, read," says Gary Krebs, editorial director at Adams Media. What does he mean? All serious students of writing must also be serious readers. You can't expect to flourish in a field you don't enjoy and also aren't very familiar with. Read everything you can get your hands on—books, magazines, newspapers, and online articles. Study what other writers are doing. The hours you invest in reading will pay you back when you sit down to write.

Common phrases of speech sometimes spark an idea. They can also make great book titles. Remember that *USA Today* article about memory loss a few paragraphs ago? The perfect title for a book on preventing memory loss was right there in the story. A memory expert said, "Use it or lose it!" Doesn't that give you a perfect image for a book? And you understand exactly what the book is about.

Let the Shows Show You

Another way to find ideas for books with large audiences is to attend major industry trade shows. There are trade shows of all stripes: food, gardening, health, fitness, computer, interior design, cars, gift shows—you name it. If you plan to write a non-fiction book on a particular topic, check to see if there's a trade show related to it. Attending a show is a great way to learn what's hot in the industry. Prowl the aisles, pick up literature, observe merchandise and trends, and, of course, eavesdrop on conversations to listen for news trends and possible titles!

Trade shows are also a prime way to find experts you can team up with to write books.

I'm Not Hanging Out, I'm Working!

Spend lots of time in bookstores. Pay very close attention to the books in the front of the store and those marked "New Releases." Get to know what's new and hot in the area you're considering writing. Become an expert on what's available.

The more you know about what's out there, the sooner you'll be able to spot what's not. When you find a hole, you've found yourself an opportunity!

Learn to Work the Bookstore Shelves

Here's another exercise that'll help you develop your skills. Go to a bookstore and choose a book category. Are there two, maybe three shelves devoted to that category? Are there any book *series* in your category? Spend as much time as you need familiarizing yourself with the books on the shelves. You might need to write down the titles. Now, go back to the store every few days and check your section. Have new titles been added? Have many books sold? Which books? Why do you think they sold?

def•i•ni•tion

A **series** is two or more books linked by a brand-name identity, such as *The Complete Idiot's Guide* or *Harry Potter,* or even the quaintly named children's books, *A Series of Unfortunate Events,* by Lemony Snicket. Publishers are fond of series because they build awareness and momentum in the marketplace. Writers like them as well because it can mean steady work. Sometimes a series begins with a single book that sells so well the audience and the publisher come looking for more.

What Isn't Selling?

When browsing bookstores, don't skip over the bargain tables. Examine those reduced-price books very carefully. If there's a big stack of sale books on bulb gardening, that might be an area to avoid. Have several titles on low-fat baking been marked down? Stay away. Learn from the mistakes of other writers about what doesn't sell.

I'm Not Surfing the Net, I'm Working

Just as you can legitimately spend hour after hour in a bookstore and call it work, you also can spend hour after hour online. Check out the news sites, the women's sites, the money sites. What seems to be the topic of conversation on chat boards? You can use the same eavesdropping techniques in chat rooms to try to pick up phrases or figures of speech that might make good book titles. And no one can catch you watching! Become a blog devotee and see what's going on in the minds of bloggers everywhere.

Surfing the online bookstores for information also helps you learn more about what's selling and why. And just like the remainder tables outside the door of a bookstore, you can tell what isn't selling online by the big, big sales ranking next to it. Anything ranked beyond 75,000 or so on Amazon.com just isn't selling in very big numbers. (In other words, the lower the number, the better the sales.) Barnes & Noble's website, bn.com, lets you see what the best-selling titles are in any given category. Thinking of writing a book about herb gardening? Type "herb gardening" into the search function, check "sort by best-selling," and there you have it! Instant research into how well the other titles are selling. Just like we asked you to try to analyze *The New York Times* best-seller list and try to figure out why those books are there, check out the Hot 100 books on Amazon.com and try to figure out what is making those books sell that very instant.

Sniffing Out Gaps and Niches

The more you can learn about what's available and how well it's doing, the better you'll be able to figure out what that category needs. Perhaps you'll notice that there's a need for a large reference volume, or maybe a small, inexpensive guidebook.

Not long after the phenomenal best-seller *The Worst-Case Scenario Survival Handbook* appeared, Workman released a book called *The Best-Case Scenario Handbook*. No, this doesn't fall into the parody category, but rather it takes the interest in one thing—how to get out of precarious situations—and transfers it to a broader, more useful category. Cookbook author and editor Fran McCullough saw something missing from the diet bookshelf. There were three best-selling books on the high-protein/low-carbohydrate diet, but none of the books offered much in the way of recipes. So *The Low-Carb Cookbook* was born!

Many a beauty and spa book has been published in the past few years, but where was the book that targeted the most stressed out group of all—mothers! Jennifer combined her idea-creating talents with a yoga instructor and a spa owner and wrote *MomSpa: 75 Relaxing Ways to Pamper a Mother's Body, Mind, and Spirit*. A new niche in a crowded but popular field was filled.

Backlist Books: Sure and Steady

If you follow all our suggestions here—if you come up with an idea for a big topic with a big audience and then sell it to a publisher—will it become a best-seller? Perhaps.

Only 1 percent of all the books published in any given year actually make it on a national best-seller list. Your book might not be one of them, but many authors out there have written books that are paying the rent, and you might find yourself in their company. These authors have books with strong *backlist* sales. A book that backlists— that sells for years—can rack up impressive sales totals over its lifetime.

Keep the word *backlist* in mind when choosing a topic for a book. Look for book ideas on subjects with staying power.

Now You Know the Game

Now, we do realize you might already have your heart set on a topic for your book. We also realize that everything we've covered here sounds a bit crass and calculating. It is. Publishing is all too frequently a crass and calculating business, and we want you to understand that. Please do not dismiss it out of hand, though.

The more you know about what makes books work on a commercial level, the better you will be able to smooth and shape the book you've already been working on. Read on to learn more about researching the market and gathering the information you'll need for your book proposal.

def•i•ni•tion

Frontlist books are books that have been published recently. Many of these are piled on tables and placed in bookstore windows. Midlist books are those acquired for modest advances, that are given modest print runs, and that have a relatively short shelf life. **Backlist** books are those that have been in stores for more than 90 days—sometimes for years. Most of the thousands of books on the shelves are classified as backlist books.

The Least You Need to Know

◆ Good book ideas can come from anywhere. Keep your eyes and ears open!

◆ Read as many newspapers, magazines, and online sources as you can, always looking for big ideas for books and titles.

◆ Spend as much time as you can in bookstores—they're gold mines of information. Study bookstore shelves carefully to see what's missing.

◆ Look for ideas with long-term staying power.

Chapter 4

Super-Stealth Market Research Techniques

In This Chapter

- ◆ The bookstore: your number one resource
- ◆ Researching catalogs
- ◆ Cracking the codes
- ◆ Surfing the Net
- ◆ *PW,* directories, and newspapers

Okay, now you've got an idea for a book. But how do you know if you've come up with an idea that will work? Be it nonfiction or fiction, there are good ways to test your market well in advance of even writing your proposal and sample chapter. Let's start with the strategies to use for nonfiction. (Fiction writers, do not despair; your turn comes later in the chapter.)

Is It a Book?

The first thing you need to ask yourself is: *does my idea have strong book potential?* What sometimes seems like a big idea for a book turns out to be only a big idea for a magazine article. Be sure you've chosen a topic with enough scope and substance to sustain a few hundred manuscript pages.

> ### Slush Pile
>
> Some topics in areas like health and beauty just can't sustain an entire book but would need tremendous padding to hit book length. And if you find yourself starting to pad, you don't have a book-worthy idea. Of course, you can sell an article on the effects of sun tans, but is that a whole book? Probably not. A short magazine article on what kinds of earring styles flatter which different face shapes would be interesting, but not for an entire book.

We know this is hard, but you need to put aside your subjectivity and take a good, objective look at your idea, just like the book professionals do. The more work you put into this step, the better your chances of success months from now, when your proposal is sitting on an editor's desk. It's heartbreaking to come to the conclusion that your book won't work, but think how much time and heartache you'll save yourself. We've all been there; every published author can name a book idea that he or she had to reluctantly abandon. It's simply part of the professional process. The investment will also pay you back when it comes time to write your proposal because you will have already done much of the required homework! Bonus!

Meet Your Customer

When you're sure you have an idea for a book instead of a magazine article, try to picture your customer. That's right, close your eyes and try to imagine someone walking into a bookstore and asking a clerk for your book. If you can't envision that happening—if your idea is too weak, too abstract, or perhaps too specialized—you need to reevaluate it.

Before working as an editor, co-author Jennifer spent several years as a book buyer for a small chain of bookstores. She met with sales reps and looked at publishers' catalogs by the hundreds. Her buying decisions were always based on one simple question: *who will buy this book?* This is also a question she asks herself today when evaluating book projects to develop. Memorize the question and ask yourself often: *who will buy this book?* And then ask yourself honestly: *How many of those folks are there? Are there enough to constitute a sizeable market?*

When your idea can pass these basic litmus tests (is it a book? who will buy it?), you are ready to move on to the next important step.

Sizing Up the Competition

Few books really are the first-ever ones published on their topic. You need to be clear-eyed about the books that have been done before in your area. Remember the technique in Chapter 3 about targeting a shelf in a bookstore and tracking the success of the books on that shelf? You now need to do this for the books that either compete with or complement your own book idea.

Just what do we mean by competition? Let's say you're planning to write a book on arthritis. The first step is to go to the bookstore and look under "arthritis" on the health books shelf. Are there two books? Four? Twelve? Get out your pad and copy down the title, author, publisher, and price of each book. Open up each book and look inside the *front matter*, the front few pages of the book, to find a copyright date; it's usually on the flip side of the title page.

Now go home or have a seat in the bookstore café, and examine all this information carefully. You've got more than just some book information here—you've got clues to your own success.

def•i•ni•tion

The **front matter** is the first few pages of the book. It typically contains (in this order) a half-title page, a title page, a copyright page, a dedication, the table of contents, sometimes a preface and/or foreword, an introduction, and the acknowledgments. Front matter pages are numbered i, ii, iii, iv, and so forth.

Title

Do the titles and other language on the covers make the same kinds of promises yours would? Are they clever and enticing? Or do they have a bland and general medical reference sound to them? We'll call your imaginary book *Accurate Arthritis Answers*. A browsing book buyer would see your book and think, *Hey, accurate answers. I need accurate answers about my arthritis problem*, and reach for your book. The cleaner your proposed title is, the better.

What's missing from the shelf? Does the market need a beginner's guide, an A-to-Z reference, or a pocket guide to your topic? Maybe you could position your book to fill the gap. Could you target your book to women or seniors to make it different from the pack?

Author

You need to know who else is writing in your chosen field. Who are these authors, anyway? What are their credentials? Do they have a big-name research school behind them? Do they have television or radio shows?

Take a close look at your rivals' credentials and see how yours measure up. Be honest with yourself. Are yours as strong as those of the authors whose books are on the shelf? If not, get to work now to improve them. Begin now to beef up your professional contacts, create workshops or public presentations on your topic, and write articles for industry magazines. By the time you're ready to shop your book to agents or publishers, you will be in a stronger position.

Publisher

Finding out who published these books can be very revealing. If all the books come from major New York houses, this tells you arthritis is a hot topic and major publishers think it is hot. If a book sells well for its publisher, that publisher might just be looking for more!

But what if the topic is covered only by small publishers or by *self-publishers?* Both of those are fine and honorable ways to be published, but let's look strictly from a competitive point of view: small publishers and self-publishers don't have nearly the distribution the large houses do. If many of the books you've found on the shelves are from small publishers, you might be able to use that information to your advantage when submitting to a larger publisher.

Speaking of small publishers, there's much good to say about them. Your book is less likely to get lost in the crowd, you may get more personal attention, and you may find your editor more accessible and open to your suggestions. Keep your eyes open to the books published by thriving companies such as Ten Speed Press or New World Library.

def•i•ni•tion

A **self-published** book is one for which the author himself has paid the bills. Many successful authors started out as self-publishers before the big houses sat up and took notice. It's a fine and honorable thing to do, as self-publisher Benjamin Franklin no doubt would have agreed.

Price

Book publishing is a price-sensitive industry. If you see four books on the shelf that are expensive hardcover books, perhaps there is a need for a small *trade paperback* on the subject. Your publisher ultimately determines the price of your book, but you can always pitch the project in a particular way. When you write your proposal, you'll need to show that you've done your homework about the way the competing books are priced. Tell your prospective publishers where the pricing hole in the market is and how your book could fill it.

def•i•ni•tion

Mass market paperbacks are those small, softcover 4x7-inch books you find in the racks at the grocery store and in the airport bookstores (they're also called rack-size paperbacks). Any other larger paperback is called a **trade paperback.** Mass market paperbacks are generally printed in larger quantities and are priced lower than trade paperbacks.

Publication Copyright Date

This information is critical when assessing the competition. Are all the books on the shelf a few years old? That means the information is sure to be at least a little outdated. That might not matter for some books, such as fiction and cookbooks, but for all types of books it means the book category could use a few new books. Better yet, you'll have little competition when you try to promote your book to publishers.

Bear in mind that the publishing process moves slowly. A book with a brand-new copyright date may well have been written as long as 2 years before its publication.

Are all the books brand new? This is also useful information to gauge. It lets you know publishers think this is a viable category, one worth pursuing (unless there are so many books the publishers consider it a saturated market).

Slush Pile

Never start a conversation with an agent or editor with the phrase "Never before has there been a book on this topic." Rather, say something like this: "To the best of my knowledge, this topic has never been covered quite in this way." You want to show that your idea is different and better than the competition, but not in a whole new category.

Staying in the Know

All this information on current books is very useful, but keep in mind that it has its limitations. Maybe some books have been selling so well the store can't keep them on the shelves. At the very moment you're scrutinizing the shelves, more new books are being shipped to bookstores. When those new books arrive, some of the books on your list may be boxed up and shipped back to their publishers!

To keep current, you've got to visit bookstores regularly. And you've got to do three more things. You have to get your hands on the announcements issues published by *Publishers Weekly* (a.k.a. *PW*). Many large bookstores carry this trade magazine, and some libraries also have it on hand. Several times a year, in large round-up issues, all the publishers announce what they plan to publish in the coming season. Thankfully, the kind folks at *PW* organize these issues by topic, so it's easy for authors to keep track of what's forthcoming in, say, paperback cookbooks or hardcover biographies. It's a tremendous source of information.

The second thing you've got to do is hang around online. After you determine which publishers publish in your area, visit their websites on a regular basis. Not every publisher has a website, though, and very few websites list all the titles a publisher has published or intends to bring out in the next season. The featured announcements will probably only focus on their top titles from their biggest authors.

Catalogs for the Asking

You've done good detective work so far. Now for your third task, you need to hit the phones. To get a better sense of what publishers are bringing out in upcoming months (particularly in your subject area), get their catalogs—no, not catalogs like the ones put out by Restoration Hardware and Victoria's Secret, but Simon & Schuster, Viking, Dearborn, and others. Identify the biggest publishers in your subject area. You already know at least some of them; you wrote down their names when doing your bookstore sleuthing. Call and request a catalog. You might also ask the booksellers you've befriended. Publishers' sales reps always leave catalogs behind with the bookseller after a sales call. Why not ask if you can sit in a corner of the bookstore flipping through the most recent ones?

The big publishers generally put out catalogs three times a year: fall, winter, and spring. Medium and small houses usually do only two: fall and spring. Publishers plan their programs according to seasons—a concept you'll read more about in Chapter 20.

How to Reach 'Em

How do you find the address and phone number for a publishing company? There are a couple good sources. The granddaddy of them all is *Writer's Market*, published annually by the folks at Writer's Digest Books. It includes an amazing array of information about publishing companies and is now available on CD-ROM. You can also access it online—just go to www.writersdigest.com.

There's also a book called *Jeff Herman's Guide to Book Publishers, Editors, and Literary Agents: Who They Are! What They Want! How to Win Them Over!* Updated annually, this book is also filled with publishers' addresses and phone numbers. Of great help is the other information Herman provides: a lengthy description of each publishing company, including the kinds of books published recently.

Many large (and many small) publishers now maintain their own websites. Just take a stab in the dark by typing in their name after the old "www" prefix and see what comes up. Or check inside a book that house recently published to see whether a web address is listed. If you come up empty there, try a quick Google search.

As we mentioned a few paragraphs back, publishers' websites usually highlight their most current titles and a few big upcoming books, but they won't list projects as far out in the future as the *PW* announcements issue or their catalog.

Go Over Them with a Fine-Toothed Comb

When the catalogs arrive, study them carefully. They'll give you a good idea of what the publishers plan to publish in the next 6 months or so. If you find a book in your category, study it carefully. Does it get a full page in the catalog? This means the publisher thinks it's a big deal. Two-page spreads mean they think it is a *really* big deal. Are big publicity and promotional plans announced? What about an appearance on the *Today* show? Just as you did with the books you studied on the bookstore shelves, analyze these upcoming books by title, price, and author.

Free Stuff on the Counter, Too!

Most bookstore chains, and even some of the independents, have book catalogs for the taking, often right next to the cash register. These in-store catalogs, as they're called, contain lots of information about forthcoming titles from a variety of publishers. And every year at Christmas, associations of independent booksellers produce gift catalogs filled with advertisements of hot new books. Pick up these catalogs whenever you see them—they're chock-full of news about the book market.

What Are the Clubs Selling?

As if we haven't talked about catalogs enough already, here's one more suggestion: try to get your hands on as many book club catalogs as you can. You know, the little catalogs that the Writer's Digest Book Club, Book-of-the-Month Club, the Doubleday Book Club, and others send out to members every few weeks. No, we don't expect you to sign up for and get lots of those "6 books for $1" deals. Just ask around and see if your friends or neighbors already belong.

Why take the time to look at these book club catalogs? Because these people know what they're doing. If you can't find their catalogs, check out the clubs' websites, which also list what books they're featuring.

Except for the highly specialized ones, most book clubs base their success on their ability to sell large numbers of books to a mainstream audience. The more you study the catalogs, the more you'll learn about what kinds of books sell in big quantities.

You should be familiar with another kind of club—the discount warehouse shopping clubs such as Sam's Club and Costco. These stores are now a big part of the book business (much to the annoyance of booksellers), and any book sold there is moving *very* swiftly.

Cracking the Code

Important sales information on competing books is literally at your fingertips—but you have to know where to look.

The secret for finding out whether a book has sold well is to look at the number of printings it's gone through. When a book is first released, the number of books printed is referred to as the "first printing." When most of those books have sold, the book goes back for a second printing, and hopefully a third and a fourth. You can tell just how many printings the book has gone through by checking the copyright page. You should see a series of numbers there that looks something like this:

02 01 00   8 7 6 5 4 3 2 1

These numbers are a code that tells you when that particular copy of the book was printed. The rightmost number of the first series of numbers (02, 01, 00) is the year of the book's printing; the rightmost number of the second series of numbers (8, 7, 6, etc.) is the number of the book's printing. If you look at these numbers, you can see that the book's first printing came out in the year 2000. That was several years ago, so if this book is still sitting on the shelf, that means it still hasn't sold out its first print run—not a swiftly moving title.

Except for hot-selling titles, most books are reprinted in steady but modest quantities. Subsequent reprintings in the 3,000- to 5,000-copy range are common. Publishers don't find it to their benefit from a business standpoint to keep large quantities of unsold books stacked in a warehouse. The spiraling cost of paper has also had an effect on the size of most reprints.

On the other hand, if you see from the code that the book is in a sixth printing, that is impressive. This is a book that is selling.

How is this printing information useful? If you find a book that has sold in big numbers, you might wonder: *could this be a hot topic that has room for another book?* If you find a book that hasn't gone into a second printing after having been out for some time, you might ask yourself: *is this a dead category I should stay away from?*

To find the answers to these questions, you have to keep asking booksellers questions, reading topical newspapers and magazines, and watching this part of the marketplace closely.

Pick a Bookseller's Brain

Booksellers are tremendously helpful and knowledgeable. If you ask, they will tell. Why not approach a friendly bookseller and say, "Hey, I'm thinking of writing a book on Topic X. What do you think? Is that a category that sells well for you? Which book in this category sells the best?" Most booksellers, the unsung heroes of the book business, will be happy to help if you catch them when they're not too busy.

Find out who is responsible for the actual section in the bookstore where you would like to see your book. Get to know that person, and learn from them what works and what doesn't work in your category.

> **Experts Say**
>
> "I love to talk to writers about what they are working on," a young bookseller told us. "It makes me feel like I am a part of the big, wide publishing world. And that is not an easy feeling to come by when you are shelving books and answering phones." Go ahead and approach a bookstore employee! Don't be shy.

Surfing for Info

The Internet holds wonderful information for writers. Not only is it a great place to do research, but you also can access lots of cool stuff to help you find out about the competition and the market for your book idea. Here are a few great sites.

The New York Times Extended Best-Seller List

Sure, you know *The New York Times* best-seller list. You check it every Sunday, don't you? But did you know there are many more books on that list than are printed in the paper? To find the top 35 best-sellers, visit the paper's website at www.nytimes.com, and go into the "Books" section. You'll learn that, for instance, although in the newspaper you'll only see 5 slots for best-sellers in the "Advice, How-To" section, there are really 15 slots.

Amazon.com

Amazon.com, the granddaddy of online bookstores, is also a good place to do research. Amazon can offer long lists of titles on any particular subject, giving you a quick look at what has been published. It, too, has best-seller lists, but keep in mind that these still reflect the tastes of folks who are open to online shopping. Just a few short years ago, the number-one best-selling title at Amazon was a book on how to design killer websites.

A fun way to waste an hour, though, is to go through all 100 of the Hot 100 and try to figure out why each book is selling well that particular hour. The Hot 100 is particularly sensitive to media; you can tell pretty quickly who was on the morning talk shows or in the major newspapers by a sudden jump in rank.

An appearance Jennifer made for an earlier edition of this book on C-Span's Book TV rocketed the rankings to number 52, a number to thrill the heart of any author. Alas, a media hit like that won't sustain sales for very long, and it was back in the humdrum 1,000s within hours.

You've noticed those reviews on Amazon.com, haven't you? Sometimes they can be useful in helping you assess the strengths and weaknesses of books in your chosen category, but do read them with a jaundiced eye. You'll start to notice that many of them seem to come either from the author's close friends or the author's sworn enemies!

Barnes & Noble

Barnesandnoble.com, or bn.com, is filled with useful info gathering tools. The "Top Book Subjects" section saves you time trying to figure out just what the hottest categories in the store are. You can also sign up to receive quarterly e-mail updates on new releases in several categories, including Christian, Business and Money, and Lifestyle. Another function lets you sort titles by new releases and upcoming releases.

Another tool we really like at bn.com is that you can type in a subject such as "natural health" (or whatever your topic is), and the site gives you the top 25 best-sellers in that category. This is very helpful when analyzing markets and putting together book proposals.

Publishers Marketplace

A hardworking book packager named Michael Cader of Cader Books has developed an incredible resource for working professionals. Check out www.publishersmarketplace. com for great research features—you can track the sales rank of as many books as you'd like to enter, keep up with who's buying what, and even learn how to post your own available projects in the hopes of catching an agent's or editor's eye. Some of the site is free and some is only available to subscribers, but we believe subscribing is worth it. For $20 a month, you will be able to access all manner of info about agents (including what they're looking for and how to best approach them) and learn on a daily basis what kinds of deals are selling. Cader also sends out a daily gossip column called Publishers Lunch you should sign up for to keep abreast of the latest news.

BookScan

BookScan is a fairly new, and fairly controversial, addition to the publishing landscape. Like the music industry's ability to track sales of CDs on a minute-by-minute basis, BookScan claims to do the same for the book industry. By typing in the ISBN of a book, you can access the total sales from the outlets that report to BookScan. Therein lies the problem, as it doesn't include large retailers such as Wal-Mart and Amazon.com. Many authors object to the fact that editors have been using BookScan numbers (as opposed to the longer-range and slower-moving in-house publisher's sales figures) to peg advances. BookScan is not for the general public and requires a hefty annual subscription to access. If you know someone inside a publishing house that does subscribe, you might be able to convince him or her to research the occasional title for you.

More Assigned Reading

As a serious student of the book publishing business, you need to keep up with news and trends. Read *Publishers Weekly*, and study the articles about what's selling. *PW* prints annual roundup articles about many of the major book categories. If you plan to write a health book, it's important that you read the health book roundup. If you plan to write a novel, be sure to read the fiction roundup. Don't stumble around in the dark; the information is there for the getting.

In addition to *Publishers Weekly*, *The New York Times* and *The Wall Street Journal* run frequent articles on books and the publishing world. Again, www.nytimes.com often features articles about books and publishing in addition to its best-seller list and book reviews. The "Publishers Lunch" e-mail newsletter includes links to major publishing articles from a wide variety of sources. Start keeping a file of important articles. You never know what you'll learn there.

But I Want to Write a Novel!

Do you really have to go through all this advance work for fiction, too?

Yes. Just as a health writer should know what's already on the health books shelf, a novelist needs to know what fiction is being published and read. Be a student of the art of writing, of course, but to succeed, you must study the marketplace, too. Learn what kinds of novels are selling well (ask a bookseller) and what kinds are not (ask a bookseller). As we write this, "chick lit" is still all the rage, and many a publisher has jumped on the bandwagon. *Hen lit*, chick lit–ish novels for women in their 40s and 50s instead of 20s and 30s, is now on everyone's mind. Religious fiction is still also selling strongly. By the time you read this, another hot trend may be selling. Make it your business to know these things. Don't bury your head in the sand (or your computer)! Get into that bookstore and learn everything you can.

You know you're an absolute original and your style is unique. But if you absolutely had to name a writer or book most like yours, what would you say? You're not doing it to compare yourself with another writer, but to establish the fact that books like the one you have written have sold well.

> **Hot Off the Press**
>
> Who are you writing for? Can you picture your audience? "I decided that I was writing for 'smart women on vacation,'" said Deborah Wessell, who writes the wedding planner mysteries under the name Deborah Donnelly. The better you can visualize and describe exactly who your audience is, the better you can write for them.

Minimize Your Rejection Rate

Why, you might ask, are we giving you all this inside information about how to come up with a good book idea? Or about how to research the market and the competing titles? Because, as longtime agents and editors, we're tired of saying "No." It's hard to turn down proposals and manuscripts from good-intentioned, hopeful writers. It is truly heartbreaking to know how much time and effort went into a book project that, from a business standpoint, was doomed from the start.

So we figure the more time and effort we put into teaching you how to come up with a book idea that will get a "Yes!" from an agent, an editor, and a publishing company, the easier our jobs will be.

Now that that's clear, let's move on to the next chapter and get back to that critical question: what do publishers want?

The Least You Need to Know

- Be sure your topic is big enough for an entire book, not just a six-page magazine article.

- Never assume your book is the first ever on the topic. There's at least one book already for every topic ever thought of, and your job is to learn from its/their strengths and weaknesses.

- Pore over publishers' catalogs, snoop around bookstores, and find out what the book clubs are hawking.

- Get with it—and get online.

- The more time and effort you spend researching the market for your novel or nonfiction book, the better your book proposal will be.

Chapter 5

What's Hot, What's Not

In This Chapter

- Trend spotting
- Literary and mainstream fiction
- Love 'em, thrill 'em, kill 'em
- Niche writing
- Cookbook niches
- Books for kids

Just what do publishers want? That's a tough question. And what do publishers want right now (for publication in 9 to 15 months)? That's an even tougher question, and possibly an irrelevant one. The awful truth is, if you sat down at this very moment and wrote a book on a topic that this chapter says is hot today, odds are that by the time you had your finished book in your hands, the topic would have cooled down—maybe to subzero.

Let's say it takes you 6 months to write the book. That's not a very long time for anyone to write a good how-to book, much less the Great American Novel. Let's say you know somebody who knows somebody with an experienced and well-connected agent, and that agent just happens to be particularly hungry at the moment. Maybe he's going through an expensive divorce, or his biggest client just got hit by a bus.

You express-mail him your ready-to-publish manuscript. He reads it that very night and sees your book on Hot Topic X as his ticket out of mounting legal bills. The first thing the following morning, he couriers copies to the hotshot editors at his favorite publishing houses.

Twenty-four hours later, he conducts an auction. Your book sells to the highest bidder for megabucks. (Why not? After all, this is a dream.) Smelling success (and desperate to recoup the investment), your publisher rushes the manuscript into production.

> **Experts Say**
>
> "Boomers want to stop the clock," says acquisitions editor Renee Wilmeth of Literary Architects. "And they will spend money on books that tell them how. As this huge group hits their 60s, you will see even more growth in the categories of health, medical fitness, and anti-aging."

Nine months later, your book hits the stores amid great fanfare—and is quickly placed on the remainder table. By the time your masterpiece is published, Hot Topic X is old news, and the public now wants to read about Hot Topic Y.

Sadly, this very scenario was played out on a large scale when all the books on September 11 came out for the 1-year anniversary. Some books sold in big numbers, but most did not. Many of the Hurricane Katrina books sold by media figures also suffered this same fate.

What's In, What's Out, by Category

What's a writer to do? Now there's a question worthy of Freud. Despite the transitory and, dare we say, fickle nature of the buying public, certain trends bear watching. So with a grain of salt and an eye on how quickly the reading public can shift their interests, let's take a look at the trends affecting each of the various book categories.

Fiction

The odds for a first-time novelist are never good, but all sorts of first novels are published each year, some to great acclaim and greater profit.

The market for fiction is as good—and as bad—as it ever was. Fiction is a star-driven game; the John Grishams, James Pattersons, and Danielle Steels have become virtual brand names publishers can count on to drive sales. An increasing dependency on this star system has created a classic chicken-and-egg scenario: which comes first, the best-selling book or the best-selling author?

Every publisher worth its bottom line wants to publish Grishams, Pattersons, and Steels. But there are only so many of these superauthors to go around—and only so many publishers who can afford them. So everyone is looking for the next Grisham, the next Steel. That's where you might just come in.

Every year does bring with it a group of new successful novelists, of course. In 2005, two of the breakout surprises were Robert Hicks' *The Widow of the South* and Elizabeth Kostova's *The Historian*. And there are always the quirky and unpredictable successes such as Gideon Defoe and his *Pirates!* series written in a Monty Python–esque style.

As you know from Chapter 2, the fiction market is divided into two general types: literary fiction and commercial (sometimes also called mainstream or contemporary) fiction. The latter includes hardcover novels and genre fiction. Genre fiction includes mysteries, thrillers, science fiction, fantasies, romances, horror books, Westerns, and the like. What's selling in these categories?

> **Hot Off the Press**
>
> The number of books a "best-seller" can sell has been steadily increasing over the last few decades. Research fellow Gayle Feldman took a close look and discovered that the 1975 best-seller *Ragtime* sold 232,000 copies. Compare that to the 2000 Grisham best-seller *The Brethren*, which sold nearly 2.9 million copies. Crunch those numbers, and you'll see a staggering twelvefold increase.

Love Is a Many-Published Thing

The romance market is booming. Take a look at these numbers from *Forbes* about just how hot romance is:

- Romance generated $1.2 billion in sales in 2004.
- Romantic fiction comprises 54.9 percent of all popular fiction sold in North America.

But, you might think, *I couldn't write those bodice-rippers*. Well, if you think bodice-rippers are the only romances, think again. Today's romance genre is a versatile one. It encompasses many series, subgenres, and hybrids, as well as mainstream titles.

Consider these subcategories, to name just a few: historical romance, time-travel romance, science-fiction romance, romantic suspense, romantic mystery, inspirational romance, multicultural romance, and young-adult romance. Then there are the new, super-sexy romances. And if you think romance heroines are generously bosomed virgins looking for Mr. Right to carry them off into the sunset, think again. Today's romance heroines run the gamut from fresh-faced junior high school girls to divorced career women.

In the late 1990s, *Bridget Jones's Diary* spawned a new breed of romance book, and many younger readers have strayed away from the bodice-rippers and toward the more contemporary novels. Imprints such Red Dress Ink and Mira are much hipper than their old mothers and feature writers like Jennifer Crusie, who writes such sexy love scenes that she told us, "I get letters from husbands thanking me for getting their wives in the mood!"

After 4 or 5 years of growth in the chick-lit category, some of those readers have gotten older and are now looking for a slightly more mature heroine. Publishers and writers have responded with "hen lit" aimed at women in their 40s and 50s. Another subgenre of the chick-lit category are novels set in the glamorous worlds of Hollywood or the magazine industry.

Experts Say

Not sure if your romance novel has what it takes? You can now pay for feedback from the professional folks at Harlequin. At their main website, www.eharlequin.com, you'll find the Romance Novel Critique Service, where you can sign up for feedback at the rate of $1 per page for a full manuscript.

If you'd like to cash in on this lucrative market, you'll have to do your homework. Don't write one single word without first consulting the guidelines from the publisher you plan to target—and without reading all the romance novels you can get your hands on.

Harlequin, Silhouette, Bantam, and other romance publishers happily provide writers with guidelines for their series. These guidelines are jammed with information on the exact word counts for their books, definitions of style, and level of sensuality permitted. They include lots of "absolute no-no's" and "absolute musts," as well as submission information. By following these rules, you'll save yourself lots of rewriting, and you'll greatly increase your chances of breaking into the romance field. Many of the romance publishers such as Dorchester (www.dorchesterpub.com) and Red Dress Ink (www.reddressink.com/writing.html) post their guidelines right on their websites, so check there first before trying to track down an address.

Love Writing About Love?

The one thing all romances have in common, from romantic suspense to mainstream historical, is that they're all stories about relationships. If you can write a love story that will move readers, this could be the field for you. Laurie Gold puts out an e-mail newsletter about the romance writing industry that you might find useful. Check out her All About Romance site at www.likesbooks.com and select "writers on writing." And if you're in the mood for some snarky fun, check out the reviews on www.smartbitchestrashybooks.com, where Candy and Sarah give books the business. It's well worth reading what they say if you plan to succeed in this market.

Beyond Hot Romance

From the early days of publishing, "erotica" has always existed in some form or another, and the twenty-first century is no exception. Perhaps writing adult books is your bag? Check out what Allure Books in Oregon has to offer and request their guidelines if you'd like to try your hand at this genre (www.allurebooks.com).

Thrill 'Em, Grill 'Em, and Kill 'Em

Mysteries, thrillers, and all their kin are more popular than ever—a fact that's readily confirmed by a quick glance at the best-seller list. At the time of this writing, four thrillers were on *The New York Times* hardcover best-seller list. Such news reflects not only the immense popularity of these genres, but their versatility as well. The mystery and thriller genres rival the romance category in both variety and readership.

Today's market is witnessing a boom in historical mysteries, medical thrillers, techno thrillers, and legal thrillers. But whether you're writing a hard-boiled detective story or an *English cozy*, it doesn't really matter. In these genres, there's plenty of room for your novel, regardless of which category it fits.

def•i•ni•tion

An **English cozy** is a type of mystery that typically takes place in England and follows a sweet old lady detective and a few of her doddering friends. They stumble onto a cold, dead body one afternoon, and the story unfolds from there. The term *cozy* comes either from the fact that you can settle in front of the fire for a cozy afternoon with one of these books, or from the tea cozy on the pot of Earl Grey you brew to drink while you read.

Nouveau Niche

The marketing types in publishing love nonfiction. Why? Because the nonfiction market is much more quantifiable—some would say more reliable—than the fiction market. Those marketers don't really know how many readers out there are going to want to read your coming-of-age novel, and they can't even begin to guess. But they can guess with slightly more accuracy how many of the nations millions of overweight people would be interested in *The Martini Diet* or whether fans of the show *Desperate Housewives* will buy related books. The same goes for all the trends—demographic and otherwise—reported in the media each day. Nonfiction publishers pay attention to what's hot, and (as we've told you before) if you want to succeed at nonfiction, you need to pay attention, too.

Hot Off the Press

What's hot in fiction, according to St. Martin's Press senior editor Ruth Cavin, are great books. "There is no formula for a good book, so write what interests you and what you think is good," says Cavin, who has worked with most of the greatest names in mystery fiction. "Write characters you can believe in, plots that make you keep reading, settings and minor characters that are interesting." Cavin, who reviews "hundreds of submissions" every year, says, "There may be more competition in terms of numbers, but not in terms of quality. I'm looking for books that stand out because of the writing, plot, setting, or characters."

Identifying a niche in the marketplace and then publishing to that niche is called— you guessed it—niche publishing. Three of the most successful niche markets right now are alternative health, spirituality, and longevity. All these niches fill a deep need for readers.

As people grow more disenchanted with conventional medicine, they're exploring alternative therapies. These same folks hope to live long and healthy lives, as witnessed by the success of Dr. Andrew Weil's book *Healthy Aging*.

This group who once turned away from organized religion is now looking for spiritual guidance as they become more aware of their own mortality. A recent article in *The Wall Street Journal* noted that, in the same way boomers changed giving birth (and sold vast numbers of *What to Expect When You're Expecting*), they are now changing death.

"Fine," you say, "but I don't know St. John's wort from St. John the Baptist, and I don't know a thing about how to live forever." No problem. There are myriad trends and niches to explore, from homeschooling to women's golf, from small businesses to eBay auctions. You don't even have to be an expert—you can always team up with one.

What's Cookin' with Cookbooks?

Long a staple of nonfiction publishing, the cookbook market has disappointed many publishers over the past couple years. "The cookbook field was overpublished," admits one long-time cookbook editor, who also reveals that many cookbook editors are looking for new jobs in new fields.

Despite this recent softening of the market, some cookbooks are finding favor with the public. "Editors say to me that superstar chefs are both overpublished and still selling," says a longtime California cookbook agent. So what is a nonsuperstar chef author to do? You can still find your niche if you work at it. The same agent suggested first-time writers could find success with "anything that ties into a product, like grilling or a panini sandwich press." Cookbooks with product or equipment ties might succeed because the publisher can persuade the manufacturer to purchase the book in bulk. A recent success has been the *Fix It and Forget It Cookbook*, with 2.2 million copies sold of a book that tells you what you can fix in your slow cooker. Literary food writing is also still selling, and it is possible to build an interesting anthology or compilation book around food like the recent book featuring stories about kitchen disasters.

The Publishing House at Pooh Corner

By definition, the children's market is a perennial one. Write for children, and you can build a body of work that will enchant the little ones generation after generation. But if you think writing for children is easy, think again. To paraphrase beloved author of *A Wrinkle in Time*, Madeleine L'Engle, writing for children means writing stories too mature for adults.

L'Engle's point has been made quite clearly by the extraordinary success of the *Harry Potter* books. These enduring best-sellers have made frequent appearances on both the children's *and* the adults' best-seller lists, and fans waited for years for Rowling's fifth book to appear. The sophisticated wordplay in the *Lemony Snicket* books also appeals to both children and adults.

What kind of books are working now? Annie Martin Bowler, the author of seven books, including *The Adventures of the Treasure Fleet,* says, "Editors are looking for snappy stuff. Our world is so fast nowadays and books need to move fast, too, in order to compete with video games and television for a child's attention. Snappy like the *Captain Underpants* books, that is what is working."

Slush Pile _____

Never send illustrations for your children's picture book with your manuscript unless you're a talented artist. Most publishers like to hire their own illustrators. Never mention the following in a query letter or proposal: "My niece (nephew, son, daughter, or next-door neighbor) is a wonderful artist whose work would really complete the book."

When you write for children, be it picture books or young adult novels, you can expect somewhat smaller advances. But with the potential of a lifetime of royalties as each generation of little folks discovers your writing, it's a much-anticipated legacy.

The children's market is as varied as the market for grown-ups. You have your pick of options, from picture books to young-adult mysteries to middle-grade nonfiction.

Picture This

Picture books have been and remain this category's biggest sellers. The classic picture book is as popular as ever, but there is an increased interest in other types of picture books as well, most notably these types:

- Picture books made into baby board books (those little books whose pages are cardboard to make turning easier for little fingers)

- Picture books for slightly older toddlers

No Kidding About Kids' Fiction

Middle-grade and young-adult books also offer writers a wealth of opportunities. Trends indicate a comeback for fantasy and historical fiction geared to this age group, even as the horror trend wanes. This is largely due to the popularity of the *Harry Potter* series.

Just the Facts, Ma'am

Nonfiction for children—particularly in the areas of science, technology, and biography—are staples of this market. If your writing can entertain as well as educate, this area might be for you.

Expert Lynne Rominger observed that, although the children's market used to be thought of as a "cousin of regular adult books, not really a money-making part of the industry," this thought has long since changed. Publishers and booksellers alike recognize the fact that every 5 years they have a new crop of customers.

Market Savvy for Success

Once you develop a keener eye for what's working and what isn't, how can you put this information to use? You should be able to spot an overpublished market and avoid it. You should be able to notice a book or two on a particular topic you've never noticed before and sense that a trend is building. And you should be able to develop more marketable ideas yourself!

Still having trouble coming up with an idea? Why not spend some time brainstorming about these two popular book angles:

◆ Devote yourself to one wacky task for a year. It worked in a big, big way for Julie Powell, the blogger who decided to cook every single recipe in Julia Child's kitchen classic *Mastering the Art of French Cooking* and morphed her blog into the book *Julie and Julia*. The same idea worked for Maria Headley in *The Year of Yes*, in which she decided to accept a date with any man who asked her out.

◆ If you can't think of an unusual way to spend a year, perhaps you could infiltrate some sort of secret society … Neil Strauss did that with his much-publicized book *The Game: Penetrating the Secret Society of Pickup Artists*.

Experts Say

For both inspiration and information, children's writer Annie Martin Bowler has turned her attentions to past winners of the Newberry Award. "I've memorized whole sections of *Charlotte's Web*," she says. What wins a Newberry? "They are always meaty topics and tend to be more serious. My goal is to win that award myself someday, so I study them as much as I can."

The Early Bird ...

Keep your ear to the ground, and you can turn today's trends into tomorrow's bestsellers. But don't dawdle; when it comes to trends, the first writer to the marketplace usually wins. Keep abreast by reading *Publishers Weekly* on a regular basis and paying careful attention to the trend articles that run interviews with editors and booksellers about what's working.

The Least You Need to Know

- ◆ Publisher's predictions can be hit or miss, but certain trends bear watching.

- ◆ If you're writing romance, get publishers' guidelines first.

- ◆ The romance field has changed dramatically, and many publishers have a need for sexier manuscripts.

- ◆ Children's books can mean small advances but long-term sales.

- ◆ Put (almost) as much effort into your market research as into your writing.

Part 2

Gone with the Wind: Submitting to Publishers

So you've got an idea for a book—now what? Here's where you learn the actual process of putting together a book proposal. We clue you in on the common mistakes new writers make so you can look like a pro on the page, right from the beginning!

From submitting professional query letters to compiling appealing proposals, the chapters in Part 2 explain what you need to get the attention of an agent or editor. Both nonfiction and fiction proposals are covered in detail. You learn the ropes on how to do either (or both!).

Chapter 6

Submit What?

In This Chapter

- ◆ The submission process explained
- ◆ A peek at book publishing
- ◆ The top mistakes new writers make
- ◆ The correct spelling of *foreword* (that thing at the front of your book)
- ◆ Plain and simple: formatting your submissions

You've come up with an idea you think is dynamite, but what now? How do you move your book idea closer to becoming the finished thing? You must begin to submit.

Submit, you say? What's that? Simply stated, the *submission* process is the process by which you let the publishing world know you have a great book available for publication.

Simply Submit

To get your book idea of a manuscript in front of the publishing decision-makers, you need to know how to make your way through the submissions process. This involves two important steps.

- **Important Step One:** The query letter

- **Important Step Two:** The book proposal

Why is the submission process broken down into two steps? To see why this came to be, let's peek in on a typical day in the publishing world.

A Day in the Life of Book Publishing

It's early morning in Manhattan, and unbeknownst to each other, an assistant editor and a literary agent are sitting next to each other on the subway. The doors open, and the two hoist their heavy tote bags onto their shoulders and head for the same towering black skyscraper. The elevators deposit them on two different floors. After greeting colleagues, they settle into small offices with their first cups of weak office coffee. And for the next two hours, on two different floors, these two hard-working members of the New York publishing world lead oddly parallel lives. Both eye the fresh stack of mail perched on their desks, and both sigh when beginning the task of opening and reading the mail.

What comes in the mail every day? *Query letters, book proposals,* finished manuscripts, editorial correspondence, newspaper clippings, promotional information—there seems to be no end to the pieces of paper that must be read. Interrupting the ritual of reading the mail, the phone rings continuously. And then, think of the e-mail that must be read daily! When Jennifer was a Random House editor, it was a struggle to simply keep up with the internal e-mail communication from her colleagues and higher-ups, let alone messages from agents and writers.

def•i•ni•tion

> The process by which a writer submits a book proposal or manuscript to a publisher is called **submission.** If the author is not using an agent, it is called an unagented submission. The initial contact between a writer and an agent comes in the form of a **query letter,** which is meant to spark interest in the project and prompt its recipient to ask for more material. The packet of information about the writer's manuscript or book idea is a **book proposal.** It contains a solid description of the book's purpose, the potential market for the book, its competition, and the author's credentials. The proposal also contains a complete table of contents, an extensive book outline, and at least one sample chapter.

This scene takes place simultaneously not only in the office of our unnamed assistant editor and faceless literary agent, but also in the offices of the senior editor, the editor in chief, the publisher, the associate editor, and even the new college intern. Let's face it—everybody wants to write a book, and everybody writes to people in publishing. So how do publishers, editors, and agents handle all this mail?

Query letters, that's how.

Quantum Query

A query letter is a simple, one-page letter. In the letter, the purpose of the book is described, and the author makes a short case for why the world needs this book. If the contents of the query letter pique the interest of the recipient, that recipient requests a proposal. If the proposal is good and the book-to-be is deemed marketable, a publisher offers a contract.

But why can't you send your entire book? Because in most cases, the harried folks in publishing haven't met you and don't know about your project. You need to try to get their attention in the easiest and fastest way possible. A query letter is the correspondence equivalent of politely tapping a stranger on the shoulder and saying, "Excuse me, do you have a minute to talk?"

> **Hot Off the Press**
>
> Top literary agent Jillian Manus likes to advise prospective authors how *not* to get your proposal into the hands of a literary agent—don't slip it underneath the stall door in the ladies room. Yes indeed, it happened to her at a writers' conference many years ago. Remember, everyone likes their privacy, and boundaries *do* exist!

Sound intimidating? Don't worry. We show you how to write a top-notch query letter that will help your project stand out. We also tell you how to put together a bullet-proof book proposal that will knock the socks off everyone who sees it.

But Before We Begin ...

We've seen it all. We've read thousands of query letters and book proposals. Don't make the mistakes others have. Here you'll learn the things you must avoid, the no-no's that will brand you as an amateur. Read them, and believe them. Commit them to memory before moving on to the next two chapters. The publishing world has rules, and you've got to follow them to get people to look at your stuff.

Experts Say

"I can always spot an amateur," says longtime agent Martha Casselman. "Instead of trying to sell me on an idea, the letter brags about the fact that she has obtained a copyright for her work, and proudly gives me the copyright date and number. What does that mean to me? Nothing. Tell me about your book; don't tell me about your housekeeping details."

Co-author Jennifer recently received a large package from someone she met at a writers' conference. Thankfully, it did not arrive postage due, but his letter began, "Although all the books I've read tell me to send just a query letter first, I've decided to take a different approach and send a complete manuscript of the book." *Arrgh!*

Not only did this fellow come off as arrogant, but he also signaled that he is not someone who follows the rules. What agent or editor wants to sign someone who clearly doesn't take direction? Not many.

And what happened to the package Jennifer received? She sent it right back, unread.

Top Ten Mistakes New Writers Make

If you take the following list to heart, you won't repeat that faux pas or others that raise red flags. Here are the few simple no-no's that can easily undermine all your hard work:

♦ Letters that contain a misspelled name

♦ Packages or letters with postage due

♦ Letters printed with outdated equipment

♦ Query letters that don't quickly come to the point

♦ Proposals that criticize other books

♦ Letters that are too flip or amusing in tone

♦ Queries that say, "All my friends think this is a great idea"

♦ Proposals that smell like cigarette smoke

♦ Queries that mention the minimum advance the writer will accept

♦ Proposals that arrive in a package filled with shredded paper or packing "peanuts"

Letters That Contain a Misspelled Name

How hard is it to call and check the spelling of someone's name? Why brand yourself a careless writer before the package is even open? A simple phone call helps you show you're serious about getting things right. Tell the receptionist you'd like to double-check the spelling of an editor's name, and they should be happy to help. Don't assume that what's printed in a professional directory is correct. For many years, Jennifer's name was misspelled in a major writers' guide.

In fact, any information you've plucked out of a publishing directory needs to be verified. Find out if the editor still works there and is still acquiring in the same areas. You can research so much online nowadays, but it's still worth it to pick up the phone, call the publishing company's main number, and ask to verify the spelling of an editor's name.

Package or Letter Arrives Postage Due

You look careless and irresponsible from the moment your material arrives if your package requires postage due. Another way to annoy your recipient is to send a package laden with little slips of paper that need to be signed to prove that it arrived. Remember, you're sending something that, under most circumstances, this person did not request. So don't make it hard for them to receive it. This includes sending unrequested materials that require a signature or a return receipt.

Author Uses Outdated Equipment

Avoid using a typewriter, a dot matrix printer, or other outdated equipment at all costs. Sounds harsh, doesn't it? But using outdated equipment signals that both you and your ideas are old-fashioned and behind the times. Can't afford the fancy stuff? Just go to one of the retail stores or copy shops that rent computer time and use a better computer system—even just to print out your proposal. You need to look as good as you can on the page. (And this means checking to be sure your printer cartridge is fresh enough to print nice and dark.) Handwritten notes are a lovely touch between family and friends, but remember, this is a piece of professional correspondence, and a casual, handwritten note would not set the right tone.

Letters That Don't Quickly Come to the Point

By "quickly," we mean in the first paragraph or two. Why is this so important? Remember our typical day in publishing? The one in which the agent's and editor's desks were piled with mail? We didn't tell you about the blinking phone message light or the 73 unanswered e-mails and the 4 scheduled meetings for that day. Time and attention are short. You need to get to the point.

Proposals That Criticize Other Books

This is a major gripe of editors. You worked hard to put together a book proposal, and your agent spent a lot of time deciding which editors should be approached with it. So why annoy the very editor you're hoping to impress?

"The author should never use the competitive analysis section to slam other books—chances are, publishers who published those books will be reading the author's proposal," says Laurie Abkemeir. As the former senior editor at Hyperion, she should know. "Also, many times the books that are being slammed are books that were huge successes. It doesn't make sense to slam something that was a big best-seller, but many authors do."

As an editor at Prima, Jennifer has also received many a proposal that pokes fun at some of the very Prima books she's proudest of. Once again, not the way to get someone to like you and your book idea. (Chapter 8 explains how to position your book in a positive light without making enemies.)

Letters That Are Too Flip or Amusing

A query letter is not a letter to a friend, your mom, or a long-lost chum. This is no time to be silly. Even if friends think you're the next Seinfeld, it's safer to write a straightforward, businesslike letter. Humor can easily work against you. So can arrogance, boasting, or conceit. How can you impress an agent if you can't boast about your accomplishments? Be confident, not arrogant. Don't worry—in Chapters 7 and 9, you learn how to do this.

Queries That Mention Your Fan Club

Don't ever write, "All my friends and relatives think this is a good idea." Book publishing is a business. And professionals in the book business aren't interested in hearing about your friends and relatives (unless they are famous friends and relatives who will be endorsing your book). They want to know about markets and demographics and national publicity.

Proposals That Smell Like Cigarette Smoke

Hey, go ahead and smoke, it's none of our business, but you'd be amazed at how the smell attaches itself to paper! An editor notices when they open a proposal that makes their eyes swim from the tobacco fumes. If you smoke, you probably don't notice it, but take our word for it: smokers send letters that smell like smoke. So just to be sure, take your disk over to Kinko's and print out your work in a smoke-free environment. Does this seem like petty advice to you? Yes. But remember, you want these publishing people to like you and your project. You need to use every little method you can to woo them.

Letters That Mention a Minimum Advance

Letters that mention the minimum advance the writer will accept or the phrase "resources needed to complete this project" expose you as a beginner. Like writers who are paranoid that someone might steal their ideas, this is the mark of an amateur. Never mention money in a query letter. Never mention money in a book proposal. When considering whether to pursue a book idea, agents and editors don't care what kind of "resources" are needed to complete your project. That's your problem, not theirs. Sooner or later, the topic of money will come up, but let them mention it first, not you.

Slush Pile

A big no-no when approaching an agent or editor is to be cagey about your idea, or worse yet, not reveal it at all. More than one amateur has expressed anxiety over sharing their surefire book idea for fear that someone will steal it. Trust us, they won't. This attitude only makes you look naïve and foolish to a publishing pro. The same theory applies to asking an editor to sign an NDA—a nondisclosure agreement.

Proposals That Are Buried in Shredded Paper

You want these publishing folks to be in a pleasant mood when they're reading your material. But years of experience in opening packages has taught us that there is no way to open one of these types of packages without getting a lapful (or noseful) of shredded paper. Maddening! You want someone to love your project. Don't risk ticking them off before they can get to it.

Can't find a padded envelope that doesn't have that shredded paper stuff in it? If your proposal doesn't fit in a FedEx letter-size envelope, it's probably too darn long. And a query letter that doesn't slip right into a regular envelope is definitely too long.

Warning, Warning …

Although this hardly ever happens, it has: a first-time writer sends off highly personal possessions along with a proposal—a grandmother's diary, baby pictures. And then what happens? It gets tossed at the publishers. Unsolicited material that isn't accompanied by a SASE (self-addressed, stamped envelope) gets tossed into the trash. So don't do it. Don't ever, ever send something you can't replace.

"I got a proposal that wasn't even a proposal exactly, it was just a scrapbook about someone remodeling their house. The original plans, scraps of fabric glued in, and lots of pictures of the progress," a how-to editor told us. "No self-addressed stamped envelope, no box we could ship it back in, it would have cost us huge money to have it packed up and sent back. So it went straight into the trash." Don't let this happen to your material.

Forward and Other Foibles

The world of book publishing is a peculiar place with peculiar rules, and it's frequently filled with peculiar people.

Even if you have learned all you can from the many books you've read, the courses and seminars you've attended, and the writers you know, there are still tiny mistakes only persnickety publishing people will notice.

Here's the big one: *forward* vs. *foreword*.

Look up these two words in your dictionary. Here's what ours says:

> **forward** (adj.) directed or moving toward the front, situated in front

So if the president of the United States has agreed to write something nice for the front of your book, you think, it must be a forward. These are introductory remarks situated in front of your book, so it would seem perfectly logical.

But no! The president is writing a *foreword*, not a *forward*, for your book.

> **foreword** (n.) introductory remarks at the beginning of the book, usually by someone other than the author

Even longtime authors make this mistake sometimes, and some publishing people feel very smug when they spot it.

As long as you have your dictionary out, let's tackle two more confusing words:

which (adj. and pronoun) what particular one or ones of a set of things or people

that (adj. and pronoun) the person or thing referred to or pointed to or understood

Co-author Sheree spends a great deal of her time combing through her clients' proposals changing *which* to *that*. What's the rule? If *that* works, use it.

A Great Example of a Bad Query

We stumbled on this tongue-in-cheek example of the absolute wrong approach and couldn't resist sharing it with you. It was written specifically to incorporate all the mistakes a new writer might make. Read it and weep. And then rewrite your query letter!

> *Book Two of the Third Volume of the Elves from Ipanema:*
> *Revenge of the Gas Lords: Part I*

Dearest Mrs. Hurst:

You may remember me from the restroom of the Writer's Conference in Bigthighs, New Jersey, in May. Actually, obviously, it was my girlfriend, Ronnette, you met—the short redhead who gave you my card and mentioned my sizzling series of fantasy novels—isn't she sassy? In any case, you told Ronnette that you don't represent fantasy. Permit me to take issue with this stance. All writing is fantasy, if you just think about it, including nonfiction, which you seem to prefer. So, I would maintain that you <u>do</u> represent fantasy. I checked your website and one of your upcoming books is titled *Eat Fit and Stay Slim*. Good Lord, if that's not fantasy, what is? So, sit down, take a bite of the candy bar I've enclosed, and allow me a moment to convince you of my *Elf* series merits.

In the Land of Ipanema all is not as it should be. Darkness spreads like giant bat wings over the innocent land, and the people, both large and small, are afraid. Emma Splink is a poor and impoverished pig herder who works for a cruel master in the small hamlet of Ipa.

Now, believe me, I would love to tell you more about the plot, but then I'd have to shoot you! Just kidding. I can't tell you more because I'm only on Chapter 9 in which Emma is ensorcelled by the crone in the woods, but then is rescued by her psychic sow, Gandalf.

As I mentioned I have studied your website (congrats on your B.A. in Literature way back in '61 by the way), and I notice that you have an interest in chick lit. Clearly you are going to love my protagonist Emma. This girl may wear chain mail and little else, but she is intelligent, short, redheaded, sassy, and determined to rescue the world. *Gas Lords* is a sure-fire *New York Times* best-seller.

I have numerous writing credentials, including my personal blog, Craig's Funhouse, unpublished letters-to-the-editor at agentwatch.com, and a fourth-place prize in erotica from the Bigthighs Alternative Hairstyle and Writing Fair.

Gas Lords is the second novel I have written in what will be a series of twelve. I must admit that the first book, *Wind from Below*, just wasn't good enough for publication. Darla, my mom, loved it. But a lot of my buddies pointed out flaws in the plot, characters, theme, and words. After two rejection letters, I put *Wind* in the desk drawer and I made a vow: I will learn from this experience. Those same agents who let loose *Wind* will not pass *Gas*.

I have sent submissions to you and 50 of your top competitors. Since you haven't replied to my calls, either at your office or at your home, I would appreciate you getting back to me ASAP.

I hope you are feeling better from the stomach upset you had at the conference, Ronnette mentioned you didn't look so good.

The Blessings of Loki, Thor, and Odin Upon You,

Craig English

P.S. Hope I'm doing this right. I'm still pretty much a newcomer to the business and probably making mistakes right and left. I wasn't sure whether to include a bio and picture, so I did. I strongly urge you to run a virus scan before opening them.

Okay, which mistakes did he make? Which mistakes *didn't* he make? He is querying an agent who doesn't handle the type of fiction he is submitting, he is way too chatty and personal, and he hasn't followed any of the protocol rules. Remember, this was written tongue-in-cheek, but it is dangerously close to what some agents see every day!

Look Like a Pro on the Page

If you've got a computer, no doubt it's loaded with the latest tricks. However, this is not the time to use them. Query letters and book proposals are not the right place to show off your fancy fonts and graphics capability. Use a basic font, such as Times New Roman or Courier. Skip the shaded boxes, cartoons, and artistic borders. Keep it plain.

Plain is also the order of the day for paper. Don't send off a query letter on scented paper, fancy marbled paper, or anything other than plain white, businesslike stock. And don't get fancy with the inks. Use plain black ink, please.

Now Where Should I Send It?

With all this talk of submitting, to whom shall you submit? It's a reasonable question. Sometimes writers submit their stuff to an agent, who decides to represent them. The agent then submits the writer's material to an editor. Other times a writer just goes ahead and submits to an editor. So what do we think you should do?

If you plan to write a book with broad national appeal, we think you should first try to get an agent. (More about agents in the following chapters—particularly Chapter 10.) If that doesn't work, you should try to submit directly.

In the next three chapters, we discuss query letters and book proposals. It's our aim to help you prepare these materials in such a way to interest an agent. And if you can't? We'll cross that bridge when we come to it, in Chapter 13.

The Least You Need to Know

- There is a well-defined process for submitting your materials: submit a query letter and then, if requested, a book proposal.

- Follow the rules, or you risk looking like an amateur—or, worse, a difficult author to work with.

- Careless errors in query letters or book proposals can undermine your other efforts.

- If you're writing a book with a large potential audience, first try to get an agent to represent you.

7

Query Letters That Sell Nonfiction

In This Chapter

◆ What's a *query?*

◆ Editing yourself

◆ An agent's five pet peeves

◆ Tips on hooking 'em

◆ Can't I just phone?

Now that we've frightened you into thinking your entire publishing career rests on a single typed query letter, how can we calm you down? By telling you this: the formula for writing successful query letters can be learned, and your lessons begin now.

This chapter tackles query letters for nonfiction books. Novelists, your turn comes up soon, in Chapter 9. We do, however, urge you to keep reading this chapter, too.

Although you learned the basic idea behind a query letter in Chapter 6, it bears repeating: the query letter is your first contact with either an agent or an editor. It is your calling card, your way of introducing yourself and your book idea to the publishing world at large.

Query? What's That You Say?

A successful query letter should contain the following items:

+ A brief description of the book

+ A brief description of the market for the book

+ A brief description of the author

Brief? Just how brief are we talking here? One page, that's how brief. Your query letter should never, ever be longer than one page. You need to distill your brilliance, your wisdom, and your expertise into one potent, page-long brew that will leave a reader reeling from its power.

Here's a quick exercise to help you distill that brew:

+ Sit down with one blank page of paper.

+ Write out a two-paragraph description of the book.

+ Write out a two-paragraph description of the market for the book.

+ Write out a two-paragraph description of yourself, the author of the book.

Okay, now pretend you're Ernest Hemingway. No, you don't have to run in front of a herd of bulls; all we want you to do is simplify your writing. Take a hard look at what you've written and start cutting out extra words. Make two long sentences into one medium-length sentence. Get rid of adjectives. Turn two wordy paragraphs into one punchy one.

Here's an example of a Hemingway-esque transformation.

About the Author, Take One

This is the first draft of the bio:

> Jennifer Basye Sander entered publishing as a way to escape a failed career in California politics. Her first book was published in 1983, *The Sacramento Women's Yellow Pages*, a directory of woman-owned businesses. She worked for

several years as a book buyer for a small, independent northern California bookstore chain before becoming an acquisitions editor for a nonfiction publisher.

As an editor, Jennifer worked with many best-selling authors, including Mary Kay Ash of Mary Kay Cosmetics, and award-winning writers such as the James Beard and IACP Award–winning food writer Elaine Corn. As an author, Jennifer's own books range in topic from travel (*The Air Courier's Handbook*) to small business (*Niche and Grow Rich*) to inspiration (*Christmas Miracles*). Her book, *Christmas Miracles*, was a *New York Times* best-seller. Formerly a senior editor at the Prima Publishing division of Random House, Jennifer also operates her own book packaging company, Big City Books, in Granite Bay, California.

About the Author, Take Two

After a short consultation with Mr. Hemingway, we now give you the revised paragraph:

> Jennifer Basye Sander first entered publishing in 1983 with the publication of her book *The Sacramento Women's Yellow Pages*. Her early success with that book led to a career in publishing that includes both a short stint as a book buyer and many years as an acquisitions editor. She worked with several best-selling authors and has herself authored many books, including the holiday best-seller *Christmas Miracles*. A former Random House editor, she is now a book packager in Granite Bay, California.

Get the idea? Write as much as you want and then go back and delete most of it. (Don't really throw it away, though; you'll need the long stuff for your proposal.) Keep the good stuff that sells you and your book.

About the Book, Take One

Let's see how that works with a description of a book. Here's a two-paragraph description of our imaginary book, *Accurate Arthritis Answers*.

> *Accurate Arthritis Answers* is a unique idea. Instead of relying on the advice of just one arthritis doctor, I plan to seek out advice from top arthritis experts around the world. Research schools, government studies, magazine and newspaper articles, and medical journals will all be scoured to cull the latest information on arthritis. Arthritis sufferers will learn about cutting-edge medical treatments, the

dramatic difference that exercise can have, and the effects of nutrition upon their affliction. Special attention will be paid to recent discoveries in alternative treatments, such as herbal therapy.

The book itself is divided into four different sections: Traditional Medicine, Nutrition, Exercise, and Alternative Therapies. Each section is written by a top expert in the field. Organized in an easy-to-understand style, *Accurate Arthritis Answers* will also contain colorful charts, illustrations, and a useful medical glossary. At 175 pages, the book will be a small and handy size for the lay reader.

> **Slush Pile**
>
> Does your pitch have a professional tone? Why not read a few book pitches from the pros to find out. At Michael Cader's website (www.publishersmarketplace.com), you can read actual book pitches made by literary agents as well as a few unrepresented writers. Click on "rights posting" to read what's being pitched and how it is being pitched.

About the Book, Take Two

Okay, how do we say that in one short, punchy paragraph? Like this:

> *Accurate Arthritis Answers* fills a real need in the marketplace. Unlike other large medical books, it is a short, easy-to-read book for the general reader. Instead of relying on the knowledge of just one doctor, it brings together the expertise of a wide range of international experts in the field. All types of treatments are examined, from the traditional medical approach to the latest research in herbal and other nontraditional remedies. Arthritis sufferers will now be able to turn to one single source for all the latest information.

Writer, Edit Thyself

Go ahead, give this exercise a try. Start writing long descriptions of your book, your market, and yourself. Then shrink them down to query size. You'll quickly learn to spot what needs to stay and what needs to go.

A one-page query letter does have more than three paragraphs sometimes. What is your strongest area? Your credentials, your book idea, or the potential market? Choose your strength, and devote two entire paragraphs to it.

Why does your query letter have to be perfect? A well-written query letter is your best shot at seeing your book published. So work on it, over and over again, until it looks right to you. This is not the time to dash off a quick little something. This is the time to set aside a week to perfect your query letter.

Writer Candy Chand has her queries down to a sweet science. "Every one of my queries is four paragraphs long," she told us. "In the first paragraph I introduce myself and my other published projects. I spend two paragraphs describing my new project and then close with one paragraph thanking them for considering it." Does it work? She's sold several projects that way, including *The Twelve Prayers of Christmas* to HarperCollins.

What *Not* to Say

Agent Martha Casselman is not alone in her pet peeves. Here are five things she (and most other agents) don't want you to put in your query letter:

- The kind of computer program you write in. (It doesn't really matter.)

- That this is an exclusive submission if it really isn't. (Don't lie.)

- Asking after her health and happiness. (She wants to know more about *you*.)

- Stating how well you can write. (Show her how well you can write.)

- Stating that if an editor doesn't want this particular project, you'd be happy to write anything he or she wants. (You're writing to demonstrate your knowledge and your talent, not your flexibility.)

Hook 'Em Early

The best query letters have a strong hook in the first two lines. What's a strong hook? Something that grabs the readers' attention and keeps them reading. Let's look at a good example, the query letter that Candy Chand used to land her book contract for *The Twelve Prayers of Christmas:*

Dear Editor:

As a published author, with my sixth book in the works, I always look forward to new and exciting projects. Therefore, at this time, I'd like to share with you a manuscript dear to my heart—a holiday picture book titled *The Twelve Prayers of Christmas.*

This festive work of flowing prose is designed to share the Christmas miracle from the POV of each of the individuals present on that holiest of nights: the donkey, the innkeeper, Mary, Joseph, the star, the lamb, the angel, the shepherd boy, each of the three wise men, and, of course, the Christ child Himself.

Upon your request, I'd be happy to send you the completed manuscript. Thank you for considering this project. I'm looking forward to hearing from you soon.

Best regards,
Candy Chand

Candy heard from an editor the very next day. Why? Let's take a closer look at this query letter:

- Candy identifies herself right away as a published author, working on her sixth book. Any agent or editor would keep reading. If you can't describe yourself this way, it's best to focus in the first one or two lines on the potential size of the audience for your topic. Candy could have described the enduring popularity of Christmas-themed gift books or the built-in marketing angles.

- She describes the book itself in one short paragraph.

- Upon request, she offers to send the completed manuscript. Remember, in a query letter, you are just describing the idea, not sending along your whole body of work.

This information all pulls together into a very effective query letter that grabbed an editor's attention. "After about a year or more of several editorial bites but no cigars," Candy explains, "I sent it to the editor at HarperCollins children's. The next morning, I received a reply requesting the material. So I sent the manuscript via e-mail. The editorial director e-mailed me back the next day after to ask if she could call me. She did call and told me she loved it and would take it to committee. Two weeks later, she called with the news that it sold. It will be published in 2007."

Experts Say

"Can they write? That's what I look at first in a query letter," says agent Andrea Hurst. "Does it draw me in? Do I want to read more? With nonfiction, I ask myself— is this a unique and timely idea? Does it fit in with my agency? Does this author have a strong platform and a sense of the marketing that is involved?" Andrea sums it up this way: concise, well written, marketable, and unique. For fiction, the author's voice must carry through into the letter and draw her into the book.

Another Approach

Here's another good approach for a one-page query letter to an agent:

Dear Bill,

Mmmm, chocolate. The bad news is it can't make you thin. The good news is it could make you rich! Investing seems like such a scary thing to do nowadays, the time is right for a reassuring book that helps investors feel at ease.

In several best-selling financial planning books, Peter Lynch has urged Americans to become better stock pickers by using what he calls "The Power of Common Knowledge" and simply paying attention to what goes on in their own neighborhood. As a longtime stockbroker and financial planner, I have taken Lynch's theory one step closer to home by advising chocolate lovers to simply walk around their kitchens, peek into their refrigerators, and look closely at vending machines for terrific investment ideas!

Chocolate Can Make You Rich: The Chocolate Lover's Guide to the Stock Market will give investors a whole new way of looking at the stock market. Forget "Blue Chip" stocks; think "Chocolate Chip" stocks instead! Chocolate cookies, cakes, candies, drinks, and more—Americans literally do eat chocolate by the ton. What stronger, more stable market can there be? When I give speeches, I like to tell my audience it's time they put their money where their mouth is!

Many investors—particularly women—are scared off by volatile, high-tech stocks in industries they don't understand, and have watched their investments plummet. With the knowledge gained in *Chocolate Can Make You Rich*, skittish investors could invest in solid megacompanies such as Procter & Gamble (who make the Duncan Hines brand of cake and brownie mixes), Hershey Foods (Reese's Peanut Butter Cups, York Peppermint Patties, and their own Hershey's brand), or Archer Daniels Midland (corn syrup producers, without which candy bars would cease to exist). More adventurous investors will learn about Starbucks Coffee (now not only the kings of coffee, but leading ice cream makers as well) or Eskimo Pies (yes, a publicly traded company!).

I have been a stockbroker for the past 10 years, ever since graduating from UC Berkeley with a degree in business. I developed my theories about "comfort stocks" as a way to make women feel more comfortable with investing, and I would like to bring my message to greater numbers of readers.

A 30-page proposal is available for *Chocolate Can Make You Rich*. Chapters include "Frozen Assets," "Sugar-Coated Investments," "Eat and Grow Rich," and many more. I look forward to hearing from you soon.

Regards,
Julia Berenson

Experts Say

Robert Kosberg is known as Hollywood's "Mr. Pitch." He pitches 20 to 50 ideas a year to studio heads. What can you learn from him for your book pitch? "Ask yourself if your idea can be boiled down to two power-packed sentences that generate excitement." Look for more ideas on his website at www.moviepitch.com.

"Mmmm, chocolate." Now there's a delicious hook! Kept you reading, didn't it?

Chocolate can make you rich? Sounds like a goofy idea, so the writer's second paragraph wisely links her idea to those of perennial best-selling author Peter Lynch—a smart way to look even smarter.

She quickly describes the book and the theory and establishes herself as qualified to write on this topic (a stockbroker for 10 years and public speaker). By describing the names of some of her chapters, she whets the reader's appetite for more. It's a good letter.

Write a Good One and Then Let It Be

Go ahead and write that query letter—as perfect a letter as you can make it. But after you drop it in the mail, leave it alone. Believe it or not, many authors can't leave it alone even after mailing it.

Agents and editors have all received them, the letters that begin, "Please disregard the query letter I mailed to you on January 22, and replace it with this version, which I think more accurately captures the essence of my book." Or "This information should be added to the proposal I sent to you last week. Please remove pages 4 through 8 and replace them with these new pages." Crazy, but true.

Do not under any circumstances attempt to do this! When your query letter disappears through the slot in the mailbox, move on to something else in your life. Don't lie awake at night wondering how you might have done it differently. It will just drive you nuts.

Online Etiquette

As in other parts of the world, publishing is going online. And although online queries would have been strange just a few years ago, they are becoming more acceptable. Agent Bill Adler Jr. enjoys receiving online queries from prospective authors. It gives him a good chance to answer quickly and not make writers wait for weeks for him to open the mail. Sheree, on the other hand, doesn't care much for lengthy online queries.

Each agent has his own policy, of course. The major guides to agents, such as *Jeff Herman's Guide to Book Publishers, Editors, and Literary Agents*, have only a few e-mail addresses listed now, but as the years go by, expect to see more of them. It's worth typing an agent's name into your search engine—some even have home pages. Sheree's website, shereebee.com, was designed to help writers.

The nice thing about an e-mail query is that you won't have to worry about choosing the wrong kind of envelope! Candy Chand has had wonderful success in e-mailing queries. "Don't be afraid to try; the worst thing you will hear is 'no.'" E-mail queries can also get a response in minutes—Candy has sometimes heard back almost instantly. Sure beats checking the mail every day for a sign of your SASE!

E-mail queries can also take a long time, or go unacknowledged all together. Remember how much e-mail those editors and agents get. Be polite in how often you check in. If you send an unsolicited e-mail query on a Monday, don't send another one on Wednesday asking if the first one was received. Give publishing people some breathing room. After a week and a half you can send another e-mail, but if that one doesn't get a response, move on to the next name on your list rather than become an online stalker.

SASEs and Other Ways to Hear Back

Remember the definition of "unsolicited submission"? It's one the agent did not ask you to send. Because you're sending something that wasn't requested, it's up to you to cover the cost of getting a reply. Always include a *SASE* with your correspondence so the agent can easily reply.

If you want to know whether your query arrived at its destination, include a small, self-addressed and stamped postcard the agent can just pop into the mail. Write something like this:

Yes, the attached query letter was received in my office on _____.

def•i•ni•tion

What is a **SASE?** It's short for a "self-addressed, stamped envelope." Never send a query letter or proposal without one. The publishing industry would go broke if editors had to pay to return all the unsolicited material they receive. If you haven't included a SASE and the agent or editor isn't interested, you will never hear an answer, and your stuff goes straight into the recycling bin. Harsh, but true.

You can also send your query letter via FedEx or UPS. This is more expensive than the good old U.S. mail, but it also lets you track your letter and ease your mind about whether it ever arrived. (Two-day express mail is considerably less costly than next-day air.)

Do not call an agent's office to ask whether your query letter arrived. You will appear anxious and unprofessional.

But They Asked for It!

You met an agent at a writers' summer camp who encouraged you to send your proposal? Congratulations. But please don't assume the agent remembers the invitation. Remind him in the first line of your query letter: "We met at the Mendocino Writers' Conference, and you asked that I send the following proposal." An agent might meet a hundred writers at conferences throughout the year (and talk to another hundred on the phone). So don't be hurt if he doesn't remember you or your book. And don't forget to include a SASE with your query.

Voicemail

And if you're anxious about a query you've mailed to an agent or editor, should you ever—*gasp*—call them to check up? Try not to. We understand the impulse, but for unsolicited queries, the protocol revolves around written correspondence. If you do break down and place a call to check up, please leave a pleasant message. Sheree has received more than one hostile voicemail message from an anxious writer demanding to know if a package has arrived or when they might hear a response. The folks who left those messages received their rejections swiftly!

Hot Off the Press

As in most businesses, assistants make the world go 'round. These unsung young folks open the mail, sort the mail, answer the phone, and otherwise keep an office running. Chances are, your query will be seen first by someone's assistant. Editorial assistants, literary agents' assistants, production assistants—be nice to them all. Today's assistant might be tomorrow's editor in chief.

The Rules

Now that we've given you the rules, please believe us when we say it's in your best interest to follow them. If you try to get around them, if you try things you think are clever or devious, it can backfire. At the very least, an agent might think you're annoying. In the worst-case scenario, you could come off as a nut—and agents are not very eager to sign up nuts! Let them know you've done your homework, you know how the routine works, and you will follow the rules.

Having said that, we must confess that sometimes people do break the rules and succeed because of it. And sometimes people win the lottery. But as a first-time writer, you improve your chances tremendously by playing it straight.

A Few Words on Rejection

We've all been there. Rejected. It doesn't feel good, but it is a big part of the business. Agent Jeff Kleinman of FolioLit has this good advice to share with writers about how best to deal with it:

"It helps to know why publishing folk reject most manuscripts. We agents, for example, generally reject manuscripts for one (or more) of three reasons:

1. "The writing simply isn't strong enough. This is the most common reason, especially for fiction. You all have heard, I know, that fiction is often a tough sell, but a lot of agents and editors are certainly looking for the next great novel. I'd say about 90 percent of the fiction projects that cross my desk, though, get rejected because the author hasn't quite taken the time to really hone his/her writing skills—really learning how to write great characters, or use dialogue, or create resonating descriptions, and so forth.

2. "The author's platform is not large enough. This is especially true for nonfiction, but also critical with fiction projects that are iffy. 'Platform' means the author's visibility within his/her target readership community—so media coverage, speaking engagements, and so forth all factor in.

3. "The project is not big enough. I'm not talking word count here—I'm talking book sales. So if the concept seems run-of-the mill ['oh, great, another coming-of-age novel—what's really special about this one that will make it stand out in such a crowded marketplace?'], or something that will appeal only to a smallish audience [Salt Lake City's monuments, for example—this could be a very useful book, but it's probably not going to appeal to folks outside the Salt Lake City area]. This is another easy reason to reject a manuscript."

So Jeff has come up with a concrete plan he encourages authors to follow when they have met with a "no" or two. Test the waters a bit, and adjust accordingly: "Now that you know why books are often rejected, see where your book fits in. Try the following, as you approach agents and/or editors: send out 10 query letters. Do *not* think of the rejection letters as being letters telling you the recipient wasn't interested in your stuff. Look *only* at the form of the letter itself.

1. If you get 10 form rejection letters in response, then something may very well be problematic in Step #1 (i.e., rewrite, build your platform, or revise your book's concept).

2. If you get one or two 'real' letters—either written on your cover letter, on the agency's form letter, or an actual addressed letter—then you're probably on the right track, so submit another 10 to 20. If, after about 30 rejects, you're still not getting the offers, seriously consider going back to Step #1 as well.

3. The more real letters you get, the more you should think you're on the right track.

"The trick is, of course, not to take the rejection letters personally. Use them as a tool to work your way through the publishing maze—you're wandering around in the dark, so think of rejection letters as the walls you bump into as you go down the hall. Don't hate the wall, or get overly discouraged because you keep banging your nose—use the wall to guide you along the way."

As hard as it is to deal with rejection, Jeff's method can go a long way toward helping you process the information and move on toward success.

The Least You Need to Know

◆ Query letters should be one page long and should contain a brief description of the book, the market, and the author.

◆ Practice being brief by editing your writing to one powerful paragraph.

◆ Don't use a query letter to air your grievances with anyone.

◆ Unless you include a SASE with your query letter, you might never hear an answer.

◆ A good query letter states its purpose up front in the first paragraph.

◆ Be businesslike. Don't try to be clever or witty. And don't use scented paper or fancy typestyles.

Chapter 8

Bulletproof Nonfiction Book Proposals

In This Chapter

- ◆ What goes into a book proposal
- ◆ Building a book proposal, step by step
- ◆ Selling your idea
- ◆ Selling your market
- ◆ Selling yourself as an author
- ◆ Choosing the best sample chapter

Congratulations! You wrote a great query letter, and an agent or editor has asked to see your book proposal! Uh, now what do you do?

The Art of Proposal Writing

In a book proposal, you're proposing an idea for a book. You *propose* to do it because, in most cases, you haven't actually written the book yet!

You Mean I Don't Have to Write the Book First?

We'd like to let you in on an industry secret. Here's how most professional nonfiction writers work:

- First, they come up with an idea for a book.

- Next, they write a book proposal 10 to 20 or so pages long.

- Then they send it off to their agent and wait.

If a publisher decides to publish the book, the writer sits down in front of the computer and writes the book by the agreed-upon deadline. But if there are no takers, the professional writer comes up with another idea and starts the process over again.

That's right. To sell a nonfiction book and get a contract from a publisher, you don't really have to write the book first. You can write it later. First, you have to write a good proposal.

Hot Off the Press _____

Some proposals are long, some are short, but Jennifer thinks she wrote the smallest one ever. It was on a mini-sticky note. Many years ago she'd written up a long list of personal goals, one of which was a reminder to "wear more cashmere." Jennifer liked the way that phrase sounded so much she wrote it on the tiny yellow note and stuck it to the side of her computer. Years later, an editor who'd seen that note on her computer years before called and asked her to turn the idea into a book! Say hello to *Wear More Cashmere: 101 Luxurious Ways to Pamper Your Inner Princess* (Fair Winds). That one tiny Post-it note has now spawned a whole series of gift indulgence–themed books. So remember, always write down your clever ideas!

But When Should I Start the Proposal?

Don't even think about querying agents or editors until you've written at least some portion of your book proposal. Not only will it give you a more solid sense of what you're doing (and help you distill it into a good query), but it also cuts down on the lag time between when an agent or editor says, "I'd love to see your stuff," and when you can actually send it. So get a jump on things and start now. Working on your proposal will also help you distill your ideas about the book, so you'll have a quick answer if an agent or editor says, "Sounds interesting. Give me an overview."

Building a Book Proposal

Here's a short list of what you should include in your book proposal. Then read on for a longer description of each key element. If you have trouble understanding any elements, don't panic. In Appendix D, as well as on the CD, we've included sample book proposals for you to read.

Read through this list once and then sit down and begin to write your own version. A book proposal should develop before your very eyes.

The parts of a book proposal are as follows:

- A cover page with the title, your name, your address, and your phone number

- A three- to five-part pitch

- A detailed table of contents

- A sample chapter of the book

- Attachments such as recent news articles about the topic or recent news articles about the author

def•i•ni•tion

Be prepared to answer the question, "What's the overview of your book?" An **overview** is another term for a summary. In the movie business, it's called a "take-away." What will your reader take away with him after reading the book? Write it out in one succinct sentence.

Your Cover Page

This is a great first step. It takes only about 5 minutes to do it, and after you've made a cover page, you can consider yourself on the road to building a book proposal. Simply create a page that—in pretty big type—has the book title and subtitle, as well as your name, address, and contact info.

If you're sending off the proposal to an agent who requested it, put your name and address on the cover page. When you have an agent and she's shopping your book to editors, she'll put her own name and address on your proposal's cover page.

After you've made a cover page, print it out and hang it on the wall next to your computer. Whenever you're feeling discouraged, glance up and see your title and your name in large

Slush Pile

Remember how business-like your query letters should be? A book proposal should be equally businesslike in appearance—no fancy graphics, colored paper, or elaborate typestyles. Your writing skills are on display here, nothing else.

type! Jennifer's office walls are covered with title pages, all designed to guilt-trip her into finishing up her projects. As a technique, it really does work.

It's important to note that we just mean a plain cover page for your proposal, not a fancy, highly designed idea for your future book. As you'll learn in later chapters, authors (and even editors!) have little control over the actual cover, so you should not invest time, energy, or money into this part of the proposal.

The Pitch

Ever heard the sales term *pitch?* In a book proposal, you're trying to pitch a book idea. The pitch section of the proposal can be broken down into five smaller parts:

- ◆ The idea
- ◆ The market
- ◆ The competition
- ◆ The publicity and promotion potential
- ◆ The author

Remember all that work you did while writing your query? Those long paragraphs describing the book idea, the market, and the author? Pull them out now and see what you can use.

What a Great Idea!

First, describe the idea behind the book. What kind of a book is it? What kind of information will it contain? Describe your book in one tight sentence and then elaborate on the idea for several paragraphs. Co-author Sheree tells her clients that this is their chance to describe the contents of their book "enticingly and thoroughly."

Off to Market

Now describe the market for your book. Who are the millions of potential readers? Why will they be interested in your book? The market section should contain as much hard data about *demographics*, trends, and other facts as you can get your hands on. Remember to avoid using the sentence, "Everyone should read this book."

The market section of your proposal could also contain information about possible nonbookstore outlets for your book. Where will these millions of potential readers be found? In gardening stores, lingerie shops, or hospitals? Let the publisher know if specialized sources of distribution can target these folks.

def•i•ni•tion

Publishers love **demographics**. Publishing is an inexact science, and the more an author can cite demographics about population statistics, the size of an age group, or personal-income levels when describing the potential audience for his book, the better the agent, editor, and publisher can sleep at night, knowing there is a market for the book.

Compete with the Best

The competition section is an easy one to write. As a matter of fact, you've already done much of the work. You've spent hours wandering the aisles of your local bookstore. At last you get to display the knowledge you've gained!

To create the competition section, list all the books already published with which your book will compete. The purpose of this section is to establish that you know what else has been done in your area and that you believe your book fills an existing need. Describe these books at length, but also be fair and balanced in assessing what you perceive to be their weaknesses. Do not attack. Remember the advice of former Hyperion senior editor Laurie Abkemeier from Chapter 6? Never use the competition section to slam other books. You never know who will end up reading your book proposal!

A secondary purpose of the competition section is to highlight books that, instead of competing with your proposed book, complement it. Complementary books can help you establish that a book like yours will succeed. Flip to the sample proposal in Appendix D or those on the CD to see how this works. Check out the sample proposals section on the CD to see how they describe other books on the topic. This helps you use the success of other books to build your case.

This is also a good place to point out how your book could cross over and succeed in two markets at once. Publishers love the dazzling idea that one book might sell to two different types of people, for example, that a Christian fiction book such as one from the *Left Behind* series might someday grow so large as to burst out into the mainstream market, or that a money workbook for couples could work in the finance niche as well as in the relationship section.

La Publicité

The publicity and promotion section is of critical importance in today's publishing market. All publishers want to know how hard the author plans to work, how many media contacts the author already has, and whether this topic lends itself to *publicity* and *promotion*. So the more you can supply here, the better. How do you find out this stuff? By paying attention to how often the media writes about your topic or about the audience your book targets.

Publicity Opportunities

Using *Accurate Arthritis Answers* as an example, quickly come up with some of the different places this book could get publicity:

◆ National magazines targeted to older Americans (such as *Modern Maturity*) and the national network of small newspapers for seniors

◆ The morning news shows, such as *Today* and *Good Morning America*, which frequently devote time to issues of health

◆ Nationally syndicated radio health shows, which are growing in popularity

◆ Health editors at all major newspapers and magazines

◆ Newsletters in retirement communities, such as the various Sun City communities around the country

def•i•ni•tion

What's the difference between **publicity** and **promotion?** The two words sometimes seem to be interchangeable. The bottom line is—the bottom line! Publicity is free. Promotion (which can mean advertising) usually costs money.

We'd like to pass along a request from tired editors at this point: "Please advise writers that a real tendency to oversell in the publicity and marketing section has become apparent," said one editor who wished to hide behind the curtain of anonymity. "Everyone claims they and their book are a [shoo-in] to be booked on *Oprah*, everyone claims that they will market endlessly—it starts to read like every writer went to the same seminar about book marketing and is parroting what they learned there." What does this mean to you? Be realistic in what you say you can and will do for your book.

Is It Especially Timely?

Are there special times of the year when your book could be promoted? Talk about the potential for gift or seasonal promotions. Are there any major events (such as an upcoming election or a hot new movie) that your book ties into? If so, mention it.

Bulk Sales?

This is also a good place to mention any possibilities you see for large sales of the book to groups, businesses, and organizations. Publishers are very interested in pursuing large, nonreturnable sales. Using the arthritis book again, here's how you could say it in a proposal:

> The pharmaceutical manufacturer behind one of the major drugs used to treat arthritis has expressed a willingness to purchase 2,500 copies of *Accurate Arthritis Answers* to use as a premium. The author also intends to seek out other large group purchases for the book.

If you already have a solid commitment for a large buy for your book, be sure to mention it. If you plan to buy a large number of the books yourself (to give away to clients or sell at speeches), mention that also. Publishers are interested in protecting their investment, and this kind of information could help tip the balance in your favor.

A Stamp of Approval

Have you approached any big-name authors or professionals who are willing to give you endorsements for your book? Let the publishers know who you plan to approach, and if you have existing ties with these folks. James Patterson is your brother-in-law? Bob Woodward lives next door? Write it down! If you do have close personal or professional ties to big-name folks, approach them now. It's even better to have an endorsement in hand when you're in the proposal stage. This, too, could help tip the balance in your favor.

Let's Hear About You!

Finally, you'll need to include information about you, the author. Here's where you can really let loose and brag about what you've accomplished in life: awards, honors, education, experience—pile it on. Let everyone know about your writing experience, publishing history (if you have one), and professional success. Do you have local, statewide, or national recognition in your field? Talk about it here. Try to position yourself as someone uniquely qualified to write this book.

Are you a skilled public speaker or presenter? Do you hold seminars or classes that relate to your book? The publisher needs to be reassured that you are not only a qualified author, but that you can also be an effective public image for the book. If you have professional photos on hand, include them. But don't send candid snapshots that would undermine your authority.

Now that you understand everything that goes into the pitch section of your proposal, you're ready to move on to the other sections.

Do You Need a Partner?

While working on this section of your proposal, please take the time to seriously consider how strong your credentials will look to the editor who is considering them. Are they as strong as they should be or could be? Might you have a better chance at selling this book if you teamed up with another expert in the field? Keep an open mind to the possibility, as that might well help you sell the project. A major best-selling economics book (perhaps the only best-selling economics book?), *Freakonomics*, was the result of a newspaper reporter teamed up with an academic. Neither could have written the book on their own!

Best-selling author James Patterson seems to publish constantly, and he does. How can he put out five books a year? He teams up with other writers. "I found that it is rare that you get a craftsman and an idea person in the same body. With me, I struggle like crazy. I can do the craft at an acceptable level, but the ideas are what I like." Patterson believes he is more proficient at creating the story than executing it. Why not use his method to form a writing team and increase your own chances for success?

Detailed Table of Contents

That's right, you'll need to include a detailed table of contents. Not only should you list each and every chapter, you also should include a short paragraph to describe each chapter or section. This is sometimes referred to as a chapter summary. Describe not only the purpose of each chapter, but also some of the content.

Sample Chapters

We've told you not to write a book until the proposal is accepted, but that doesn't mean you shouldn't write at all. A good proposal contains some good sample chapters, so get to work on a few. Including a good representative sample chapter is important. Not only is the writing itself important, but so is the topic. A well-chosen sample chapter can be a powerful thing. Just as the query letter was a way of introducing yourself to a stranger (and presenting yourself in the best possible light), so, too, is the sample chapter. It gives you the opportunity to influence the way you're perceived. It's important that the chapter you include is representative of the rest of the book in style, content, and length. It's not unusual to include Chapter 1, but if Chapter 1 is not representative, send in one that is. Better yet, include Chapter 1 plus a later representative chapter. We'll give you a great example.

Write What They'd Enjoy Reading

When we were trying to get the contract to write the first edition of this very book, *The Complete Idiot's Guide to Getting Published*, we needed to write and submit a sample chapter. With all the possible aspects of getting published to choose from, which do you think we chose? Publicity. We wrote a sample chapter about book publicity and how important it is for authors to work hard to publicize their books. We included lots of information about how hardworking authors can make a big difference in the sales success of their books.

Send an Upbeat Message

Why did we choose that topic? Because we wanted to send a positive message to the publisher: that these two women, Sheree Bykofsky and Jennifer Basye Sander, know what they're doing. They understand how to make a book sell. They will work their tails off to make this book succeed.

Why choose a chapter with a negative tone (like one that talks about the high rate of book returns or the changes afoot in the publishing business) when we could do something positive? Not only was the chapter on an upbeat topic, but it positioned us as go-getters. Hey, we got the contract, didn't we?

So what should you choose for your sample chapter? Choose something that will help the reader. And the reader, in this case, is not the general reading public, but the agent or editor reading your proposal. Give that person a sample chapter that will make him feel great or learn something new. Don't choose a chapter that will leave him depressed and reaching for a box of tissues. Here is an excellent opportunity to make him feel good about you and your ideas. Look at your material and see if any section will get the editor or agent nodding their head in recognition or agreement. Help them say "yes" to you!

The Kitchen Sink

The very last thing that goes into your proposal is important: evidence of your and your book's credibility. Here is an opportunity to include all the media attention you and/or your topic have gotten and that you've been saving up. With an impressive bundle of clippings, you can establish yourself as an expert, and you can establish your topic as big.

Hot Off the Press _____

Creating a successful book proposal is a lot of work. Here is some good news, though: once you're a successfully published writer with an agent and established reputation, you can write shorter proposals. Some authors only e-mail an idea to their editor and end up with a contract!

Newspaper and Magazine Articles

Did we say *recent* articles? It's important to include only articles from the last 5 years. If all your clips date from years ago, an agent or editor will wonder what happened to your career in the meantime.

Slush Pile _____

No gimmicky presents should accompany your proposal unless they relate to the book itself. So a proposal for a book on chocolate truffles probably won't be harmed by sending along a box of samples. But don't send a box of truffles with your proposal for a book about world peace.

It's also important that the articles you include about your topic be recent. If you include dated material, it might appear that the topic itself is old news and that the book wouldn't sell.

Be careful about the quality of the clippings you send. Ripped, smudged, or messy-looking clippings will do you no good. You are a professional, and you need to look like one. Be sure you include only clear copies that are readable, neatly presented, and of a reasonable length. It's better to send nice new copies rather than large original clippings from a newspaper. And because you'll be making many copies of your proposal, making photocopies is cheaper than buying up 20 copies of the newspaper with your article in it.

Video Clips

Videos, whether on videotape or on CD/DVD, of you being interviewed on a major television program are great to include as well. Short clips are best, though. Don't go overboard, as agents and editors will rarely watch an hour-long video. A professionally edited and labeled video clip is best. Worst is sending the wrong video, like the one of your children in the bathtub. Be sure to label your video clearly with your name and address in case it gets separated from your proposal.

Has all this proposal talk left you feeling overwhelmed? In Chapter 11, we fill you in on some folks who can help: *proposal doctors* and *book doctors*.

def·i·ni·tion

Some folks out there are known as **proposal doctors** or **book doctors.** You can hire one of these "doctors" to help you write your proposal. They are mostly former editors or longtime writers, and you will see their advertisements in the back of writers' magazines. You might also ask an agent for a recommendation.

Proposing Your Self-Published Book

If you have a self-published book that you're now trying to sell to a publisher, you must include a copy. Also include a brutally honest description of the sales and distribution of your self-published book. Did we say "brutally honest"? We mean it. Be sure to specify not only how well your own edition sold, but where and how you sold it—whether out of the trunk of your car or at Barnes & Noble. Under no circumstances should you fudge, puff up, or exaggerate how well it sold. Trust us—if you lie, you will be caught. And that will be the end of your chances of selling the book. It may work to your advantage if your book sold well to a limited audience (for example, through your newsletter) but never made it to the major bookstore chains. That way, if a publisher *does* release your book, it will appear fresh to a bookstore buyer and not seem like old news.

More than one self-published book has sold successfully to a major publisher. Two big examples are Robert Kiyosaki's *Rich Dad/Poor Dad* and Richard Paul Evans's first book, *The Christmas Box*. Both were self-published originally and then picked up by major houses. Kiyosaki's book has been on *The New York Times* best-seller list for more than five straight years, and Evans has produced six best-selling novels since his first effort.

Time to Get Writing!

Do you have a handle on what exactly a book proposal is now? It might seem daunting at first, but we know you'll get the hang of it. To help you learn from actual proposals, we've included several both in Appendix D and on the CD. Also included is a book proposal template that will walk you through the steps with a fill-in-the-blank format. So what are you waiting for? Get to work!

The Least You Need to Know

- A book proposal is a 10- to 20-page description of the book, with supporting information.

- Professional nonfiction writers write a book proposal first; if it sells, then they write the book. You can do the same.

- The more compelling the information you provide about the market, the greater your chance of finding a publisher.

- Choose a sample chapter on a topic that will leave the reader (the editor or agent) with a good feeling.

- Include clean copies of recent newspaper and magazine articles about yourself and your topic.

- Do not send gifts or attention-getters with your proposal.

Chapter 9

Fun with Fiction

In This Chapter

◆ You've got to write the whole book first!

◆ Query, query, query

◆ Writing a novel synopsis

◆ Now you've got an agent on the line!

◆ Summarizing your novel

When writing nonfiction, you can sell your book before you write it. No such luck with fiction. Fiction is a different ball game with a more complex set of rules. It's harder to play and harder to win—but the rewards are enormous. The most successful novelists become, in effect, the brand names of the book business: King, Grisham, Rice, Crichton, Patterson, Steel … Although Jennifer and Sheree have been updating this book every few years, the names of the biggest fiction writers really hasn't changed much. Okay, Anne Rice switched from writing about vampires to writing about Jesus, but that's about it.

As the late best-selling author James Michener used to say, "You can't make a living [writing novels] but you can make a killing." Win in the very competitive field of fiction, and you can win big. How big? According to an article about his investment habits, James Patterson makes $40 million a year. *Forty million.* Is that big enough for you?

In this chapter, we tell you how to write query letters and book proposals for fiction. But before we do, let's look more in-depth at the wide world of fiction.

So I Have to Write the Whole Book First?

Yes, to sell a work of fiction, you have to write the entire book first. Why? Because fiction requires more craftsmanship.

To write nonfiction, you need to know how to organize information in a clear and entertaining way. But writing fiction requires a mastery of myriad techniques. From pacing to character, plotting to dialogue, more skill is required to pull it off. Moreover, a novel has a beginning, a middle, and an end—and lots of complications along the way. Publishers can't tell from an outline and a sample chapter alone if you can sustain a narrative and keep readers turning the pages for 250, 500, or maybe even 1,000 pages.

You have to supply them with proof, which is in the completed manuscript. You need to have written an entire novel before you can approach an agent to represent you. Agents, too, need to know you can keep it up for hundreds of pages. Then, with your masterpiece in hand, you can prove you've written a page-turner. You might become the successful novelist you—and your mother—always dreamed you could be.

Want Support? Mingle with Other Writers

Writing may be a lonely business, but getting published doesn't have to be. Join a writers' organization so you can keep abreast of new markets and trends and make valuable contacts with agents and editors.

If you're completely antisocial, don't despair. Many writers' organizations have online chapters you can join (see Appendix C for some good resources to pursue). You can cybernetwork without leaving the privacy of your own computer.

You can also sign up for a writing class at your local college, which will help you make friends and contacts even as you polish up your writing skills. Here again, you don't have to leave home if you don't want to; a number of writing classes and seminars are available online, run by writing organizations, local universities, and online "distance learning" centers such as www.ed2go.com.

> **Hot Off the Press** _____
>
> Agent Jeff Kleinman had great success in placing the Robert Hicks' novel *Widow of the South*. Once published, the publicity department had great success getting coverage for this first-time novel. Why? Jeff believes it was because the novel revolved around a real place—an antebellum mansion in the South—and a real woman—the plantation owner who turned her front porch into a Civil War battlefield hospital. "There was a house they could go to, halls they could walk down—it helped so much with the media interest." Is that a method you could use? Then be sure some elements of your novel in the plot or the characters can be seen and felt today.

And Then I Have to Write the Whole Book *Again?*

You and your mother are not alone. Agents and publishers like nothing better than successful novelists. Like the Energizer Bunny, successful novelists just keep on going and going and going. They sell, sell, sell. New York literary agent Ethan Ellenberg, who represents fiction writers in all genres, puts it this way: "A successful novelist can write 10 or 20 books over 10 or 20 years."

That's the long haul, and the long haul is what publishers are looking for when it comes to fiction. It takes time and money to build an audience for a new novelist. Publishers are willing to spend that time and money when they believe they are building a new brand name for their house. Brand names attract a huge audience, whose loyalty sustains through book after book after book.

Once that audience exists, though, the sky's the limit. People who read fiction read their favorite writers, i.e., their favorite brands. And when they find a new favorite writer, they read everything that writer ever wrote—as well as everything he or she goes on to write in the future. They also like to tell their friends and recommend the book to book clubs they belong to! This makes successful novelists an excellent investment for publishers. It more than makes up for the initial investment required to build an author's name.

That's why it's not enough to show the publishing world you can write one great novel. You have to convince 'em you can do it over and over and over that you, too, are in it for the long haul and you can keep 'em turning pages through 10 or 20 books over 10 or 20 years.

Most important, you have to convince 'em you aren't just a good writer, but you're also a good storyteller.

The Never-Ending Story

Literary agent Don Maass, author of many novels as well as *The Career Novelist: A Literary Agent Offers Strategies for Success*, advises aspiring novelists to make the distinction between good writing and good storytelling. Artful language does not make good storytelling. Conflict does.

"John Grisham is not known as a great stylist, but he's a great storyteller," says Maass. "Take the opening scene of *The Firm*. It's just a job interview, but it's riveting because of the conflict. In a Grisham novel, there's conflict on every page, and conflict keeps readers turning the page."

Forget Dickens!

According to Maass, the biggest mistake many fiction writers make is to rely on nineteenth-century storytelling techniques—techniques that no longer engage today's fiction readers.

"I see so many manuscripts that begin with long, rambling descriptions, descriptions that would be great in a novel published in 1890, but not in a novel published in this era of MTV," says Maass.

What works today is the novel that's written cinematically. Film and TV storytelling have become the vernacular for audiences the world over. Not only does cinematic storytelling resonate with your readers, it also attracts film and TV interest, which not only increases your appeal to prospective publishers but ultimately increases your potential audience exponentially.

Elmore Leonard, author of dozens of best-selling novels over more than 30 years, admits it was the film version of his novel *Get Shorty* that made him truly famous.

"When I meet somebody, and I tell them I'm a writer, and they've never heard of me—I ask them if they've seen *Get Shorty*. 'Oh, yeah,' they'll say, 'great movie.'"

With the success of the movie *Get Shorty* and then the book and movie sequel *Be Cool*, Elmore Leonard won a new audience—an audience far greater than the book audience. The movie also brought Leonard more readers, making him a bigger brand-name author than ever. (For more on adapting novels to the screen, see Linda Seger's *The Art of Adaptation* or catch the Bravo TV show *Page to Screen*.)

Writing in a cinematic way helps you get your start in the book business and sets the stage for crossing over into other media as well.

Read, Read, Read

So where do you go to learn twenty-first-century storytelling techniques? Surprise! Go to a bookstore.

"The best course is also the least expensive," says Maass. He advises his clients to study today's great storytellers. "Read, study, and analyze. Then write your own powerful stories—stories with conflict on every page. Tell the best damn stories that you can."

We'll take Maass's advice one step further: read books about writing written by writers you admire. We like Barbara Shoup and Margaret Love Denman's *Novel Ideas: Contemporary Authors Share the Creative Process.* It includes long interviews with best-selling authors such as Tony Hillerman and Wally Lamb and goes into great detail about plot, dialogue, developing characters, and, of course, dealing with editors!

Writing Is Rewriting

Joyce Carol Oates likens writing the first draft of a novel to "building a house." The second draft, she says, is when "you decorate it." As she writes and publishes with blinding speed and shows no signs of slowing down, her metaphor is worth adopting as your credo.

Just as a house is not a home until you've moved in, furnished it, and invited friends and family over, a manuscript is not a novel ready for public viewing until you've rewritten it. Be prepared to do at least three drafts:

- ◆ A first draft to get the story down
- ◆ A second draft to refine the story, capitalize on its strengths, eliminate its weaknesses, and layer meaning and theme
- ◆ A final polish for language and style

As we've noted, writing good fiction isn't easy. Don't panic if you know your work needs revising but have no clue where or how to begin. There are people out there who can help you figure out what you need to do to make your story shine.

Take It to the Next Level

The days of Maxwell Perkins—the famously nurturing and hands-on editor at Scribner's for Ernest Hemingway, Thomas Wolfe, F. Scott Fitzgerald, and others—are gone. Gone are the editors who discover a diamond in the rough in the *slush pile*

def•i•ni•tion

The **slush pile** is where all the unsolicited manuscripts are piled, waiting to be returned.

and then spend months, even years helping the writer rewrite until the manuscript is ready for publication. Editors today don't have the time or the energy for that sort of intensive editorial work that their predecessors such as Perkins gave to such raw young luminaries as Fitzgerald, Wolfe, and Marjorie Kinnan Rawlings.

If you're thinking agents have taken over where editors have left off, think again. While it's true that some agents do develop close working editorial relationships with their authors—Al Zuckerman and Ken Follett come to mind—most do not. Agents are first and foremost salespeople; their job is to sell your work, not edit and revise it.

Still, you can find professionals who can help you make sure your manuscript is publisher-ready before you send it out the door. Find an experienced editor who will critique your work, suggest revisions, and help polish your prose. Ask your writing friends and any publishing professionals you may know in the book business for referrals; you can also look online and in industry publications. Be sure to choose an editor who has experience in your genre. Remember that word-of-mouth is the usually best recommendation; ask for references. Rates vary, but you'll find ballpark ranges for editing fees in the *Writer's Market*, at the National Writers Union, and online. Also check out Appendix C, which lists lots of good resources.

Ready, Set, Query

Okay, so you, the great storyteller, have written a great novel with an engaging protagonist. There's conflict on every page. The ending not only satisfies your readers, but it leaves them screaming for a sequel. You've pounded out several hundred pages readers won't be able to turn fast enough—and rewritten those pages until they sing.

Congratulations, you wrote a novel. Now take that 12-pound doorstop and put it away where you can't see it (and the dog can't eat it).

What? After we insist you write the whole novel first, now we tell you to put it away?

Exactly. The last thing anyone in publishing wants to do is read a 12-pound manuscript from an unknown writer. Agents and editors are drowning in them. All those publishing cartoons you've seen in *The New Yorker*, the ones with the editor sitting behind a desk mounded high with papers, are true. You have to sell these people on the idea of reading your hefty tome. That's where your query letter comes in.

Targeting your queries should reveal better results than the shotgun approach. Seek out those editors and agents most likely to appreciate your story, and query them first. You'll find their names on the acknowledgments page of your favorite books and/or the books most like your own. You can also find them in industry publications such as *Publishers Weekly* and the online Publishers Lunch, both of which feature deals made in the fiction business. Find out who's representing/buying novels like your own—and put them at the top of your to-be-queried list.

Did you read Chapters 7 and 8? They were good introductions to what comes next, especially for you. (If you didn't, go read them now.)

Introducing the Mighty You

Your query letter is your major sales tool. It's a one-page letter that sells an agent on taking a chance on you. Your query must convince your quarry to invest several minutes, hours, and even days evaluating your novel—all this on the off-chance that the time invested will pay off. Remember, few pay agents a salary. They invest hundreds of hours looking at stuff in the hopes that they can find a writer who will someday bring in the dough via royalties.

All that in one page, huh? It can be done. The trick is to keep the query simple, sweet, and sell, sell, sell. Here's how you break it down.

First Paragraph: What Kind of Book You've Written

You've written a 55,000-word mystery set in Jamaica at a Club Med titled *Dead Men Don't Date*. Skip the cute introductions; get straight to the point by describing the genre, your concept, and a sentence or two about the plot.

The only exception is if you've met the agent at a writers' conference or you've been referred by a mutual friend or colleague. If so, mention that first. As with every business, publishing is a business of people. Any kind of personal connection counts.

Second Paragraph: What Your Book Is About

Dead Men Don't Date is a story about young, unpublished romance novelist Melissa Manhattan, who escapes the cold, slushy, January streets of her native New York City in search of sun, sex, and a multibook contract at a writers' conference in Aruba—only

Slush Pile

You won't make it very far if you do any of the following: hand-write your query letter, fail to send it to an agent who represents fiction, spell the agent's name wrong, or spell anything wrong. And please, don't say "fiction novel." It's repetitively redundant.

to wake up and find the publishing industry's leading sleaze-bag agent dead in her king-size Club Med bed. Through a combination of wits, pluck, and an uncommon knowledge of deadly voodoo poisons, our girl Melissa solves the murder, saves the life of the biggest independent romance publisher in the business, and lands a six-figure contract as well as a very attractive and well-connected publicist—not to mention bringing the murderer (a disturbed ghost-writer driven to the edge after years of putting his sexy prose into lesser writers' mouths) to justice.

Third Paragraph: Why Only You Could Write This

You grew up in New York, where your mother worked as a secretary at a big publishing house. You spent your summers in the Caribbean helping your father with his life's work, the cataloging and classifying of voodoo poisons. You have met a sleaze-bag agent and personally know two ghostwriters committed to mental institutions for the foreseeable future.

Fourth Paragraph: Other Impressive Stuff

You studied creative writing in college and wrote your Master's thesis on "The Importance of Poisons in Agatha Christie's Poirot Novels." After school, you worked for a couple of years as a reporter for the *Bronx Cheer*. You have published a number of short stories in the mystery magazines, both print and online. You serve as president of your local Sisters in Crime chapter. You are already hard at work on book two of the Melissa Manhattan series, *Dead Men Don't Call You Back*.

Fifth Paragraph: How to Reach You

You would be happy to send a copy of the manuscript for review; the agent should feel free to contact you at home or at work anytime. You have also enclosed a SASE— as well as your cell phone number and e-mail address. You look forward to hearing from him.

How Hard Can That Be?

Writing an effective query letter ultimately depends on salesmanship. For some reason, many people who can write great novels cannot write a decent sales letter. So if you feel your efforts to sell yourself and your work on paper fall flat, don't despair. Enlist the help of a copywriter friend or colleague to help you punch up your pitch. If you don't know anyone with that skill, hire someone. Look in the Yellow Pages or online for freelance advertising copywriters.

Remember, this one-page query letter is your foot in the door. It's worth investing more than a little time and money on perfecting your query. So when the door opens up a crack, you want to slip in a Gucci loafer, not those old sneakers you wore to paint the front room.

Also be sure to enclose a SASE, and sign all the query letters yourself.

An Invitation for a Proposal!

You come home from a hard day at work to see the message light blinking on your phone. Could this be the call? Has your query letter hooked an agent?

"I'd really like to see more," the agent says. "Can you send me a proposal?"

A proposal for a novel? If you read the chapter on nonfiction proposals, you now know all the different types of information that go into one of those. But what on earth do you put into a fiction proposal?

Very little, actually. Here's what goes into a fiction proposal:

- A *synopsis* of the novel

- The first 50 pages of the novel, or the first 3 chapters, whichever is longer

- Information about the author

def•i•ni•tion

Before an agent or editor will read your whole novel, he will want to read your synopsis. A **synopsis** is a 10-page long summary of your novel, written in the present tense, in the third person. It spells out the plot of your novel in an effective and readable way.

Unlike a nonfiction proposal, you won't have to spend countless hours analyzing the competing titles. Novels are generally understood to stand on their own, not to compete directly with similar novels on similar themes. You won't have to do research and include data on the market for the novel. The market is understood—it's people who read fiction.

So let's see how to put together a synopsis.

Summarize, Please

Why do you need to write a synopsis if you've already written the whole novel? Here again, it's a question of time. Agents and editors aren't going to plow through your 12-pound manuscript to see if your plot is full of holes. They can figure it out by skimming a 1- to 10-page synopsis. They also don't have room in those cluttered offices for an extra 30 chapters when they can tell in 50 pages or less that your characters play like cardboard cutouts and that your pacing is wildly uneven.

Like the query, writing a synopsis is an art all its own, with its own set of rules.

Hook 'Em Again?

Entertaining and scintillating? How can you condense an entire novel into a few pages, much less be entertaining and scintillating? Granted, it's not easy to breathe life into such a stilted narrative, but it can be done. Many writers spice up their synopses with snippets of dialogue and small bits of scenes. Whatever you can think of doing to add flair to your synopsis, do it.

Approach the writing of your synopsis as if you were writing a treatment for the movie adaptation of your novel. Not only will a cinematic style ensure that your synopsis is engaging and compelling, it will make it that much easier to sell the film rights later.

Sample Synopses

Did you join the local writers' group for your genre? Do you attend workshops as part of a romance writers group or a mystery writers group? Or do you meet with a group of local writers at the Starbucks down the street to swap tales? Ask your friends if they have sample synopses you could see. Study these synopses and then write one for your book that outshines them all!

If they're interested, some agents, such as co-author Sheree, will request the whole manuscript in lieu of a proposal. Even then, it's necessary to include at least a one-page synopsis and bio. Sheree likes to request the whole book for several reasons:

- So she can finish the book while it's still fresh in her mind if it's got her hooked after Chapter 3

- So **she can** be sure the novel is complete

- So she can be sure the novel keeps her attention through the end

Exclusivity

There's a lot of confusion about this topic. When an agent asks for exclusivity, it means she wants to be the only agent to consider your manuscript (see Chapter 11). If an agent does ask for exclusivity, be sure she gives you a reasonable time frame for a response. Ask exactly what she expects, and be sure you understand her terms, as each one might be different. Sheree usually offers a 4-week turnaround for a proposal or manuscript in exchange for an exclusive first look at a manuscript.

Giving an agent exclusivity does not mean you are then required to use that agent if the agent likes your manuscript. She is still going to have to click with you. The agent should show some passion for your project, offer you terms for representation that you find reasonable, be able to give you references, and be able to do whatever is reasonably necessary to make you comfortable that he or she is the best agent for you. If not, move on to the next!

The Least You Need to Know

- With fiction, you must write the entire novel before trying to get an agent or a publisher.

- Be sure to rewrite and polish your manuscript before sending it out. If you need professional help to take your first draft to the next level, hire an experienced editor to advise you on the rewrite.

- Write your novel in a cinematic way to increase its marketability.

- Never send the entire manuscript unsolicited; try first with a short query letter.

- Your query letter should include a short description of your novel.

- Your proposal should include a 1- to 10-page summary of the novel and either the first 50 pages of the manuscript or 3 complete chapters.

Part 3

Romancing the Stone: Getting a Book Contract

Whether your goal is to find an agent first or to go directly to a publisher yourself, the information is all here in Part 3. Here you find great tips on how to find agents and even how to get agents to find you! But if that doesn't work, you learn the protocol for approaching publishers without an agent. Whether children's publishers, university publishers, or even self-publishing, there is much to be learned about the different styles of publishing books.

We also help you understand two critical areas of the publishing process: what goes on in an editorial meeting and how to understand a standard publishing contract.

Chapter 10

What's an Agent for, Anyway?

In This Chapter

◆ Why writers use agents

◆ Why agents and editors "do lunch"

◆ How agents negotiate contracts

◆ Some common contract pitfalls

◆ How agents help you stay on the publisher's good side

You've written a tantalizing query letter, and your bulletproof book proposal is put together. The outline for the book (or the entire novel itself) is solid and waiting for a buyer. You're ready to go. But wait! You worked darn hard on all this—why should you cut an agent in on the deal now? Because writers write, and agents sell.

Whether you write fiction or nonfiction, it's hard enough going about the business of writing without also having to deal with the actual business end of it. Very few writers are really equipped to both let their imaginations soar on the blank page and at the same time concentrate on trying to market their work.

Here are a few quick reasons why writers use agents:

◆ Contacts

◆ Contracts

◆ Money

◆ Guidance

◆ Subrights

Friends in High Places

Agents devote much of their time to cultivating contacts with editors and publishers. They do lunch; they circulate at book parties; they attend conferences; they share cabs. Agents make it their business to get to know *acquisitions editors* at all the major publishing houses. Agents learn what kinds of books each and every editor likes and, more important, just what kind of book each editor never wants to see again!

def•i•ni•tion

The editors who are responsible for bringing in new books are called **acquisitions editors**. They are often called senior editors, but they may also be editors or editors at large. The titles vary from house to house and generally depend on the level of responsibility or the amount of experience an editor has.

Each publishing house has its specialties. Some large houses publish a vast array of books on a vast array of topics. Random House, for instance, has a mind-boggling number of imprints, each with a different personality and focus. A smaller publisher such as New World Library, on the other hand, is known for spiritual, New Age, and personal-growth titles. Agents keep track of who publishes what, who went out of business, and even which publishing companies seem to be nicer to their authors than others. This is the sort of specialized knowledge an agent can use to sell your book to the right publisher. And editors do jump ship a lot. They change jobs, change careers, go on maternity leave, and quit to write their own books. A good agent tracks the circulation patterns of all the editors while remaining a constant contact for the author.

When Agents and Editors "Do Lunch"

Lucky for agents—particularly poor, starving agents—this is the only business around where the buyer wines and dines the seller. This expensive practice alone should help convince you of the important role agents play in the publishing business.

Publishers value the knowledge, judgment, and wisdom of agents enough to ply them with meals. Just as authors can't effectively do their job of writing while also being their own agents, publishers can't do their jobs of acquiring and editing while at the same time screening a million writers and projects.

When an editor agrees to take a look at a project an agent is representing, he knows this is a professional project worth considering. The editor is relying on the fact that an agent is not likely to take on a project (investing hours of her own time, office help, and supplies) she doesn't believe to be of the highest quality. Editors rely on agents to do quite a bit of the screening and selecting for them.

What do they find to talk about during these long publishing lunches? That is where all your hard homework, all the information you dug up about the audience, the market, and the potential for your book comes in. The agent works to sell the editor on the potential of your book, combining her knowledge with the information you've supplied. In the publishing business, unwritten books are the stuff of dreams. Who knows where the next big thing will come from? Every agent, every editor, and every publisher hopes she has found it.

Experts Say

You might wonder how, if agents and editors are friends, they can negotiate contracts. "Agents and editors share such a love of books and the arts in general, that it's natural that they would become friends outside of work," says Natasha Graf, editor at McGraw-Hill. "While there's always an understanding of professionalism when it comes to negotiating contracts and acquiring projects, I think it can benefit the author if the agent and editor are friends. The agent really learns what the editor likes and then can try to match the author with the right person for the project."

A Hope and a Prayer

Does a book have an intrinsic value? Well, no. The value of an *intellectual property* is determined purely by taste (the editor's) and perceived need. It isn't like a diamond or a vacuum cleaner, something that has an expected value in the marketplace.

A book is more like Jackie O's toilet brush or Mark McGuire's seventieth home-run baseball: it's worth whatever someone is willing to pay. So over lunch, agents get editors excited about the books they have for sale. Agents also listen closely as the editor describes the kinds of books he hopes to find.

def•i•ni•tion

What is an **intellectual property?** A house owned by a college professor? No, it's a legal term for, according to the *Random House Legal Dictionary,* "copyrights, patents, and other rights in creations of the mind; also, the creations themselves, such as a literary work, painting, or computer program."

"Is That the Best You Can Do?"

Well, the lunch meeting between your agent and the prospective editor was a great success. The agent sends over the proposal, the editor reads it, and eventually the editor calls your agent to make an offer. This doesn't happen that same afternoon, however.

Profit or Loss?

In Chapter 14, you'll get an inside look at what happens during editorial meetings. But before then, we'll just say that the editor needs to get the support and approval of a whole bunch of other folks—and to do what's known as a *P and L* (profit and loss statement) before he makes that call to your agent.

This profit and loss statement is used to estimate in advance what a publisher can expect to earn from the publication of a book.

Any Other Takers?

Agents often meet with several editors to raise interest in a project from several publishers. Let's pretend your agent has submitted your brilliant proposal to editors A, B, and C. Editors C and B are polite, but editor A is the only one who calls the agent with an offer. Editor A wants to be sure he is not "bidding against himself." If there is only one bid on the table, the agent does not have much leverage to get it raised. Agents do have a trick or two up their sleeves to try to maximize the publishers' offers and get the best possible deal for their author. This process is referred to as an auction and can take place over the course of an afternoon or a few tense days.

def•i•ni•tion

P and L stands for a profit and loss statement, which takes into account all the money that must be spent on a book, balanced against the money that can be expected from potential sales. A publisher hopes the P column outweighs the L column by a desired profit margin.

Let's not forget that an agent's work is done on "spec"—her income is solely based on *commission*. No sale, no commission; low sale, low commission. Your agent earns no money at all from representing you until your book is sold to a publisher. Then, depending on your

def•i•ni•tion

Literary agents work solely on **commission,** a percentage of the book's income.

agreement, she receives anywhere from 10 to 15 percent of your royalties and 15 percent of your advance. So it's possible for an agent to work long and hard, only to earn nothing if your book isn't sold. You can see why an agent will always try to get the best deal possible for you, the author—because at the same time, it's her deal, too.

Money, Money, Money

So the editor wants your book. Great! You get the call from your agent and begin dancing around the room shouting, "Show me the money!"

Just how much money can you expect? This is a sticky subject. Sadly, most American writers have rather small average yearly incomes. Around $10,000 a year is typical, and that may reflect a number of different income sources (magazine and newspaper articles, freelance copywriting, etc.) in addition to book royalties.

How much money you can expect depends. We've seen first-time advances for non-fiction books range anywhere from as low as $5,000 to as high as $100,000. You may only hear about the mega-advances, but that might be because they're so unusual, that makes them news. At a single meeting, a major publishing house might allocate $2 million to acquire 5 books—with $1.9 million going to a single title. A smaller publishing company might allocate as much as $50,000 to acquire 5 or more titles. If you really have a great background—a platform that includes a large speaking schedule, a newspaper column, a high-profile name, or a tremendous idea—the number will reflect that.

Experts Say

Life in New York has become so frantic that the traditional leisurely lunch hours have become a time to cram in as many meetings as possible. According to *The New York Times*, some agents and editors are doing multiple lunches in an effort to find that big book before someone else does. How does it work? A big agent sets himself up at the table and meets with one editor over the salad course, another editor over the main course, and yet another editor for dessert and coffee!

Megamarkets

The number could also be higher if you establish a ready market for your book. With *Christmas Miracles*, co-author Jennifer was able to establish how well Christmas books sold, how well books on miracles sold, and how well inspirational short-story books such as *Chicken Soup for the Soul* sold. All that research paid off—as did the passionate pitch her agent, Sheree, made at a Women in Publishing Christmas party.

Advances for Fiction

Advances for first-time novelists are generally on the low side, but if your book is perceived as a best-seller candidate and an auction ensues, the advance could go off the charts. From time to time, an unknown writer hits the million-dollar jackpot. It happens.

def•i•ni•tion

The money paid to an author upon signing a contract is called an **advance against future royalties.** That's money up front that will have to be earned back once the book is available for sale. An author's royalty account starts as a negative figure that reflects the advance. When the royalties earned surpass the amount advanced, an author begins to receive more money.

Double Indemnity

When agents negotiate contracts, the size of the advance is just one of many complicated issues. In Chapter 15, you'll walk through a typical publishing contract piece by piece.

Rely on Your Agent

Although agents negotiate contracts on behalf of the author, the agent does not sign the contract. The author does. But you shouldn't sign the contract until the agent is happy with it, until you have read it completely, and until you understand it. Your agent is there to explain the quirks of the contract. Don't be afraid to ask about any and all details.

Publishing agreements are sticky wickets, but thankfully (for agents and authors), they are all pretty much the same. An experienced agent is aware of the traditional traps and loopholes. Nobody, including most lawyers, knows publishing contracts like an agent. Agents know just when to push and when to back off.

Let's Do Another One, Just Like the Other One

Agents sometimes maintain "boilerplate" contracts with the publishing houses with which they do business. What does this mean to you? On other contracts, the agent has already gotten the house to agree to more free copies or a better royalty rate on special sales, or she's eliminated the option clause (which ties up the first look at your next book). The agent then has a boilerplate she can use with that house for future contracts.

> **Experts Say**
>
> Author and former lawyer Tim Perrin says that whenever you receive a first offer from a publisher, you should always say, "Oh? Is that all? I was thinking more like ...." Then name a figure substantially higher than what you've just been offered. "It's never failed for me," says Perrin. "I don't often get double or triple the amount first offered, but I always get a substantial increase. I make more money in those 10 seconds than I do in any part of writing."

After the Deal Is Done

So your contract has been negotiated and signed, and you and your editor have a direct relationship. Your editor will now guide you through the publishing process. Is your agent's job finished? Not by a long shot.

An agent is an experienced publishing player. She can help you learn the ropes so you, too, will be an experienced player. After the contract is filed in a drawer, the agent takes on these tasks:

- Getting the most from the publicity department
- Examining your royalty statements
- Ensuring you get paid properly
- Selling subrights and licenses for your book
- Assisting you and the editor in solving any major problems that might arise in revising or finishing the manuscript
- Being your book's greatest advocate

Good Cop/Bad Cop

And the best part of all is that your agent can be the bad guy. As an author, you want your editor to love you. You want to shy away from any kind of behavior that could damage your relationship with your editor. (More on this later in Chapter 19.) But what if you aren't happy?

Your agent can do the job! Call and tell him your concern, and ask him to speak on your behalf. You can sit back and let your agent air your complaints in such a way that you don't jeopardize your relationship with your publisher. Your agent is the bad cop. The agent can do the yelling (about the crummy cover design, the lack of a publicity campaign, or the slow royalty checks) while you sit back and bat your eyelashes.

> **Slush Pile**
>
> Don't ever pick up the phone and call the editor directly about a contract issue. This will make both your editor and your agent angry. Relax, and let your agent do her job.

Publishers are people, too. Even if your book is the best thing since *Gone with the Wind*, those with the power to help you will not put forth their best efforts if you alienate them. At any given time, a publishing house has lots of different books to peddle, so don't give it a reason to spend less time on yours. Your second most important job as a writer (after writing the best book you can) is to make the publisher love you and your book. Be as pleasant as you can. Let your agent do the unpleasant things.

Substance in Subrights

When an agent places a book with a publisher on behalf of an author, the most basic right the publisher acquires is the right to publish the manuscript in book form in the English language. Every other right associated with the book is considered a subright. Some typical subrights associated with the book are audio, video, book club, movie and—most important to an author with an agent—foreign rights.

Most agents maintain subagents in territories outside the United States for foreign sales and subagents in Hollywood for movie sales. When an agent withholds foreign or movie rights from the publisher, this means that—with or without the help of her subagent—the agent can license those rights directly to foreign publishers and movie studios.

If the agent and her subagent share a 20 percent commission for such sales, as is typical, this puts 80 percent of each sale (less taxes) directly into the author's pocket. When publishers keep movie, foreign, and other subrights, they may keep 25 to 50 percent of the sale and apply any proceeds against the author's unearned royalty account, thus depriving the author of additional monies for valuable subrights. Occasionally, it's to the author's advantage to allow the publisher to control subrights, such as, for example, when the publisher gives the author a fair percentage and aggressively goes after those sales.

Should You Get an Agent?

Now you know the full story. An agent's role goes far beyond brokering a profitable deal with a publisher.

We're not saying you need an agent because co-author Sheree is one. (And we're not saying that because Sheree is Jennifer's agent, either!) We're both writers, and we know a lot of other writers. We have seen all that can happen to writers in the rough-and-tumble world of book publishing. Get yourself a good agent, and you will have less to worry about.

Even in-house editors, like Jennifer, who know the ins and outs of the publishing business, use agents when they become authors.

How the heck do you find an agent? Move on to the next chapter, and we'll show you where they hide!

The Least You Need to Know

- ◆ Agents do many things, from negotiating a contract to guiding you through the publishing maze.
- ◆ Agents get to know editors and what kinds of books they want to publish.
- ◆ Books are intellectual properties and are worth what the highest bidder will pay. An agent is better equipped to handle the bidding.
- ◆ Standard boilerplate publishing contracts favor the publisher, not the author. An agent knows the ins and outs.
- ◆ Agents can help you maintain a good relationship with your editor and publisher.
- ◆ When an agent controls the subrights, the author is likely to make more money.

Chapter 11

Finding and Working With an Agent

In This Chapter

- Where do they hide, those agents?
- Tips on choosing among the many
- Fiction or nonfiction?
- Agent etiquette
- Landing a live one!

With any luck, we convinced you in Chapter 10 that you need an agent, particularly if you are a first-time author and want to sell your book idea to a large national publisher. If you've decided an agent is the way to go, read on. In this chapter, we tell you how to find a good one.

Members of the Club

So how do you tell if an agent is the real thing? A large percentage of established agents in the business are members of the Association of Author's Representatives (AAR), the largest professional association of literary and dramatic agents for authors. To get a list of all its members or search for an agent by name or interests, visit the association's free website at www.aar-online.org or write to PO Box 237201, Ansonia Station, New York, NY 10023.

What does this list tell you? That the agents listed are what they say they are: experienced literary agents. To become a member of the AAR, you must be a well-established agent with several contracts negotiated on behalf of authors with major publishing houses. In addition, you must agree to abide by the AAR's strict Canon of Ethics. You must also pass a rigorous application and screening process.

Hot Off the Press

In their Canon of Ethics, the members of AAR pledge loyal service to their clients' needs. A member's accounts must be open to the client at all times with respect to the client's transactions, and members promise not to represent both buyer and seller in the same transaction. The AAR believes that the practice of agents charging clients or potential clients for reading and evaluating literary works (including outlines, proposals, and manuscripts) is subject to serious abuse that reflects adversely on the profession. Current and future members may not charge for reading and evaluating literary works and may not benefit from the charging of such fees by any other person or entity.

Just How Much Is This Gonna Cost?

It costs nothing to have an agent who's a member of AAR read your material. Other agents may charge reading fees. Most of the reference books that list agents note whether they charge a reading fee, and if so, how much.

Reading Fees? No

The fact that an agent charges a reading fee does not necessarily mean he or she is taking advantage of you. In fact, if you ever got a glimpse at the towering stack of unsolicited material that floods into agents' offices every day, you might understand the idea behind a reading fee. Remember, agents don't make any money at all until they sell your project.

But the AAR believes that reading fees can easily lead to corrupt practices (like charging for books they might never read, or charging for needless editing or ghostwriting on a book they knew was not salable), so do try to stay away from paying a reading fee.

Slush Pile

Rather than paying reading fees to an agent, hire yourself an independent editor, or sign up for a writing class if you want your writing evaluated. Agents either represent you or do not represent you. We don't think you need to pay someone to evaluate your work in exchange for representation. And by all means, do not pay an agent a fee to represent you or to place your manuscript with a publisher. Agents collect commissions, not fees.

They're Agents, Not Readers

Not only do most literary agents not charge reading fees, but they also do not provide "reader's reports." An agent will simply tell you whether your manuscript is suited to his agency. If the manuscript doesn't interest him enough to represent it, he certainly won't take the time to tell you what he thinks is wrong with it. But if he does want to represent your book, he will take the time to help you make it better.

The hard truth is this: if all the agents you approach who don't charge fees turn you and your project down, it's pretty likely that the publishers are going to have the same reaction. So if this happens, spend your money on a good book doctor, a writing class or seminar, or an independent editor. All these will help you improve your work and its chances of someday being published.

Hot Off the Press

"Book doctors should respect your confidentiality," says Jerry Gross, a book doctor himself. If you use a book doctor, no one needs to know about it. Other than the confidentiality question, what else should you ask a book doctor before hiring one? First and foremost, be sure she is skilled in your area. "If you are writing a sci-fi novel, be sure the book doctor critiques or edits sci-fi novels, too. You don't want someone with an expertise in romance novels." Ask for references—and check them! And always be suspicious of someone who "guarantees" that if you work with her, she will get you an agent or a publisher. Jerry Gross is a member and co-founder of the IEG (Independent Editors Group). His website is www.bookdocs.com.

Where to Find Help

Many good book doctors and freelance editors can help you with your proposal, and agents sometimes can give you the names of such people. So might members of local writers' groups. Then there's the Editorial Freelance Association (EFA), a nonprofit organization whose members are all freelance editors. Check out EFA's website at www.the-efa.org, or call 212-929-5400. Another good group of editors can be found at www.wordsintoprint.com.

Screening Agents

Are all good agents members of the AAR? Are all members of the AAR good agents? Many good agents are not members of the AAR and don't charge fees. But evaluating them may prove difficult without checking with an association.

After an agent has offered to represent you, but before you sign up, feel free to ask for names and phone numbers of other clients. The agent should happily let you speak to some of his clients to get a better sense of who they are. If an agent is reluctant to hook you up with any other clients, take this as a red flag.

> **Slush Pile**
>
> You owe it to yourself and your book to be rigorous in your evaluation of a potential agent. Do most of your early research through books, online, and via any personal sources you might have. Don't call and ask agents for their biographies or the names of potential clients until they have offered to represent you. After they have offered to represent you, it is perfectly proper to ask questions.

Not sure what kinds of questions you should ask an agent before agreeing to let him represent you? Here are a few questions that will help you sound him out:

- How long have you been in business as an agent?

- Do you have specialists at your agency who handle television and movie rights?

- Do you represent other authors in my area of interest?

- What is your commission?

- Do you issue 1099 (nonemployee) tax forms at the end of the year?

- What kinds of books have you sold lately?

Where to Look for Agents

So where else do they hide, these agents? Co-author Sheree would like to say that all the good agents have offices in New York City (guess where she has an office?), but she would be lying. New York agents might have an easier time accessing New York editors face to face, but excellent agents live all around the country. Agents outside the Big Apple make frequent trips to New York. They pack their appetites in their carry-ons and gang up their breakfasts, lunches, dinners, drinks, and coffee dates with as many publishers as they can.

Besides checking the membership list of the AAR, you can find agents several other ways.

Look in a Book

Three great books list agents: *Literary Market Place (LMP)*; *Jeff Herman's Guide to Book Publishers, Editors, and Literary Agents*; and *The Writer's Digest Guide to Literary Agents*. The *Literary Market Place* is an expensive professional reference. Though it's full of information, only one of the many sections in it is devoted to agents. The agent listings in the *LMP* don't give any information beyond name, address, phone number, and whether the agent is a member of the AAR.

Jeff Herman's Guide to Book Publishers, Editors, and Literary Agents is put together by literary agent Jeff Herman. He's been doing it for the last 10 years or so, and he includes lots of personal and professional information about the agents he lists. Each agent listing includes the agent's description of the type of book he or she likes to represent and the type of book he or she never wants to see again. If you're just beginning your search for an agent, Herman's book is great. Be sure to get the most current edition available because the listings change every year.

The Writer's Digest's Guide to Literary Agents lists more than 500 agents who "sell what you write." It's concise, is kept up to date, and is an excellent resource not just for finding agents, but also for learning about the publishing industry.

Face to Face

A great way to find an agent is through a recommendation from a friend or colleague, particularly a published friend or colleague. But what if you don't know any other writers? Get thee to a writers' conference!

In any given month, somewhere around the country, a writers' conference is being held. Most organizers of writers' conferences arrange to have a few agents on hand for potential authors to meet. These meetings are invaluable. Not only do they give you a chance to shake a live agent's hand, but you also can often arrange for personal appointments with agents to discuss your project. This is time you wouldn't be able to get from them on the phone with a cold call. If you're serious about writing, writers' conferences are never a waste of time. They're especially useful for authors who write in a particular genre, as some conferences specialize in genres, such as mystery, romance, and sci-fi. The Guide to Writers' Conferences & Workshops at www.shawguides.com is a fabulous source for writers. It provides more than 600 detailed conference and workshop descriptions, including upcoming dates, faculty, and programs. We've included a list of conferences, many of which co-authors Sheree and Jennifer have addressed, on the CD.

Making the Most of Writer's Conferences

All writer's conferences are not created equal. Many are large affairs with lots of writing craft workshops and keynote speakers. Many exist for the simple purpose of introducing prospective authors to lots of agents. Whatever their purpose, there is much to be gained from almost every conference. At the very least, it is a place where authors can learn about the writing and publishing process and meet other authors at different stages in the process.

The important thing when attending a conference where agents are present is not to rush yourself to the point where you think you need to finish the novel you started last Thursday or write a book proposal in 1 day just because you'll have the opportunity to discuss it with an agent. Agents are used to getting mail and e-mail in their offices long after the conference is a distant memory. If they're not in business that long, you'd be wise to select another agent, anyway.

> **Hot Off the Press** _____
>
> When you do get a chance to meet an agent at a writer's conference, how does it work? It can be likened to speed dating, in which you have a limited amount of time to make a good impression. Most appointments are for 15 or 30 minutes, and you should arrive with your best material in hand and a well-practiced speech about your project and why it should be published. Like a speed date, this is not the time to go into heavy background on your life, but rather stick to what will sell your project and you as a potential client. It also gives you a chance to see agents up close and get a feel for who you'd most like to work with.

Frequently conferences do present authors a chance to pitch their work to agents. Please keep in mind that pitching your work is not necessary, though. The purpose of the pitch is to see if the agent wants to see your proposal or manuscript. It's important to be concise. Just say enough to achieve that goal. So many times, Sheree says, an author will start off with a wonderful pitch and then ramble on and on long after Sheree exhibited enthusiasm and requested the material. If an agent requests your material, stop pitching and just find out where to send the material and what to expect in terms of a response. You may be great at query letters and your book may be fabulous, but if you're someone who tends to get tongue-tied in a one-on-one, skip the pitch and absorb information. You don't have to pitch anyone at all. Most books that end up in bookstores are the result of a written query or proposal and never got verbally pitched by anyone.

And if editors from publishing houses are present at the conference, listen to whatever they have to say but don't pitch your books to them. Before approaching editors, learn about the publishing process and try to find the perfect agent who will do the pitching for you.

> **Experts Say**
>
> "Writers need to remember that the writing you do *about* your writing is as important as the writing itself," says Katharine Sands, agent at the Sarah Jane Freymann Literary Agency in New York City and agent provocateur for *Making the Perfect Pitch: How to Catch a Literary Agent's Eye.*

"I'd Like to Thank My Agent"

Don't know any writers? Can't get to a writers' conference? Well, you can open a book, right? That is a great place to find agents! Take a book, any book, off the shelf. Open it to the acknowledgments page. Not all books have such a page, but many (if not most) do. This is where the author thanks his family for their patience, his editor for her guidance, and his agent for all those lunches.

Looking in the acknowledgments is a great tactic for finding an agent, particularly when you need to find one who represents books in your area. Writing a health book? Look inside the health books you admire. Writing a romance novel? Check out recently published romances. This method helps you find the agent who might be open to your type of writing. Does the author thank everyone in the world but her agent? Hmmm … must have been an oversight.

Eeny, Meeny, Miney, Mo …

So you've looked inside your favorite books. Your list has arrived from the AAR, and you met eight great agents at a writers' conference last weekend. You've highlighted, cross-checked, and pondered the selections. You know which agents represent your area, and the list is longer than George Clooney's little black book. Do you have to just choose one? No! You're in luck. It is perfectly acceptable to send *multiple queries*, or queries to more than one agent at one time.

Still, you want to be somewhat selective about whom you send your precious queries to. What if they all responded at once and they all said "Yes"? Select your hottest prospects first.

Exclusive Territory

When an agent does respond and requests more material from you, she might also ask for an *exclusive* for a limited amount of time; 3 to 4 weeks is standard. (See the later "You Hooked One!" section for more on exclusives.) What does an exclusive mean? It means that for the next 3 to 4 weeks, she can study your material closely and not have to worry that you might be swiped out from under her by another agent.

If an agent chooses you, do you have to choose her? No. But realistically, if someone does want to represent you and offers you a reasonable author/agent agreement (and if she doesn't seem obnoxious), well, why not? Don't try to interest an agent you really don't want. You will waste both your time and hers.

The Good Agent

The best things to look for in an agent include the following:

- ◆ An established reputation
- ◆ A reputation for selling books in your field
- ◆ Accessibility by phone (after she's become your agent)

♦ A manner that lends itself to comfortable communication

♦ A passion about her work—and about yours

If you can't find all these qualities in an agent who responds to you, move on down your list until you do.

Are You Really Ready?

How do you know when you're ready to begin querying agents? You're ready if you have two things: a well-written query letter and a polished proposal for nonfiction or a polished manuscript for fiction. If these elements are in place, get started!

Fiction

If you're writing fiction, don't even think about querying agents until you're satisfied that your novel is the best it can be. You'll hear from time to time about first-time novelists selling a novel for a million dollars. It happens, but rarely. What you might not realize, though, is that although this is the first book that writer has sold, it's probably not the first book he has written. Many writers write 2, 3, or 10 novels before selling one.

Novelists write and write, regardless of whether they'll get published. True novelists usually get published, eventually. But don't send something to an agent just because you worked hard on it or are sick of looking at it! Send it because it's good. Don't ask an agent to decide whether it's good; ask discriminating colleagues, teachers, and editors for their honest opinions first. Take praise from family and friends (who may be biased or who don't want to hurt your feelings) with a large grain of salt.

Slush Pile

No matter how brilliant you think your book idea is, if you don't have the written material to back it up, you will fail. Do not approach an agent or a publisher with an idea for a book until you have something in writing—your writing!

Sometimes novelists need to put their novels aside and let them sit for a while. Then they go back to them with a fresh perspective and reevaluate them. Very often authors come back to their first novels years later and say, "Oh my gosh, what was I thinking?"

Nonfiction

For nonfiction, you can submit before you've got the entire book written. As you learned in Chapter 8, nonfiction is usually sold on the basis of a book proposal, a table of contents, and a representative sample chapter. If a publishing house likes what it sees in a proposal and decides to publish it, you have a deal. There are several models for paying out advances—some publishers pay half the advance upon signing a contract and half upon receipt of an acceptable manuscript. Others might break that up into smaller sums for milestones such as a third on signing, a third on completion of the first half of the book, and a third upon delivery of the manuscript. A manuscript is deemed acceptable when it matches the promises in your proposal, as reflected in the contract description.

When you have a good nonfiction proposal together, go ahead and start querying agents. If you haven't yet started your sample chapter, don't worry. Start it soon, but don't let it hold you back. If an agent is interested in your query and then asks to see more, you don't want her to have to wait too long. She might forget you!

> **Slush Pile**
>
> Although most nonfiction books require only a book proposal, there is one instance in which you will need more. Creative nonfiction books that are literary memoirs (such as *Angela's Ashes*) require a more fictionlike approach. You can't sell creative nonfiction with a bare-bones nonfiction proposal. Like a novel, you might need to write the whole book or a substantial portion first.

Try, Try Again

What if an agent looks at your proposal and tells you it still needs more work? She might tell you exactly where she thinks it is weak and how to improve it. Or she might think your proposal is so weak that you need to hire help and suggest that you work with a book doctor. (See more on book doctors earlier in this chapter and also in Chapter 8.)

Big Name, Superb Credentials

You might not have to wait until a proposal is done before querying agents. If you have superb professional credentials, such as a recognizable name, you might not have to wait. Write a strong query letter and see what kind of reaction you get from agents. It might be that an agent will be able to link you with a co-writer for the project. The agent might also be able to guide you in the proposal process.

Shopping Yourself

If you decide to try to place your book first without an agent, don't shop the project to all the publishers in town and then try to find an agent after you have a stack of rejection letters in hand, no matter how good your project is. Agents can't go back to the same publishers; if a publisher has passed on a project already, an agent will feel awfully foolish when the editor points it out—and it will come back to haunt you. Come clean with agents about which publishers have passed.

> **Slush Pile**
>
> If you use a book doctor or other kind of professional in preparing your proposal, and the book finds a publisher, you need to be sure your finished book does not disappoint the publisher. If the publisher bought your project based on a proposal that had help, be extra sure your book meets or exceeds the expectations set in that proposal. Don't promise one thing and deliver another. Many publishers have been burned by books that didn't match the quality or content of the proposal. In cases of extreme differences in the quality of writing between the proposal and the finished manuscript, the publisher has the right to hire a book doctor to fix it and charge the cost to you.

Return to Sender

Don't send your unsolicited query letter via certified or registered mail. The agent will think he's being sued! Seriously, you don't want to look overcautious or paranoid. Portray yourself like the professional you are.

Once again, we remind you of the importance of including a self-addressed, stamped envelope (SASE) with your correspondence to agents. This simple step can make all the difference in hearing back. If you leave out the SASE, the agent might assume you need no reply if the agent isn't interested. If that's the case, it's better to say so than to look sloppy.

Hold My Calls, Please

Unless (and until) you have an agent/author agreement with an agent, do not try to call a prospective agent on the phone. It will backfire. Approach agents the way they want to be approached: with a query and a SASE.

Agents need to evaluate your writing, not your speaking. So give them what they need and more: a great query letter that will pique their interest right away.

You Hooked One!

An agent received your query letter, read it, and then picked up the phone and called you! Hurrah! This is a good sign. But don't jump the gun and start writing your Pulitzer Prize acceptance speech yet. When an agent is intrigued by your query, she might call you to find out more about the project. She might also be calling to learn more about you as a person.

If the agent does want to go further, she might ask for an exclusive. Remember, this is when you assure her that she is the only one considering your project for a particular length of time. It's hard to say no to an agent on the phone, and that's why it's so important for you to have done your research before deciding which agents to query. You don't want to go to the dance with the wrong partner!

Another Darn SASE?

When an agent responds to your query and asks to see more material, include a SASE with your proposal. There's more at stake here, in fact. You're sending a lot of material, and you want it back if the agent decides to pass. To be sure your package was received, send it via an express service such as FedEx or UPS. You can track it by phone or online without calling the literary agent and looking anxious. The good old U.S. mail is just fine, too. According to statistics, 99.9999 percent of all mail is delivered properly.

For packages that weigh more than 1 pound, include return postage, either loose stamps for the proper postage or a check to cover the cost of an express service.

The Least You Need to Know

- ◆ Members of the Association of Author's Representatives (AAR) abide by a professional code of ethics and don't charge a reading fee.

- ◆ Find an agent through the membership of AAR, directories that list agents, or writers' conferences.

- ◆ Looking in the acknowledgments section of books you admire in your genre could lead you to a great agent, too.

- ◆ With nonfiction, query agents when your proposal is finished. With fiction, query when your novel is finished.

- ◆ Always include a self-addressed, stamped envelope (SASE) with any correspondence to an agent.

Chapter 12

What You Can Expect from an Agent

In This Chapter

- ◆ When an agent calls to represent you, what then?
- ◆ The agency/author agreement
- ◆ Is it okay to call now?
- ◆ Dealing with rejection letters
- ◆ Every author's first question
- ◆ How agents sell books

Was that a dream? Did an agent actually call and say, "I want to represent you"? You wrote a good query letter and you have a great idea, so stop pinching yourself! Right about now you might want to run to your agent's office and pop open a bottle of champagne, but you and your agent both have more work to do. If you thought your agent worked hard for you before, wait until you see what he or she is going to do for you now.

A Day in the Life of an Agent

What exactly do agents do all day? Let's peek in on Sheree's typical day:

An agent has to like doing a lot of things and doing them all at once. In the course of a day, I play many roles as an agent: editor, salesperson, social worker, and much more. On any given day, I may evaluate writers' works, call editors and pitch new projects, follow up on pending proposals publishers are considering, talk to a writer who is upset that her editor is quitting the business, receive an offer or two and haggle for more money and better terms, and negotiate the fine points of a contract already in the works. I do this all while the e-mails and the phones bring a new, never-ending stream of demands. Fortunately, I enjoy being busy.

Today was a typical day. It started out with a pile of papers on my desk and phone calls from yesterday that needed to be returned. Soon the big bag of mail arrived. I paused to see if there was anything particularly interesting, and yes, I struck pay dirt—literally. Right on top was the telling envelope that revealed an acceptance check for a book I thought would never see the light of day—a book on astrology. I rubbed my eyes in disbelief. The author had died tragically just before the book was due, with only three chapters to go. After many complications, the publisher had hired a writer (for a flat fee) to complete the last few chapters. She understood the author's idiosyncratic voice and the editor had an expertise in the area, so they were able to complete it so it would seem as if the author herself had done it. It was a sad and unusual situation, but it was still gratifying that the book would finally be published after everyone's hard work.

No time for reverie, though. Publishers called to ask questions about projects and register their interest; others called to make offers (my favorite calls). As Tim Perrin wisely advises, whatever they offer, pause and say, "Is that all?" There were a few contracts to negotiate, a few authors with requests ("Where are my contracts?" "Should I hire a publicist?" "Did you see that horrible cover?" and the ever popular, "When is the publisher sending the [expletive deleted] money?").

One thing I love about being an agent is successfully troubleshooting problems—well, in hindsight, anyway. It's extremely rewarding to save books from the cutting-room floor and keep authors and publishers from shooting each other.

A famous radio disk jockey whose career I followed all through high school and college called to see how I liked his proposal (based on my ideas). My associate and I had some feedback for him, as we were as eager as he was to get this into shape quickly so we could begin the process of submitting it to publishers. That is one of the special pleasures of being an agent. I'm not talking about hobnobbing with celebrities and teen idols; I'm talking about being in a position to come up with an idea, seek out an expert, and bring that idea to readers in the form of a book. Richard Roeper's *Ten Sure Signs a Movie Character Is Doomed* is based on my idea, and just last week I saw an installation at a museum in Milwaukee that inspired a book idea. I searched out the artist on the Internet (that was easy!), sent him an e-mail, and, wow, I got a positive response. He is interested in working with me. *Gulp.* I'm glad I wrote to him before I realized how important he was. His lengthy bio listed Emmys and other prestigious awards. Luckily, I hadn't been too intimidated to contact him. Most agents are continually on the lookout for high-profile folks they can approach with ideas.

As usual, several editors called with a shopping list of titles in search of authors. I am so pleased they think of me when they have such projects. I have placed at least 30 great authors with series books at the request of the publisher. Many if not most series titles (like the one you're reading!) come to fruition this way.

After I looked through the mail, read some queries and rejections, and glanced at some requested manuscripts, I fired up the computer to check my e-mail. There they were: the usual 100 e-mails of which only a small portion could be deleted out-of-hand. Here's something interesting: my Chinese agent is asking if we'd like to accept two offers from Chinese publishers for two of my authors. Hmmm … we just double-checked and saw that these two authors had already published with this agent in China. What's up? It turns out that there are at least two languages in China, and the rights are sold separately. So we are, happily, free to accept these offers. What do you know? A book can be sold in 10 countries and in 11 languages (at least).

As you might guess, my to-do list (I'm a Virgo) is miles long and the phone is ringing. Remember, every day my day looks like this, and so does the typical day of other agents in the business.

That's a typical day for an agent. Whew! But remember we said *you both* have work to do. So put down your champagne glass, because you have some things to take care of as well.

99 Percent Ready

It's rare that the manuscript or book proposal you sent in is 100 percent ready to go. Chances are, the agent will want to discuss some fine-tuning and changes. At the very least, you'll need to change the cover page to your manuscript or proposal. Remember, it has your name and address on the bottom. Now that you've got an agent, you'll need to drop your own information and add his.

"I Really Like It, but ..."

Fixing the cover page—that's no problem. But is this agent passionate about your project? Does she believe in your book? It's imperative that the person who is going to represent you to publishers feels confident about your book's prospects. If the agent has any doubts going in, you want to know about it.

Let's say your agent loves your project, but maybe she also has some changes she needs you to make before sending your book out to publishers. After all, what an agent sends out is her calling card. She must maintain a good reputation with publishers to stay active in the business. You must make your work as perfect as possible.

> **Slush Pile** _____
>
> Spelling mistakes are unacceptable under any circumstances. With the advent of "spell check," there is just no excuse for finding misspelled words in your manuscript or book proposal. But be careful—even spell checkers can work incorrectly. Read your manuscript for spelling and usage first—then use spell check.

Be Open to Changes

The agent might feel that the competition section of your proposal needs work. This might mean you need to strengthen your facts or do a quick double-check to be sure you haven't left out major titles.

She might also feel that you've been too hard on the competing titles and might risk alienating the publishers of those books you've maligned (who might have otherwise become your publisher).

Your new agent might also make recommendations on your author bio section. Perhaps you've been too humble about your accomplishments. Or perhaps you've been a touch arrogant and need to tone it down.

Whatever the agent suggests, feel free to discuss it with her. This is very important: discuss all changes. If an agent makes suggestions to your manuscript (about combining chapters, say, or dropping a section), you don't have to agree. Do not make any changes to your work you don't feel 100 percent good about. If you can't get the agent to see things your way, or vice versa, then perhaps this is not the agent for you. True, you've both wasted your time, but thank Heaven you discovered it early.

On the other hand, the agent does have quite a bit of experience in this area. Do try to be open-minded and understand what your agent's suggesting (and why). The agent has your best interests in mind and is trying to make your project as salable as possible because you really have only one shot at it. If the agent sends out a project that wasn't quite ready to go and everyone who sees it turns it down, that's the end of the road. Publishers seldom want to see the same project twice.

Love at First Sight

Now let's say you and your agent are completely simpatico. You see eye to eye about the book and agree on what's necessary to touch it up and make it ready. The conversation you had about your book energized both of you. You like the agent's manner. You can talk to her. She listens. Great, so what's next?

Call Other Authors

The agent might suggest that you call one or two of her other clients for a reference. This is a great way to learn more about what the agent is like to work with on a long-term basis. Take the numbers; it wouldn't hurt to call. In fact, if the agent doesn't offer this, you should bring it up.

Great Expectations

This is also a great time to find out more about how the agent works. Ask the agent to describe how she plans to sell your book. What's the process? And what more does she need from you? Here are a number of good questions to ask your agent:

- ◆ Will I need to make copies of the proposal or manuscript? How many copies?
- ◆ How many publishers do you plan to contact?
- ◆ Will I get copies of the rejection letters?
- ◆ Do you call the publishers to let them know my proposal is coming?
- ◆ Do you plan to submit to several publishers at once, or only one at a time (exclusively)?

Are there any wrong answers to these questions? Not really. But it's better to ask in advance about how the agent works than to grumble about it later.

The Agent/Author Agreement

The answers to "who does what?" might be found in the agent/author contract. This is an agreement the agent sends to you after you have agreed that she may represent your book.

Most times, the agent/author agreement covers just the one book. Ideally, an author hopes that one perfect agent will represent him forever. Just as ideally, agents long for clients whom they can represent profitably forever. But at this stage of the game, take it one book at a time.

In many ways, this is a trial run with an agent—an engagement, not a marriage. Maybe you're really just dating for a while. Hopefully, the relationship will turn out well—the agent will sell your book, and you two will get along famously. But you'll also want to continue to monitor the relationship after your book is successfully sold. Is the agent still communicating? Is she still passing along information as she receives it? If not, maybe the relationship should end.

Read the Fine Print

Examine the agent/author agreement carefully before you sign it. Be sure you understand all the terms and that they are acceptable to you. (You might want to look at the sample agreement on the CD.)

One of the things you might notice is that there is typically a charge for expenses such as postage, messengers, copying, and other office expenses. Most agents require that the author pay for these expenses. This charge is not to be confused with the reading fees discussed in Chapter 11. Some agents put a cap on such expenses. For instance, co-author Sheree caps these fees at $150 per book. Realistically, however, it could cost an agent several hundred dollars to sell a single book.

How are these fees collected? If your agent sells your book and receives an advance check from the publisher, the office fees are deducted (along with the agent's commission) before a check is sent to you. And if an agent hasn't had any luck selling your book after trying for a year or so, don't be surprised if you receive a bill in the mail one day.

So be sure you know what the fees could be. If the agreement doesn't mention office fees, ask.

"Hello, It's Your Author!"

You shouldn't call agents during the query process, but now that it's official, go ahead and call. You have a right to expect reasonable access to your agent, not to just shoot the breeze, but to be kept informed of everything the agent does on your behalf. Expect progress reports from time to time.

Your agent will be pleased if you respect his time. Call only when you need to, and try to group your questions. Better yet, send an e-mail or a fax with all your questions, and ask your agent to call you.

Do we make agents sound scary? They aren't really. But they are busy people who, like us all, have developed particular ways of working. You will get along nicely with your agent if you just accept that fact.

What's Going On?

Up to this point in your writing career, you have been in control. But from the time an agent starts to try to sell your project, the agent is now pretty much in control of what happens.

Here's what you hope is happening: the agent is calling editors to pitch your book. He's talking you and your book up as he lunches with editors. Throwing humility to the winds, he has all the top editors clamoring to see what you've written. He has written a glowing cover letter, which accompanies your proposal as it goes out to publishers that request it.

How long does the process take? It takes several weeks for editors to respond. The cover letter your agent sent along with your material might have requested a response within a certain time period. Sometimes agents include a sentence similar to this: "I'd like to have all offers in by January 30." But even with a clock ticking, editors tend to move slowly. (In Chapter 14, you'll get a glimpse at the inner workings of a publishing house to better understand the process.)

What is your agent doing while the days slip by without an answer? Making follow-up calls to check that the proposal arrived. The real purpose of the phone calls is to remind editors of their early interest in the project, of course. But so as not to appear pushy, more subtle tactics are employed.

Ante Up

If a publisher calls to express an interest in acquiring your book, the agent once again works the phones. Calls are placed to all the publishers that received the proposal, and the agent says: "Publisher X is interested in that book you liked so much, and I wondered if your house was still interested." This way, the editors are once again prodded into action. And such news might result in a larger offer because the second (or third or fourth) bidder has to beat what's already on the table.

The Rejection Blues

Realistically, most responses will be in the form of *rejection letters*. Even the best writers get rejection letters, so if it's any consolation, you're in fine company.

def•i•ni•tion

When an editor declines to pursue a book project, she sends out a **rejection letter**. Rejection letters sent directly to authors say little more than "no thanks." But rejection letters sent to agents might contain more information about why the editor turned it down.

Slush Pile

Rejections do hurt. But don't respond with a rebuttal in writing or a nasty phone message. You can easily make enemies in the publishing world with such loose-cannon behavior. Your agent will not be pleased, and editors will not be pleased. Try a big bowl of ice cream instead.

An agent can help you overcome the sting of rejection letters. Plain and simple, those letters hurt. They hurt you as the author, and no matter how many rejection letters your agent has seen in her career, they hurt her, too. Talk about it with your agent.

Should you even see your rejection letters? Yes. Here's what you can learn from them:

♦ How many publishers have seen your work

♦ Which publishers have seen your work

♦ What kind of a relationship your agent has with publishers

♦ What kinds of criticism your project is receiving

All this information will help you get better and will help increase your chances of getting published in the future. Are all the letters saying the same thing? If all editors say they don't see a market for your book, that might tell you something. If all the editors say there are too many similar titles already out there, that, too, might be sending you a message. And if it makes you feel better, pin your rejections up on the wall and toss darts at them.

One of Sheree's clients once asked for the original copies of two of his rejection letters. In one, the publisher said the proposed book was "too specific." In the other, the publisher said that the book was "too general." The author framed the letters side by side in his office. You'll be pleased to know this story has a happy ending: another publisher thought his proposal was just right, and his book was published!

No matter what you wind up doing with them, try to learn from those letters—and learn to deal with rejection. Consider it a personal growth experience.

Going Once, Going Twice ... Sold!

What if several publishers let your agent know that they plan to make an offer for your book? To get the best price for it (in other words, the biggest advance), your agent will plan an *auction*.

Here's how an auction works:

♦ Your agent chooses a date and alerts the interested publishers.

♦ Your agent may establish a *floor*, a minimum bid, or reserve the right to decline unacceptable bids.

♦ On the day of the auction, your agent calls the editors for their bids. (Not all editors will end up bidding.)

♦ As the number rises, the agent continues to call editors and inform them of the latest price.

♦ At the end of the day (or days), the editor with the highest bid gets your book.

def•i•ni•tion

When an agent has all interested publishers submit their bids on the same day, it's called an **auction**. This is the best way to get a high advance. The agent might also specify a minimum bid, called a **floor**.

An auction day can be very exciting for both the agent and the author. You'll find it hard not to call your agent every few minutes to check on things. Let your agent call you, though. She needs to keep those phone lines clear for editors with big checkbooks!

"How Much Can I Expect?"

This is the dreaded first question every new author asks an agent. And it's a question that's impossible to answer. The size of an advance depends entirely on the perceived size of the book's audience. It depends on how much the publishing house loves your book. It depends on how unique your book is. It depends on how many publishers are interested in your book. It depends on the timing of your book, too, and how many competing titles are out there.

Other factors that can affect the size of an advance include whether the publishing industry is on an upswing or a downswing. The size and power of the publishing house that wants to buy your book figures in, too. Another factor may be whether that publishing house had a good year or a bad year. It may also depend on whether the publisher had a fight with his spouse or whether it is raining outside. Who knows?

Nibbles

If an editor is interested in your book, chances are she'll call your agent before making a formal offer. This lets the agent know you've hooked at least one fish! Chapter 14 is filled with material about how editors pull together information before making an offer, but in this chapter, let's just say that the first offer is never the best offer. Your agent works hard to try to get the offer increased.

Reeling 'Em In

As the author, you should be included on the action surrounding your book. Your agent will want to keep you abreast of interest, offers forthcoming or on the table, and any anticipated closing date. You should definitely be included in the conversation about money. This does not mean that you, too, will talk to the editor. Money talk goes on between an agent and an editor; it does not include the author. But you do get to approve the final deal—congratulations!

Breaking Up

You worked hard to get yourself an agent, and you did get one! Now that agent has sold one or two of your books, and you're feeling … well, feeling like maybe you want to get a new agent. Like any relationship in life, dealings between writers and agents don't always work out smoothly forever. So can you change agents?

Yes, you can change agents. Most relationships between writers and agents go from book to book. If you want to change in between books, it should be fine. However, changing agents while a deal is being negotiated is verboten. And even if you've changed agents, the publisher will continue to send monies through the agent of record for a book as long as that book is in print.

The Least You Need to Know

- ◆ Know what you can expect from an agent who wants to represent you.

- ◆ Familiarize yourself with an agent/author agreement.

- ◆ An agent might ask you to make changes to your work, but you don't have to agree.

- ◆ Rejection letters sometimes have much useful information you can learn from.

- ◆ The size of an advance is totally unpredictable, but what is certain is that your agent will work to get you as large an advance as possible.

Chapter 13

Submitting Directly to Editors

In This Chapter

- If you can't get an agent—or don't want one
- University presses, small publishers, and niche publishing
- The world of children's books
- Basic submission guidelines
- Should you self-publish?
- Information on publishing electronically

What do you do if you can't get an agent? Or what if you simply don't want to use one? Can you try to work directly with a publisher without the extra layer of an agent? Sometimes. In this chapter, you discover how to work with editors directly and some of the specialized situations in which agents aren't required. You also learn how to make a professional submission without out an agent.

It's entirely possible to get published without the help of an agent. Many writers have done it. In fact, in some areas of the publishing business, agents rarely, if ever, are used. Where? At university presses, scholarly publishers, regional publishers, some small presses, midlist nonfiction, and many children's publishers. Are these the only areas in which you can try without an agent? No, you can try to approach anyone on your own, but these are the areas of the business that might be most open to you working alone.

Let's take a quick look at the world of academia first.

The Ivy Leagues

University presses are a world unto their own, with specialized methods of editorial selection and approval. Acquisitions editors who work for university presses crisscross the country attending professional conferences of all sorts—literary, anthropological, medical, sociological, and the like—to stay on top of what the issues are and who is tops in the field. When they familiarize themselves with the leading scholars in their field of publishing specialty, the editors cultivate relationships with them in the hopes that these experts will someday write for them. To put it bluntly, in most cases you don't call such editors; they call you.

> **Experts Say**
>
> Planning to turn your dissertation into a book? Then you need to buy a copy of *Revising Your Dissertation* (UC Press, 2002), which will guide you through the process of turning your dull, dry academic treatment into a lively read for the general public. The expert folks at UC Press in California know a thing or two about both academic and trade publishing.

You can submit without being "summoned." How do you do it? First, send a query letter to the acquisitions editor describing yourself and your book and then wait for the editor to respond. All the same rules for writing query letters (as you learned in Chapter 7) apply. Do not leave out your self-addressed, stamped envelope (SASE). University presses have even less money than other publishers and surely cannot afford to pay the return postage on all the unsolicited material they receive!

Curriculum Vitae

An editor at a university press will take a long, hard look at your educational and scholarly credentials. If you don't have the right ones to back up your book, the chances are slim that a university press will take you on.

If an acquisitions editor does respond to your query, she might ask you to send in a "prospectus." Don't panic—that's just a book proposal by another name. Why the world of scholarly presses uses that term is unclear; perhaps it just sounds more scholarly.

Readers and Referees

Unlike a trade publisher with its pub board and editorial meetings, folks outside the university press primarily judge the fate of a proposal.

If the editor likes what she sees in your prospectus, and if your credentials are up to snuff, your material is then sent to a reader. *Readers* are also known as *referees.* These are well-known professors and other experts who are qualified to judge your material from a professional standpoint. As the editor is seldom academically qualified to pass judgment on a manuscript, readers perform this critical task.

How many readers or referees will see your material? Perhaps only one, or as many as three or four. It depends on the topic and the input from the first reader. Readers might sometimes recommend your book "with reservations." The editor then comes back to you and asks for changes or a response to the reservations.

def•i•ni•tion

University presses use **readers,** or **referees,** to help with the acquisitions process. These folks judge manuscripts in their fields of expertise. They either are paid a fee or are paid in kind with free books from the press.

Read More About It

The average print run from university presses is lower than a trade publisher, but you might find that university presses have a longer-term commitment to keeping their books in print.

An excellent way to learn more about the world of university presses is through a book published by the Modern Language Association. Known as the *MLA Style Manual and Guide to Scholarly Publishing,* this is the standard guide for graduate students preparing theses. Over the years, it has grown to include information on how to get published.

At a recent annual conference of the Modern Language Association, many in the academic world decried the difficulty of having their scholarly work published. Do fewer presses, fewer opportunities to publish, yet the same "publish or perish" atmosphere exist on campuses? Is academic publishing on the verge of disappearing, as so many at the conference fear? Not likely, but it is a specialized industry in which it is very difficult to succeed.

Small Can Be Good

Some of the success stories coming out of small publishing companies show that small can indeed be beautiful. Don't kid yourself—New York is not the only place where book publishing gets done. Thriving presses exist all over the country, from Tennessee and Louisiana to Washington and Vermont, and from New Mexico to Colorado. One of the strongest-selling business books in the last decade, *The Millionaire Next Door*, didn't come from Random House or Simon & Schuster. It came from the Longstreet Press in Atlanta. The long-time best-selling career guide *What Color Is Your Parachute?* comes from Ten Speed Press in Berkeley, California. Are both *small publishers?* Technically, yes.

Mini-majors, a new term in publishing, refers to publishers such as Running Press in Philadelphia; Adams Media, based just outside Boston; Chronicle Books in San Francisco; and Workman Publishing in New York. They're not big publishers with sales of hundreds of millions of dollars, but they're independently owned, medium-size companies with solid sales in the $20 million to $50 million range.

def•i•ni•tion

How small is small? Instead, ask how large is small, as the case may sometimes be. The term **small publisher,** or small press, is used loosely but generally is applied to publishing houses with sales of less than $10 million a year. **Mini-majors** are publishers with $10 million to $50 million in annual sales.

Small publishers and the mini-majors are generally more open to dealing directly with authors than the New York houses are. And it can be somewhat less intimidating for a first-time author. Many a big-name author (including Deepak Chopra) got started with a small publisher before achieving fame with a larger house (much to the chagrin of the smaller publisher, who took a chance on an unknown).

When you work with a publisher that has a small staff, you can sometimes have a closer relationship with the editor, publicist, and other people working with your book.

Small publishers are seldom in the business of paying big advances, so cast aside your dreams of the big bucks up front if you're pursuing this route. The occasional small publisher might only offer authors a one-time payment for work-for-hire, but this is rare.

Before you can get your foot in the door at a small publisher, though, you need to introduce yourself in the same way you would to an agent—with a compelling query letter.

The Name Game

The best way to get your query letter read is to address it to an actual editor. How do you find out who the editors are at these small presses? Here are three ways:

 ◆ Look on the acknowledgments page of other books from that publisher; authors often thank their editors.

 ◆ Look in the *Jeff Herman's Guide to Book Publishers, Editors, and Literary Agents* or in the annual *Writer's Market* published by the same folks who do the *Writer's Digest* magazine.

 ◆ Call the publishing house and ask which acquisitions editors acquire books in your genre.

 ◆ Read the free e-zine *Publishers Lunch* to learn the names and e-mail addresses of editors and who is buying what. Sign up at www.publishersmarketplace.com.

Query an Editor

The query letter you should use with a small publisher is essentially the same as outlined in Chapter 7. The only difference is that you're not trying to sell an agent; you are trying to sell an editor.

Review the advice in Chapter 7. Remember to keep your query letter short and to the point. But also remember that the purpose of a query letter is to sell yourself and your project. Talk up the market, and talk up your commitment to seeing the book work. Also include a SASE. A word to the wise: if you are approaching editors directly because you have been dropped by your agent or had an unsuccessful experience with agents, keep that info to yourself. Starting your query to an editor off with a rambling explanation of why you don't have an agent will backfire.

Will you hear back from an editor at a small publisher? Yes, if you have included a SASE. How long it will take to hear back is anyone's guess. But if you neglect to include a SASE and your query doesn't interest the editor, you will never hear back. Your letter will be tossed, and you will wonder forever if it ever even arrived. Resist the temptation to call and ask whether your query letter got there. Even at small presses, an editor's day is hectic, often with no time to return phone calls about unsolicited queries, proposals, and manuscripts.

> **Experts Say**
>
> Have you been dropped by your agent, who was unable to sell your project after a year or so? You're not alone. Mark Victor Hansen and Jack Canfield were dropped by their agent, too, just before the *Chicken Soup for the Soul* book sold to Health Communications. "Biggest mistake he ever made," they laugh.

Negotiating on Your Own

If an editor responds to your query and requests a copy of your proposal or your manuscript, you're one step closer to success. What happens then is described at length in Chapter 14. The acquisitions process for a small publisher is the same as that for a large publisher.

If the small publisher makes you an offer, then what? You can negotiate on your own, but if you decide to do so, you'll need to learn a lot in a hurry. An excellent book by Mark Levine, called *Negotiating a Book Contract*, can help you.

Chapter 15 walks you through some of the basic points in a publishing contract. Some editors are also quite patient in explaining contract points to first-time authors.

> **Hot Off the Press**
>
> Lewis Buzbee, a San Francisco writer and college professor, sold his book *Alone Among Others: The Pleasures of the Bookstore,* to Jennifer at Prima Publishing on his own, without an agent. What did Jennifer find most compelling about Buzbee's proposal? The fact that he included letters of support for the book idea from publishers' sales reps. These are folks who have a terrific sense of what sells and why, so early approval from this group carried a great deal of weight in her decision. Could you pull this off, too? Get to know booksellers, sales reps, and anyone else in the publishing world who might help you get a leg up in the process if you are doing it on your own.

An Agent, at This Point?

If you have an offer in hand, getting an agent should be no trouble now! Those same folks who weren't interested in helping you before would be happy to help you now that there's an offer on the table. But do you need an agent?

If you don't think you can do a good job of negotiating on your own behalf, perhaps you should get an agent involved. At this point, the editor may be happy to refer you to an agent she's worked with before. Ask if the agent is willing to take a lower commission, though, because you got the deal on your own.

If the publisher tells you it doesn't like to work with agents, be on your guard.

The Hunt Is On

Small publishers and mini-majors sound great, but how do you find them? They're right there on the shelf next to the big boys! As you spend time in bookstores familiarizing yourself with the players in your category, you will begin to spot the small publishers on your own. Many of them are listed in *Jeff Herman's Guide to Book Publishers, Editors, and Literary Agents* and in *LMP*.

If you're game, give it a try; small publishers just might be right for you.

Tight Niches

A discussion of small publishers has to include the "niche" publishers—the ones that specialize in one tight-niche market. A niche market can be anything from mountain-climbing books (The Mountaineers Press) to books on the occult (Samuel Weiser, Inc.), and from Northwest travel books (Sasquatch Books in Seattle) to Southern travel books (Pelican Publishing Company). The more familiar you become with your area of specialty, the more you will notice niche publishers that cater directly to your market.

Don't spin your wheels trying to interest a large publisher when you can go directly to a small niche publisher that specializes in your area. These are the experts in the marketplace and will understand right away whether your book is marketable and how best to do it. Niche publishers are very careful about the books they publish. The decision process will be slow, but if a smart niche publisher produces your book, the sales could be steady for years to come, and possibly greater than what might have been achieved by a large publisher that didn't have the same niche approach.

Once Upon a Time …

Children's books are another area in which you can sometimes deal directly with a publisher. Keep in mind that children's books include both picture books (written with an author and illustrator) and YA (young adult) novels and series. Some agents, such as

Andrea Brown, specialize in representing children's books, but a large portion of children's authors do not have agents.

def•i•ni•tion

There are several different types of **children's books:** illustrated books, easy readers, and chapter books. Illustrated books are the lovely big picture books small children love to "read" over and over again. Easy readers are books of the "see Jane run" variety, and chapter books are longer books for more experienced readers.

How do you approach a children's book publisher about your idea? With a query letter! Look for the names of editors in *Jeff Herman's Writer's Guide to Book Publishers, Editors, and Literary Agents* or the more specialized *Writer's Guide to Children's Book Editors, Publishers, and Literary Agents.* Or you can call the publisher to ask for the names of its acquisitions editors and their areas of specialty. But if you do call, just get the name from the receptionist and politely hang up. Resist the urge to ask to speak to an editor directly at this point. Remember, in the early stages of getting published, all the work's done by written letters, not phone conversations. You must first prove that you can write.

You may also call the company and request its submissions guidelines, or visit its website and search around until you find the submission guidelines. This will also help you know if it even accepts un-agented submissions. When you receive the guidelines, follow them down to the letter. Do not get fancy and decide to try another approach. Guidelines have been developed over many years of publishing experience and should be heeded.

Slush Pile

Do not send an illustrated manuscript to a children's publisher. Illustrated manuscripts go first to the publisher's art department to be evaluated, not to the editor. If it doesn't meet with the art director's approval, it is rejected. Your actual words themselves will never be seen or read. Submit only a manuscript. In children's publishing, the publisher traditionally matches authors with illustrators, rather than buying a complete package from an unknown.

Be warned, however, that many children's publishers have ceased accepting unsolicited manuscripts altogether. These companies still will accept query letters from first-time authors, though. Many aspects of the children's book publishing industry can be quite different than regular publishing. If you plan to try to get a children's book published, pick up a copy of *The Complete Idiot's Guide to Publishing Children's Books, Second Edition.*

Experts Say _____

"I recommend so many writers to the Society of Children's Book Writers and Illustrators, it should pay me a commission!" laughs author Debra Keller. "The benefits of membership are tremendous: a list every August of all children's book publishers, the names of their editors, the submission guidelines, and what they are looking for." You don't need to have been previously published to join. Contact the SCBWI at 323-782-1010 or check out www.scbwi.org.

Poetry

Poetry is still one more category that usually does not require an agent—and most agents do not represent poetry. If you would like to have your poetry published, our best advice is to scour the poetry shelf in the library or bookstore and read more than one book on getting poetry published. Identify appropriate magazine, journal, and poetry book publishers, and query them according to their specific guidelines. Some books list appropriate publishers, but an even better technique is to read books and magazines of poetry. Ask poetry teachers as well as published poets for advice. Don't get discouraged before you start. Poetry gets published all the time—just not very often via agents.

To Self-Publish or Not to Self-Publish?

If you've had no luck with agents and no luck submitting directly to publishers, what options do you have left? Is the only way your book will ever see its way into print if you pay for it to be printed and bound?

Self-publishing is an old and honorable pursuit, and many of the literary world's glossiest names have published their own work at one time or another. Think we're just trying to make you feel better if this is your only option? Nope, this is the actual truth. Margaret Atwood, Virginia Woolf, Pat Conroy, Ken Kesey … the list could go on forever. But how can you decide if self-publishing is right for you? After all, writing a book is an art. Self-publishing a book is a business.

To decide if self-publishing is the right route for you, go back to a question in Chapter 1: why do you want to write a book? Which of those goals can be satisfied by self-publishing your book? Pretty much all of them could be except for fame and fortune. Sure, it has happened that a self-publisher has gone on to fame and fortune, but it is a fluke.

Do You Have What It Takes?

Not everyone is cut out to be a self-publisher. It requires lots of money, creativity, ingenuity, dedication, and entrepreneurial zeal. Do you have what it takes? Asking yourself these five questions might help you find out:

◆ Is publishing my book so important to me that I am willing to pay thousands of dollars to see it happen?

◆ Am I willing to accept the fact that I will probably never see that money again?

◆ After my book is published, am I willing to invest countless hours attempting to distribute, publicize, and market my book?

◆ Am I thick-skinned enough to take it if my book is criticized, ignored, or rejected by booksellers and/or the media?

◆ Am I persistent enough to keep going if I get that kind of treatment?

Hot Off the Press

If you're submitting an electronic query to editors or agents, check for viruses first! One hapless children's book author e-mailed a query to a long list of agents and editors (leaving the CCs showing so everyone knew it was a blanket submission) that included a vicious virus that attacked whomever opened it. Publishing folk around the country were furious. Her next submission will need to be under an assumed name ….

Speaking of Speaking ...

One of the best reasons to self-publish a book is to augment your speaking career. If you're already giving talks to rooms full of people, it might be quite easy to sell them a book you just happened to bring with you. Skip the headache of bookstore distribution, and keep all the money. Sounds great! And it can be done with a self-published book.

Several excellent books are already available on how to self-publish a book. We really don't have enough room here to do a thorough job of covering the process, but here's a quick look at the steps you need to go through.

1. Find a copy editor and a proofreader.

2. Get the book designed and typeset.

3. Have a cover designed.

4. Find an affordable short-run printer.

5. **Arrange for** your book's distribution.

6. **Market and** publicize the book.

Experts Say

Why not learn from the best? Best-selling author Mark Victor Hansen periodically teaches a popular weekend seminar called "Mega Book Marketing University." He also runs a Mega Speaking event focusing on ramping up your speaking career. And he should know—millions and millions of people bought his *Chicken Soup* books, and his financial self-help book *The One Minute Millionaire* was a best-seller right out of the gate. For information on scheduling, or to purchase audio recordings of the event, check out his website at www.markvictorhansen.com or call 949-759-9304.

Proof Positive

If your self-published book is a success, can you sell it to a larger publisher? Certainly! You have to stop selling it yourself then. If you can show a solid record of sales success with a self-published book, both agents and publishers will take you very seriously.

On the other hand, some best-selling self-publishers have just stuck it out instead of selling to a larger publisher. They might also ride it to the very top to cut a bigger deal with a large publisher. *Rich Dad, Poor Dad* spent month after month on the business best-seller lists at the end of 1999 and into 2000. The author continued to publish under his own imprint, pocketing the larger portion of the proceeds himself instead of taking a royalty arrangement from a publisher. The book itself attempts to teach lessons in wealth creation—apparently the author had learned the lessons pretty well, because when he finally did sell to Warner Books, he made quite a bundle! In late 2005, author Robert Kiyosaki announced his book had been on the best-seller list for a solid 5 years straight.

Oh, Don't Be Vain!

Self-publishing is a fine and honorable pursuit, but we think vanity presses are a rip-off. We recommend staying away from anyone called a "subsidy publisher," or anyone who acts like he's willing to publish your book as long as you pay the costs.

The contract from a vanity press looks just like a standard publishing contract, but with one critical difference: a clause states that you have to pay for producing the book. If you're offered something like this, run!

The Electronic Edge

Many adventurous writers are experimenting with new forms of self-publishing: e-books and on-demand printing. Companies such as Xlibris (which is owned by Random House, so they know a thing or two about professionally produced books) have set up systems whereby writers can either make their materials available online to prospective purchasers or print up smaller quantities than would be possible with most printers.

Like traditional self-publishing, though, it remains the author's responsibility to generate sales for what he has written. Just because your work is available online as an e-book doesn't mean a reader is going to buy it, unless you somehow create demand through publicity.

These companies have even more to offer: online classes and seminars taught by publishing professionals. Check out the website at www.xlibris.com.

As with the rest of the online world, changes happen with blinding speed. So even if this route never occurred to you, go and check out these companies anyway. Who knows what services they're offering today?

Another great resource for publishing e-books is Joe Vitale, a successful e-book author and marketing consultant. Check out his site at www.7dayebook.com to learn his method.

You're on Your Own

You now know many of the circumstances in which you can try to get your work published without an agent. When submitting on your own behalf to any kind of publisher (whether a children's publisher, a niche publisher, or a small publisher), be as businesslike as possible. Review the chapters on queries and proposals before you begin to compile your materials, keeping in mind that you are directing your information to a book editor, not an agent.

Editor Jere Calmes at Entrepreneur Press attributes one of his most successful book series to an "over-the-transom" submission. Here is what he likes to see in a query from an author: "A proposal no longer than 40 pages, and a very detailed table of contents. Not just the name of the chapters, but several sentences for each chapter that truly detail the information. And the more testimonials you can round up—meaningful testimonials from people who know your work and have commented upon it—the better."

An editor like Jere has the same concerns as an agent: the potential market for the book, the author's credentials, and the uniqueness of the idea. Just as an agent's career depends on finding successful authors, so, too, does the editor's career flourish when she finds great writers whose books sell well. Editors are looking for new writers. Help them find you!

The Least You Need to Know

♦ It is possible—and quite common—to approach university presses, children's publishers, and small publishers without an agent.

♦ Learn the names of the editors, and approach them directly with short query letters.

♦ Respect the system: queries first and proposals later (if requested). Don't try to call editors directly before they've had a chance to review something from you in writing.

♦ When you have a deal in hand, you will be able to get an agent, but ask for a reduced commission.

♦ Self-publishing requires both money and dedication, but it can be emotionally rewarding and can perhaps help boost your career.

Chapter 14

Behind Closed Doors

In This Chapter

- The first hurdle: the editor
- The pub board meeting
- Competition and sales projections
- Production costs and P and Ls

So far, on your mission to get published you wrote a great query letter and a superb book proposal. An agent called you up and offered to represent you. Or no agents called and you decided to take up the task yourself. Twelve copies of your proposal have been sent to twelve editors at the twelve publishing houses best suited for your book. Your fingers are crossed, and you are saying your prayers nightly. What happens now?

Hurry Up and Wait

Several things could happen:

- The editor opens her mail one day and discovers your proposal. Intrigued after reading just a few paragraphs, she sets it aside on a stack of material she plans to take home and read more thoroughly.

◆ Your agent may have placed an advanced call to the editor to get him excited about the proposal before he reads it. Your proposal arrives in the mail, and the editor thinks—*Ah, yes, this is the book Mr. Agent described. I must take a look at it right away; it sounded perfect for our list.* He glances at a few pages and sets it aside on a stack of material he plans to take home and read more thoroughly.

def•i•ni•tion

The word *list* is used to describe the books the publisher or editor plans to publish in the near future. "It's on our list," an editor might say, or "We have a few holes on our list that need filling"—these phrases are music to an agent's ears. Perhaps *your* book is just perfect for their list! The list is usually a preplanned template of books (or types/prices) of books editors have committed to their bosses and their bosses have committed to their bosses for planning purposes. In any given year, an editor is responsible for bringing in a set number of titles for the list (or plan).

◆ Your agent might have gone to lunch with the editor the day before. Over a spinach salad, your agent pitched the editor a number of book projects from several clients. The editor expressed an interest in seeing one or two of them (including yours!), and the agent messengers them over that same afternoon. The editor sets it aside on a stack of material she plans to take home and … you know the rest.

However it got there, your proposal is now inside the doors of a publishing house.

Experts Say

Editors don't read much at the office. Yes, they do read query letters, but most of the real reading gets done at home. When Jennifer was an editor, she was also the mother of two small boys. Rather than read at home, she would go to lunch with large stacks of manuscripts and queries. Many of her rejections were a bit smudged. Don't be hurt if your material comes back smudged and coffee stained; it means an editor took the time to read it thoroughly!

"Sorry, Not Right for Our Needs at This Time"

Sadly, the story could easily end right here. The editor might not put your proposal on the stack she plans to take home. Perhaps she took a look at your proposal and then put it in her reject pile.

Why? Well, for any one of a number of reasons. You might not make it as far as the editorial meeting for these reasons:

- It is clearly not appropriate for that publishing house—your book is about the history of fighter pilots, and this publisher publishes only vegetarian cookbooks.

- The publishing house already has a book on that topic, and it hasn't sold well.

- The publishing house already has a book on that topic, and the author of that book plans to do more in that area.

- The editor doesn't think a large market exists for your book.

Most rejection letters do not include any actual reason why your book was rejected. The standard line is "Thank you, but this is not right for us." Why don't editors write more? Two reasons: they don't have the time to analyze, critique, and then write to you; and they don't want to invite a response or rebuttal from you. Try to take your rejection letters in stride.

Who knows, you might end up selling your book eventually to that same editor at a different house. The book series Jere Calmes of Entrepreneur Press bought after it came over the transom actually came over the transom of a different house! It was turned down when he pitched it there, but after changing jobs and joining another house, he pitched it and was successful the second time. So be nice to editors—be very, very nice!

Hot Off the Press

Publishing is a people business, and the people who work in publishing are people just like you. Sometimes they're tired, cranky, and not in the mood to buy books. If your book proposal has been rejected by one editor, don't take this as a sign that your project is doomed and will never be published by anyone. Who knows, perhaps it just was a bad day at the office when your material crossed that editor's desk. Keep trying, and go on to the next publisher.

Consider This

But if your book does make it onto the stack to be read further, then what?

Editors do quite a bit of investigating before bringing your proposal to a meeting. An editor might call your agent to ask questions or request more material. An editor might call you directly to learn more about you, the market for the book, and your plans to promote it. Editors also do more hands-on investigation: prowling around bookstores to examine the competing titles, asking friends in the industry how well that category is selling, checking sales numbers of similar books on BookScan, or cruising online to see if there is much interest in the topic.

> **Slush Pile**
>
> The phone rings, and it's an editor asking about your book. Although the questions may all relate to the book itself, the editor might have another motive. How well you present yourself on the phone is critical to your book's future success. Editors want authors who can handle themselves easily with interviews and the media. If you are tired, distracted, or otherwise unprepared to sound good on the phone, it is better to beg off and reschedule the conversation.

If the editor likes what he sees in the proposal, what he hears from you, and what his own research turns up, the next step is for him to present it to his colleagues and superiors for possible publication.

Committee Decisions

As powerful as many of them are, editors do not make the decision to publish a book on their own. That decision rests with a group of people sometimes called the *pub board* or *editorial board*. The editor who likes your book is only one voting member of this group. Other members usually include some combination of other editors; the publisher; and folks from the sales, marketing, and publicity departments. The process works something like this:

> **def•i•ni•tion**
>
> Unless it is a one-person publishing house, your proposal will be presented to an **editorial board,** or **pub board.** This is a group of people who collectively make the decision about what titles to publish.

- An editor is intrigued by your proposal and decides to present it to the pub board.

- The editor brings your proposal to a meeting.

- The editor makes a short presentation about your book and attempts to drum up interest and enthusiasm.

- The editor answers questions from other members of the group. Sometimes the editor needs to do further research and presents the book in more detail at a future meeting.

So that's it. The fate of your book can be decided in about 10 minutes. But if you get past this point, then what happens? Does the editor call to say that he wants to make an offer? No, not yet.

Hot Off the Press

"At Andrews McMeel, our first meeting is just with the other editors," explains Lane Butler. "It is more informal; with no sales or marketing staff in attendance there is less pressure. Collectively we look at the proposals and ideas not only for content, but also for ways in which it could be made stronger. We meet at least once a week and every editor gets a chance to present one or two projects they really like. After that first meeting a proposal would go on to the acquisitions group, which does include sales and marketing."

How's It Gonna Sell?

Even if an editor has successfully lined up support in the meeting, there is still more work to be done. Remember, publishing is a business, and in business, the bottom line is king. So the editor has to work up the numbers to see whether publishing your book will pay off. How is this done?

Editors often ask the sales department for help. Experienced sales folks can help the editor figure out what the typical orders would be for the proposed book. How many copies would Borders buy? Barnes & Noble? Target? Is there a chance Wal-Mart would pick it up? Small independent bookstores across the country? They add up all these numbers and hope the result is big.

Slush Pile

The power and influence of the publishing sales department has grown in the last decade. Although in years past, the typical sales department wouldn't find out what was on the list until the sales conference, it is now often included in the front-end decisions about what to publish—either just before or just after the book is approved. If the sales department doesn't think it can sell a book to its customers, the book doesn't get published. End of story.

The publicity department may also be polled at this point. The editor talks with the publicity folks about whether the topic of the book (or the name of the author) lends itself to publicity.

The editor might also pay a visit to the production department to check on the typical production costs for a book of this type.

All these numbers are plugged into the P and L, the profit and loss statement. If the numbers look good, the editor reports back to the pub board. And then maybe, just maybe, the title will be approved and the editor will get the go-ahead to make an offer.

The Meeting Begins

Let's take a close look at what goes on in one of these meetings. This gives you a good idea how all the information you dredged up for your proposal comes into play.

It is a Tuesday afternoon at Big Publishing Company, Inc., and all the members of the pub board are gathered in a conference room. The editors carry armloads of book proposals and other materials. In any given meeting, the fate of 10 or more books is decided. Each editor has high hopes for the books he has decided to champion.

Batter Up!

Editor 1 leads off with her first proposal: a book of affirmations and prayers for breast cancer survivors. She describes the focus of the book, the reason the world needs this book, the qualifications of the woman who put it together, and the impact the book could have on the women who read it.

The sales manager speaks up with a question: "How many books already exist on this topic? And just how large is the market? What are the current figures on breast cancer occurrence?"

The editor has carefully read the proposal and knows the answers to those questions because the author did her research well. It was all right there for her.

The publisher wants to know: "There is a strong title already on the subject from another publisher. How will this book be different enough to find an audience? I worry that the bookstores won't see a need to order another similar title."

Once again the editor answers the questions and concerns with authority. The author of the book has researched the competing titles, talked to bookstore managers about the need, and lined up the support of a major breast cancer survivors group. A solid proposal has all the answers.

So the pub board is interested in considering this title. What happens then? The editor spends the next few days making the rounds of the departments to gather more information on how much it would cost to produce this book and how many copies they can expect to sell. She calls the agent or the author with any questions about the proposal she couldn't answer herself. She distributes copies of the proposal to those interested in reading.

When the editor has rounded up all the answers, she once again makes a short presentation at a pub board meeting. If the numbers are right, the group decides to go on to the next phase: making an offer to publish the book.

Next Up!

Editor 2 gets a turn. He begins his presentation on a book about the history of baseball cards. "This will be the first-ever book on the topic," he says proudly, pointing with confidence at that claim in the proposal.

"Oh, come on!" says the publicity manager. "I am a collector myself and own at least two books on the history of baseball cards."

The editor stammers and flips quickly through the pages of the proposal, looking for something to salvage the situation. "Ah, but this is the first time that the cards will be organized by player position rather than team! That is really unique!"

"Just like the book I have on my shelf," the publicity manager snickers.

Another book bites the dust.

Hot Off the Press

The worst thing you can do in a book proposal is lie. If you lie or fib about your qualifications, if you lie about the competing books, or if you lie about the sales history of your other books, you are headed for disaster. Editors never forget and will certainly not forget if they are made to look foolish with information you supplied. Think you can try to fool one editor at one house and then move on to the next if that fails? Don't be surprised if your first editor moves, too. A bad reputation spreads quickly and is hard to shed. Always play straight.

Let's Pretend

You can see how critical the information you provide in your proposal is to your future success. When compiling a proposal, pretend that you, too, are a member of a pub board. Put yourself in that person's shoes, and try to anticipate all the negative or hard-hitting questions that might be asked. Then supply the answers in your proposal. Give the editor something to work with.

Jere Calmes likes to think of an acquisitions meeting as a grown-up version of show and tell. "The editor has to tell people why they want to publish your book, so give them as much to show as possible!"

Second Chances?

Is there ever a second chance? If an editor flops with your proposal once, can he ever try it again? Seldom, but it happens. It has nothing to do with begging or pleading on your part, though.

If the editor has truly fallen in love with your book project, he might go back to square one. He might poke around some more in the marketplace, ask more questions of friends in the industry, and try to gather ammunition to convince the skeptics that this book would succeed. If the information he gathers is compelling enough, and if his own commitment to the book is strong enough, it just might work the second time around.

But if the answer was "no" and the editor doesn't have the heart or the interest to re-pitch the project, you have probably come to the end of the road—the end of the road with that publisher, anyway. If you've been in touch with the editor prior to their editorial presentation, chances are they will fill you in on what kinds of problems they ran into. Use this valuable information and try to make changes to your proposal or plans before you submit it again to another house.

Congratulations are in order, though. Only a tiny fraction of book projects ever make it to the pub board stage, so you have succeeded. Keep trying. If one editor was interested enough to pitch it, another one will be, too.

They Like Me! They Really Do!

What if the answer is "yes"? Go ahead and pop open the bottle of champagne. The editor succeeded with the pub board and got the go-ahead to make you an offer—way to go! Now what happens?

The editor will call you, or your agent if you have one. The conversation will sound something like this: "I've got good news! We'd like to publish your book. I'd like to make you an offer of an advance against future royalties of …."

Money, Money, Money, Money

The editor doesn't make the decision to publish on her own, nor does she decide the size of the offer on her own. In the pub board discussion or in a one-on-one with the publisher, all decision-makers determine the range of the advance. The editor then has the authority to call either the agent or the author (if there is no agent involved) to make the offer.

Understand that a smart editor will never make her highest offer first. This is particularly critical information to have if you're working without an agent. If the editor has been approved to offer $18,000, she might first offer $15,000 to give herself room to go up. It's a basic negotiating tactic. So brush up on your own negotiating skills and ask for more.

> **Hot Off the Press**
>
> Some editors like working with first-timers—especially first-timers who are willing to learn how publishing works. On the other hand, the first-timers (typically arrogant business guys) who think they can come in and make publishing work like other businesses are frustrating—this includes contract terms, processes, marketing, etc.

The Numbers Game

The size of the advance could vary from small to large. Who knows? There's no way to predict exactly how much you'll be offered. If you have an agent, chances are that he will immediately ask for a larger figure. (Remember, the more you make, the more your agent makes.) If you don't have an agent, should you ask for a bigger number, too?

It never hurts to ask, but ask for a reasonable increase over what's being offered. You might also risk looking like an egotist if you counter with what the editor thinks is an unreasonable sum. And you only risk being told, "No, we won't go any higher." On the other hand, if you are just thrilled that someone wants to publish your book, take the offer.

Other Considerations in the Offer

Do you need to bone up on negotiating techniques to deal directly with an offer? Thankfully, publishing isn't a particularly cut-throat business. In Chapter 15, we walk you through each contract clause and let you know which ones are easiest to negotiate and change.

Congratulations, you are getting published!

The Least You Need to Know

◆ Editors present proposals to a pub board made up of representatives from several different departments.

◆ If the sales department is not enthusiastic about a book idea, it seldom goes any further.

◆ The better the information in your proposal, the easier it is for an editor to gain support for your book.

◆ Never lie, exaggerate, or exclude important information from your proposal; it can only hurt you.

◆ If you get a "yes," you'll be offered an advance, which you (or your agent) might be able to negotiate upward.

Chapter 15

The Party of the First Part

In This Chapter

- Boilerplate contract clauses
- "Half-and-half" advances
- The 12 major flex points
- Rights, royalties, and remainders
- Bonuses and other contract sweeteners

An offer is in and a contract is coming. Your book project is becoming more real by the moment. Someday you really will be able to walk into a bookstore and see your book on the shelf.

But first, you have to sign a contract.

We are not lawyers. After working with hundreds of contracts over the years, however, we do have a fairly good handle on what it all means. In this chapter, you learn the meaning behind many of the standard clauses found in a publishing contract. Then we give you the inside scoop on which clauses we have found to be more negotiable than others.

Whereas **and** *Therefore*

Regardless of the size of the publishing company, most contracts are essentially the same. Some are considerably longer than others (40 pages is the longest we've seen), but the basic points are the same. Each contract begins as a *boilerplate contract*, a kind of skeleton contract waiting to be negotiated and changed.

What's the purpose of a book contract? A publishing company wants to publish a work you wrote and needs to have a legal document that does the following:

def•i•ni•tion

The publisher's standard contract is referred to as a **boilerplate contract.** It's the standard contract that's always used, and it has not (yet) been modified with any changes you might request.

♦ Gives the company the right to publish and sell your material in agreed-upon territories

♦ Outlines the monetary arrangements

♦ Establishes your right to grant the company the rights

♦ Spells out the responsibilities of the author and the publisher

♦ States a time length for the agreement

Pretty simple, isn't it? Then why does it take so many darn pages to establish those simple facts? Is that because lawyers bill by the hour? Perhaps. But the business world grows more complicated by the decade, and new legal issues crop up all the time. Let's take a close look at 15 major clauses in a publishing contract.

Most all points are negotiable. And editors will tell you which ones are not (like the indemnity and warranty clauses). So if you want something, ask for it. You might not get it, but at least you asked—and you might get something more than you had before. Negotiating a publishing contract is all about choosing battles—be prepared to let a few things go, and decide in advance what they will be. In the following sections, we fill you in on which points are the easiest to get changed.

Slush Pile

So you don't have an agent. Do you need a lawyer? Actually, most lawyers have little knowledge about the quirks found in publishing contracts. An editor won't be pleased to hear from your lawyer, either, if he or she is not familiar with a publishing contract. To find a lawyer who specializes in publishing, contact the Author's Guild (see Appendix C).

The Work

One of the early paragraphs in a contract defines what is generally called the "Work." This, of course, is your book. Your book is henceforth referred to as the "Work." You get to be the "Author." The company is forever known in contracts as the "Publisher."

In this paragraph, the subject matter of the work is defined. If you're writing a novel, it's defined as a work of fiction, and the general focus of the book is mentioned. If you're writing a nonfiction book, the work is described as "a Work of nonfiction whose subject matter is as follows …." The expected length of your finished manuscript is also stated.

Why is this here? The publishing company needs to be sure the book you turn in is the book it had in mind when it signed you up. This clause protects the publisher from signing you up to write a novel about the Civil War, only to have you turn in a nonfiction memoir about your childhood in New Orleans.

> **Experts Say**
>
> As the author, you are not selling your book rights to the publisher; you're merely licensing the rights. When you license a right, you continue to own it for the life of your copyright, which is 95 years. The publisher may exercise certain rights that you grant him only for the term of the license. After that term has expired, those rights revert back to you.

Copyright

Standard publishing contracts state that the publisher will register the copyright to the work in the name of the author. Beware of any contract that asks you to assign all rights to the publisher or one that stipulates that the publisher is the copyright holder. Unless the author gives the right away, he or she owns the copyright by virtue of having written the material. In fact, the minute you put pen to paper and write something original, it is copyrighted material without you even so much as filling out a form.

Tentatively Titled

This section of the contract might also contain a zinger, a phrase that refers to the book as "tentatively titled." Tentatively titled? But you thought of your title years ago, and it is all over your queries and proposals. How can the publisher refer to it as tentatively titled?

Sorry, but most publishing contracts allow the publisher the right to change the title of your book. Some state that the title can be changed only "by mutual agreement."

Your delivery date (the day your manuscript is due) also appears in this early section of the contract.

The Advance

Ah, the money part. This is where the publisher spells out exactly how much of an advance you will receive. The language reads something like this: "As an advance against all monies accruing or payable to the Author under this Agreement, the Publisher will pay to the Author the sum of ___, payable as follows …." Payable as follows?

Regardless of the size of your advance, do not expect to receive it in one lump sum. Those glittering sums you read about in the paper—like the millions retired politicians like Rudy Giuliani are offered—aren't paid out all at once, either. One arrangement is for two payments: one payment on signing the contract, and the second tied to the completion of the final manuscript. (Some of the big ones have final payment tied to publication.) The language and terms for the final payment vary widely, with some publishers paying when you turn in the manuscript on your delivery date, and other publishers not paying until the manuscript has been edited. Those are the most common advance payouts, but not the only ones. A few publishers have gone to three payments of one third each, with the final payment upon publication of the book. Others pay one third upon signing, the second third upon receipt of one half of the manuscript, and the final third upon receipt of the remainder of the manuscript. If it's your first book, they might tie a payment to completion of revisions.

Why won't they just write you a check for the whole sum? The publisher needs to know that you will follow through and turn in a manuscript on the topic and in the style you promised in your book proposal. The best way to do this is to hold back part of the money until that happens. The publisher also wants to be sure what you turn in is publishable—hence, the second payment is generally linked to receipt of an acceptable manuscript.

Grant of Rights

This is where you, as the author, grant and assign the rights to your work to the publisher. This is what gives the publisher the legal right to publish and sell your book.

In addition to the right to sell your book in bookstores and other retail outlets, this clause may also grant the publisher the right to do these things:

- License the work to book clubs

- Sell the English-language book in foreign countries

- License foreign-language editions of the work

- Produce or license electronic versions or multimedia versions

- Produce or license audio book versions

- Produce or license hardcover, trade paperback, or mass market paperback versions

- License newspaper and magazine excerpts or serializations

- License movie rights

- License commercial or merchandising rights (maybe even coffee cups and T-shirts)

- Produce other sundry items, such as Braille versions or a play based on your book

Sounds like a lot of rights, right? This is a complicated section, one agents love to tackle in detail. Publishers believe they should be granted all these rights to be given a chance to earn back the money invested in your book—and they often have whole teams of people focused on selling these rights—called subrights (see Chapter 10). On the other hand, agents like to retain as many rights as possible on behalf of the author to obtain extra income for both of you!

There is some flexibility in this clause. Although most rights categories call for a 50/50 split of monies received between the publisher and the writer, you can negotiate the percentage with the editor. The most common change has to do *with first serial rights.* (This is when a section of the book appears in a magazine before the book is published and available in stores, authors can sometimes get 90/10, with the 90 in their pocket!) It's not unusual, either, for foreign rights to be split 75/25 in favor of the author. Be aware, though, that the less money the publisher receives, the less likely they will try to market those rights.

Royalties

In the royalty section of the contract, the publisher defines exactly what the author receives from the sale of the book. There are two different ways to calculate royalties:

- As a percentage of the retail price printed on the book

- As a percentage of the publisher's net, the actual cash the publisher receives from the sale of the book after discounts have been deducted

There are two major types of royalties: retail (based on the cover price of the book) and net (based on the after discount price of the book). Royalties based on the retail price usually range from 7 to 15 percent or more. Royalties based on net may start higher, at 10 percent, and escalate from there. Your contract should clearly state what type of royalties you receive for each copy of your book sold. Whether a publisher pays net or retail royalties is a policy set by their financial advisers. Changing from net to retail is not typically a negotiation point.

The royalties clause might also be where you find information on what share (or "split") the author receives of any subsidiary rights income if any of the rights the publisher is granted earlier in the contract (book clubs, mass market paperback, and so on) are sold.

You also find information on how many free copies of the book the author receives after it is published, and whether the author can buy more copies at an author's discount.

Delivery of Manuscript and Corrections

The hard, cold truth is revealed here: the date by which you must turn in your completed manuscript. It might be a few short months, or it might be years away.

What happens if the date arrives and the publisher does not receive your finished work? The contract includes language to the effect that the publisher has the right to terminate the contract, generally upon written notification of the author by the publisher. If this happens, the contract states, the author is obligated to repay the publisher any sums advanced to the author.

The contract also includes language that allows the publisher to reject the work as unpublishable, or to request specific changes to the manuscript. The contract should state a process by which the author can address the changes. If the publisher still feels that the manuscript is unacceptable, the contract can be terminated.

Once again, this language is included because the publisher needs to be protected against receiving a shoddy product. In the case of nonfiction books, the publishing house probably made its decision based on only a proposal and a sample chapter. If the book ultimately turned in does not offer the proper information or isn't written professionally, a publisher can pull the plug.

Other Deliverables

The contract outlines the publisher's expectations regarding photographs, illustrations, maps, and charts. Who pays and when it needs to be turned in is spelled out in this section.

Options

The publisher is taking a chance on your book. If it becomes a success, the house might want to publish more of your work. In the *option clause*, the contract states that the publisher gets the first crack at your next work, the book you write after the book under contract. The language gives your publisher the exclusive right to consider your next work and describes how long the publisher has to make an offer. It may also say that if your publisher bids on the next work, you cannot sell the next work to another publisher for a lesser sum. It also specifies the earliest date the next work can be submitted for consideration.

The clause might also cover competing works. The publisher doesn't want you to publish a similar book with a different publisher that would compete with this one.

The option clause and the noncompete clause can sometimes cause trouble for working writers. Later in this chapter, you find some ways to deal with this issue.

def•i•ni•tion

Most contracts contain an **option clause** for the author's next work. This means that the publisher gets first crack at the next book you write, or the next book of the same type.

Author's Representations, Warranties, and Indemnity

In this clause, you, as the author, are assuring the publisher that the work is original and that you have the "sole and exclusive right to make the grant of rights set forth herein …." You also are assuring the publisher that you are not slandering, libeling, or invading anyone's privacy with your work.

If legal action arises from the publication of your book, this clause allows the publisher to stand aside and point directly to you: "He's the one you want; he wrote the words. We just printed the darn thing." This clause might also outline the legal procedure if a lawsuit arises. Some publishers carry libel insurance; some do not. This clause is also going to point out that in the case of a lawsuit, the publisher will manage the defense and provide the legal team. This is because most large publishers have legal teams who know publishing law inside and out and are going to have the best idea of how to handle a situation.

Although you might or might not agree with the wording in these clauses, this section of the contract is often not up for negotiation.

Obligations of the Publisher

You have promised to deliver a manuscript by a certain date, and in this clause the publisher promises to publish the manuscript by a certain date. Other than exceptions mentioned in the contract (such as labor strikes, acts of God, or other circumstances beyond the publisher's control), if the publisher does not publish it, what then? There should be language that allows the author to terminate the agreement and keep the advance.

Accounting

You've already been informed about the amount of royalties you'll receive, but when exactly will this be paid to you? The contract has a paragraph that outlines the schedule. Some publishers pay twice a year; some pay only once a year. This section should also include language on what happens in the case of overpayment (if the publisher's accounting department accidentally sends you too much money!) or if audits are requested by the author. It is within any author's right to request an audit if inadvertent irregularities in payments arise.

Overstock, Out of Print, or Reversion of Rights

If your book goes out of print, or if the sales dwindle down to nothing, what then? The answers are found in this section of the contract. Most contracts state that if the book goes out of print for a particular length of time, the rights revert back to the author.

This clause also gives the publisher the right to sell your book at *remainder* prices, if need be.

def•i•ni•tion

When a book ends up being sold at a steeply discounted price, it is called **remaindering**. Books are sold for pennies on the dollar to remainder companies (who then sell them back to bookstores for the bargain tables). Before a book is remaindered, most publishers offer the author the chance to buy copies at bargain prices.

Assignment

After you sign the contract, your heirs are legally bound by it as well. This means that if you die, the publisher still has the rights to the book. This clause also allows the publisher to assign the rights to your book to a new company if your publisher sells the business.

Bankruptcy

This clause covers the possibility of the publisher's bankruptcy, not yours. Your book rights are an asset now, and according to most contracts, if the publisher goes bankrupt, the author may buy back the rights to the book or the publishers assets will be sold. But it may leave the publisher the right to sell any remaining copies of the book in inventory without paying any royalties.

Agency Clause

If you're represented by an agent, there will be an agency clause in your contract. If you are not using an agent, this clause won't appear.

The agency clause names the agent as the person to whom the publisher should send all monies accruing to this book. The agent will then subtract her percentage and pass on the balance to you. As long as the book remains under contract to this publisher, the agent receives the royalty check. What happens if you and your agent someday have a falling out and part ways, or if you decide to change agents? You are committed to the agent stated in your contract. You won't be able to call the publisher and ask them to start sending checks directly to you or your new agent. The checks for this title will still go to the agent listed in the contract unless both you and the agent send a letter to the publisher.

Electronic Rights

The term *electronic rights* is very broad. Several things are meant when one speaks of electronic rights, so it is important to look at each right individually:

◆ **Verbatim electronic rights.** The right to make a book available online, non-interactively, or on a handheld device such as a Rocket eBook, a palm-sized e-book reader. This is also known as "electronic display rights."

◆ **Database.** An electronic collection of writings (such as an anthology or a cookbook).

◆ **Interactive.** An electronic version of the book that is enhanced by a third party (the publisher, for example) with material such as audio or video elements or illustrations that allows the reader to manipulate the text. Publishers increasingly either are insisting on keeping this right or are retaining the first option of exploiting it. Even when an author does keep this right, it is important not to compete with the published version of the book. The publisher might get angry and might have cause to litigate, and it is not necessarily beneficial to the author.

◆ **Print on demand.** This refers to short-run printing. New technology has made it possible to use an electronic file to print a small number of copies of the book, as and when they are needed, relatively inexpensively. In the past, it was very expensive to print a small number of books; even 1,000 was considered small. Now books can be printed one or a few at a time. When publishers control print on demand, they either use it to authorize wholesalers or retailers to print copies as needed, or do so themselves. When authors control print on demand, they can publish books themselves through services such as those offered by Xlibris. Authors cannot hold back print on demand, however, when they sell to a publisher. It is really only useful after the rights to a book have reverted back to the author.

For the average unpublished writer, self-publishing, whether through electronic print on demand or otherwise, does not bring you income, nor does it establish you as a successful writer—and you may end up with a garage full of books. Print on demand, therefore, seems to be most valuable to published authors whose books no longer generate enough sales to warrant standard print runs, but who have found an audience. Another value to print on demand applies to promotional speakers or people who make a living giving seminars: these authors can sell books from a table in the back of the room. This is a cheap way to make professional-looking books available.

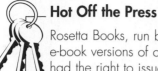

Hot Off the Press

Rosetta Books, run by a New York agent, ran into trouble when they began to issue e-book versions of old classic titles. Random House wasn't pleased, as they felt they had the right to issue old version of books by writers such as Kurt Vonnegut. But the contract didn't cover electronic rights, because back then, the argument was, no one even knew of such a thing. After much legal tussling, Random House and Rosetta finally settled by agreeing to work together to produce the e-books. The perfect ending.

So Is Anything Negotiable?

Hey, most things in life are negotiable, including (sometimes) contracts. As we mentioned before, we've each spent hundreds of hours working with publishing contracts, so we know a thing or two about where publishers might be willing to make changes. Don't take this as legal advice, but rather as guidance from two learned colleagues. Here are the 12 major flex points:

- Who pays for the index
- Who pays for illustrations, photos, and similar parts
- What sales territories the publisher has the rights to
- Splits and serial rights issues
- Commercial and dramatic rights
- How many free copies the author receives
- The delivery date
- The author's expense budgets
- High-discount/reduced royalties clauses
- Joint accounting
- Next work and option clauses
- Reversion of rights

We've seen publishers make concessions in these clauses many times. Let's examine them closely.

Who Pays for the Index?

Most contracts call for the author either to provide the index or to pay for a professional index. Ever tried to do an index? Forget it. We recommend asking that the publisher pay for the index, or at least split the cost with the author. Indexing can cost several dollars a page, so the bill can be steep. If the publisher won't pay the entire amount or won't split the cost, ask for a cap on the cost. If you end up having to pay for the cost of the index, be sure it comes out of your future royalties so you don't have to pay for it out of your advance or out of your pocket.

Who Pays for Illustrations, Photographs, and Other Such Things?

For books in which photographs play a central part, the cost is usually borne by the author. When designing the book, if the publisher thinks photographs add to the book (food photography, for instance), the publisher should pay. The publisher usually pays for illustrations that decorate the book, but the author pays for illustrations for necessary charts.

Be sure you understand who pays for what, and feel free to ask the publisher to pay a larger share. Sometimes the author needs to deliver only what is known as scrap art: rough sketches of suggested art for the publisher to have drawn professionally.

The Sales Territory

The publisher will, quite literally, ask to publish the book in every language throughout the whole world—not just the United States and Canada, but tiny territories you've never even heard of. It wants the right to publish the book in the English language throughout the whole world, and it also requests the right to license foreign publishers to translate the book into other languages.

Some publishers do exploit these foreign rights well; others routinely distribute in the United States and Canada and let all the other territories languish. If you have an agent, your agent might want to keep foreign rights on your behalf and try to sell them directly to foreign publishers, so she will try to retain this right for you.

When publishers license translation rights, they split the monies received from foreign publishers with the author. If you don't have an agent, at least ask if there is any flexibility regarding the split. Some contracts call for a 50/50 split between the publisher and the author on the money from the sale of these rights, but you can always ask for a better cut. "How about 75/25, with 75 percent going to the author?"

Splits and Serials

As with the size of the territory, there are two questions with regard to serial rights. One, who controls the rights? Two, what is the split? If you have an agent, she might want to try to keep control of the *serialization* rights. But if you (or your agent) don't have the contacts to try to sell *first serial* rights to a magazine or newspaper, you might as well let the publisher's rights department try. But again, ask about the split. It's not unusual for the author to receive 90 percent of the money from a first serial rights sale.

def•i•ni•tion

When an excerpt from the book appears just before the book is published, this is a **first serial.** Any excerpts that appear after the book has been published are known as second serials. These strange-sounding terms come from the word **serialization.**

Commercial and Dramatic Rights

These are the movie and play rights. Do you see your book as a perfect movie of the week? Or as the basis for a Broadway musical? Then either fight to control these rights all yourself, or reduce the publisher's split.

Free Author's Copies

Most publishing contracts give the author a scant 5 or 10 free copies. Hey, you've got a big family! Your mom wants one, your great-aunt, your old next-door neighbor … You need more free books, and you can probably get them. This is an easy place for an editor to give up a little something. Ask for 25, anyway, and see what you get.

Publishers usually are generous with free copies used for publicity or review purposes, so if you have good opportunities for promoting the book yourself, ask for some free publicity copies.

Try to get at least a 50 percent discount on the cover price for any additional books you want to buy. If you plan to give lots of speeches and sell books, try to get an even better quantity discount. Bear in mind that you'll have to pay the shipping charges on these purchases and that books are heavy objects. You need to factor in the shipping costs when deciding what makes up an attractive per-book purchase price.

The Delivery Date

By the time you get to the contract stage, the publishing company might already have a pub date in mind. But you can always try to get a little extra time here—a few weeks or an extra month or so. Be kind to your editor, though. If you don't need the extra time, don't ask for it.

Expense Budgets

These are fairly rare. Expenses are assumed to be the author's responsibility—that's what an advance is for. Sometimes cookbook authors get baking allowances to help with the cost of buying ingredients. And sometimes the authors of anthologies or compilations can get a *permissions* budget. It never hurts to try, though.

def•i•ni•tion

If you're using material to which you do not own the copyright, you need to secure the proper **permissions**. To quote or reprint from newspapers, magazines, or other books, you must contact that company's permissions department. Sometimes a fee is involved, which generally falls on the author.

High-Discount/Reduced Royalty Clauses

These are tough. Publishers claim that the deep discounts so prevalent today have cut into their margins and that they need to reduce royalties to stay in business. Agents (and authors) claim that it reduces royalties to practically nothing. Always try to get some concessions in this area. Publishers will also ask for reduced royalty rates on small print runs. You can try to negotiate the size of the print run that triggers this.

Slush Pile

This chapter is not all you need to negotiate a contract. If you don't have an agent, then consult a literary lawyer, or at least a good book, such as *Negotiating a Book Contract*, by Mark Levine. The Author's Guild in New York can also be a good resource, if you want to join.

If your royalties are based on net and not list price of the book (see the section on royalties earlier in this chapter), you or your agent might want to ask for a higher starting royalty rate. Or perhaps ask that the royalty rate escalate as the book sells more copies—for example, a starting percentage on the first 10,000 copies sold, a higher percent on the next 5,000 copies, and the highest percentage on all copies sold in excess of 15,000.

Joint Accounting

Joint accounting? What's that mean? It means nothing on your first book. It means a great deal if you publish a second book with the same publisher, however. With joint accounting, all monies from both of your books go into the same big pot. So if you haven't earned out the advance on your first book and your second book does really well, the publisher will ding your account for the negative royalty balance on the first one. We think each book should stand on its own, and we recommend asking to get this clause eliminated.

Options Clauses

If you and your publisher get along well, you will want to work together again. If you don't get along, you don't want to be legally bound to offer it your next book.

If you are a working writer with lots of books in the works and in various stages of publication, this needs to be stated in the contract. Some contracts actually seek to prevent you from signing another contract with another publisher until this book is published—and publication can be months (even years) after you've completed the manuscript. If this is a problem, speak up.

Electronic Rights

Unfortunately, as the field of electronic publishing is changing so rapidly and rights appear to be more lucrative, publishers are becoming less willing to budge from their very stringent boilerplates on the matter. They want to keep a great big bag full of rights.

Following is an electronic clause that we feel is fair to the author:

> **Experts Say**
>
> Publishing lawyer Bob Stein says, "Authors should look very, very carefully at all electronic rights clauses to ensure that they are compensated for any uses made or authorized by the publisher." He adds, knowingly, "Publishers vary considerably in their willingness to negotiate these provisions."

> "Electronic book" rights, which for the purposes of this agreement shall be limited to the right to digitize, reproduce, transmit, display, download, or otherwise transfer, manufacture, publish, distribute, and/or sell the verbatim text of the Work, or a portion thereof, in an electronic format in any media and by any means, on any platform now known or hereafter developed, but without

enhancement (such as video, extrinsic illustrations, audio, or any other contributions not present in the printed edition of the Work). Any such display, transmission, or transfer of more than a single chapter of the Work must be encrypted to prevent unauthorized reproduction. Publisher acknowledges and agrees that such grant of electronic display rights does not include any grant of electronic version or interactive multimedia rights, and that such rights are expressly reserved to Author.

Reversion of Rights

Some contracts state that as long as the publisher keeps the book in print somewhere (even if it's available only in New Zealand), the rights will not revert to the author. It is generally in the best interest of the writer that the rights to the book revert when the book is out of print in book form in the United States. Ask and see.

It's becoming more important to note that the availability of print on demand copies or electronic copies have the potential to keep a contract in effect forever if it is not expressly excluded from the definition of "in print."

Publishers might say this is beneficial to the author, but it prevents the author from having the book reissued by another publisher who might promote it, which actually might happen if a new book by the author becomes successful. It also hinders the author's ability to reuse the material in other, newer works on the same subject. In any case, it is just as easy for an author to make her book available through print on demand as it is for the publisher, and the author can keep 100 percent of the profits without having to earn out an advance.

If you can neither keep the print on demand rights nor get the publisher to exclude print on demand from the out-of-print clause, then at least request vociferously that a clause be added stating that unless the book sells a certain number of copies (for example, 250) in a royalty period, the work shall be considered out of print. Many publishers are finding this to be a fair compromise.

The Least You Need to Know

- A publishing contract grants the publisher the right to publish and sell your book.

- You should receive a small payment, a royalty, on every copy of your book that is sold.

- Exactly what rights are granted to the publisher is open to negotiation.

- Under most contracts, the publisher has the final decision regarding the book's actual title and the cover artwork.

- Some contract terms are more negotiable than others, such as free copies to the author, first serial rights, and merchandising rights.

- If you plan to negotiate on your own, get help from a literary lawyer, or get a good book on publishing contracts. The family lawyer probably won't be much help here.

Part 4

War and Peace: Working with a Publisher

Congratulations, you've got a publisher! But now what happens? In Part 4, you get a complete overview of the actual book publishing process and learn about how to work effectively with all the players. From meeting deadlines, to formatting disks, to keeping an editor happy, to understanding the retail book process, it's all here.

You also learn the basics of book publicity, a critical element in the future success of your book.

Chapter **16**

I Signed a Contract—
Now What?

In This Chapter

- Deadlines, deadlines
- That first advance check
- Assembling attention-grabbing sales materials
- Why haven't I heard from my editor?
- What your book is going through
- The loud ticking of the clock

Now you've done it—you've signed a book publishing contract. That means now you have to produce a manuscript. No more talking about how "someday" you plan to write a book—you have to *now*. In fact, you are legally obligated to write one. This was the very thing you sought so hard, but now that it's happened, it can be intimidating.

Allow us to repeat what we believe is the central message of this book: the book publishing business is a business, and to succeed in book publishing as an author, you must be businesslike.

You wrote a businesslike query letter. You put together a businesslike proposal. You conducted contract negotiations in a businesslike manner. Now you must continue to behave in a professional manner during the next phases of the process. No artistic suffering, no writer's block—and the dog can't eat your manuscript. Remember to use professional behavior at all times and in all interactions with your publisher.

Deadlines Loom

Deadlines can sound so final—and they are. When a contract specifies a deadline for a completed manuscript, it's not just an arbitrary date. It's a date that needs to be met because of these reasons:

- ◆ You need to maintain a good working relationship with your editor and publisher.

- ◆ Your publisher has to plan for the publication of your book in advance so it can be sold and marketed.

- ◆ If you do not meet the deadline, your chances to be published might disappear.

Think back to those idyllic days when you first decided to write a book. You were completely in charge of the schedule for the project. You decided when you would sit down and write, when you would wander down to the bookstore for a low-fat cappuccino and a little bit of research, and when you'd finish up the query letter.

But those leisurely days are behind you. After you sign a contract with a publishing house, you may no longer do things at your own pace. You must meet the deadlines specified in the contract. You also have to think about something else—meeting the exact *word count* or *page count* specified in your contract.

def•i•ni•tion

Some contracts specify a **word count** for the completed manuscript. This is the minimum number of words your manuscript should contain to live up to the contract. Some contracts might specify a **page count,** the minimum number of pages that must be in the manuscript. And sometimes there is a maximum word count or page count, which ensures you don't promise *Life's Little Instruction Book* and deliver *War and Peace.*

Ready, Set ...

Why is meeting deadlines so important? The minute a book is scheduled for an upcoming season, the following wheels are set into motion:

◆ The book is scheduled for publication.

◆ The catalog copy writers begin to write.

◆ The cover designer begins to design.

◆ The accountants begin to forecast costs and expenses.

◆ The sales department starts planning the best way to sell your book.

◆ The publicity department begins to think about publicizing your book.

◆ The subrights department begins to think about who they can sell foreign rights to or which magazines might pay to excerpt.

◆ Your editor makes plans for editing your book.

So as you can see, this is no longer just a solitary endeavor for you, your imagination, or your computer. A large structure has just been put into place that depends on the timely arrival of your fully completed manuscript.

We'll examine some of these things more closely in later chapters so you have a better understanding of the sales process, the publicity process, and the editorial process. But for right now, keep that image in your mind—the image of a cast and crew of several people all waiting anxiously to begin working on your book.

This image isn't meant to scare you. But on those days when you just don't feel like working (even if you know it will set the project back a week or two), remember what's happening inside the publishing house. The entire house is expecting you to meet a deadline.

More Time, Please?

You tried hard to meet the deadline, but the book just won't be done on time. What can you do? You can ask your editor for an extension on the deadline—that is, an officially sanctioned excuse note.

"Don't wait until the last minute to ask for an extension," warns editor Steve Martin of Sage Publishing. "Better to recognize your need for extra time as early as possible and ask accordingly." If you don't warn your editor that you won't make the deadline and then call the day your book is due … well, this is not a good thing. No editor wants to hear bad news at the very last minute. Plan ahead, but don't count on an extension, and never ask for an extension of an extension. Do try to get your editor to put the extension in writing. Read your contract, and be sure you're aware of what will happen if you ask for more time. At many houses, the failure to meet a new deadline can be grounds for cancellation.

> ### Slush Pile
>
> Bear in mind that if you need to ask for an extension on your deadline, the reason is immaterial. The editor doesn't really care if your computer crashed, your house was destroyed in a mudslide, or there has been a death in the family. This sounds cruel, but it's true. One excuse is no better than another. If the book is late, the editor is in trouble. It doesn't matter why.

Where's My Advance?

You signed a contract promising to deliver a completed manuscript by a certain date. The publishing company also signed that contract and promised to send you an advance. But it's been weeks, and the money isn't here. You have to meet a deadline; shouldn't there be some deadline they have to meet, too?

> ### Slush Pile
>
> Editors don't cut checks; the royalty department generally does. No matter how sympathetic your editor is that you haven't yet received a check, she cannot write one for you. She might be able to walk down the hall and ask, nudge, or lobby, but she cannot write the check. So don't hold your editor responsible because the check hasn't arrived yet.

The simple answer is "no." The company should be timely, but it can take many months sometimes to see the first of your money. Welcome to the world of business.

It seems awfully unfair, doesn't it? Yes, but try to be businesslike about it. If you have an agent, let your agent nudge the editor about when the first payment will arrive. If you don't have an agent, tread as gently on the topic as you can. You're just starting out in your relationship with your editor—don't jeopardize it now. Should you threaten to stop working on the book until you get your first check? Once again, the simple answer is "no." Yes, it stinks that you're working hard to meet a deadline and the money hasn't yet shown up. But it's better for your book (and your career) to keep working. If you threaten to stop working, you only hurt yourself.

> **Hot Off the Press**
>
> When does a contract become a signed contract? Most publishers send a contract to you to sign, then you send it back for them to "countersign." It might have to be countersigned by more than one person in-house. After the publisher countersigns the contract, a check request for your "on signing" advance is processed. The publisher will also send you a copy of your contract. Your contract then will go to the royalty department, where they will set up an account for your new book and process the check. Depending on the department and size of publisher, this entire process can take up to 4 to 6 weeks.

The Sizzle for Your Steak

You and your editor have had a conversation or two about your book, and she has asked you for quite a bit of backup material. This might seem like unimportant stuff to you. Shouldn't you concentrate on writing and not have to worry about sending off the bunch of newspaper clippings and magazine articles she's asked for?

As you learned a few paragraphs ago, much is happening at the publishing house while you work away on your book. One of those things is *hype*.

The fate of your book may depend on several things, including how excited the salespeople are, how sexy the catalog copy is, and how jazzed up your editor is.

Bend Over Backward

While you're working hard to meet your manuscript deadlines, you also need to work hard to supply the things the folks at the publishing house need—particularly *when* they need it. If someone from the publicity department calls for a copy of the newspaper profile you included in your proposal, make another copy and send it. Don't ask to get a copy from your editor. If someone from the editorial department calls and asks about where you went to school, answer the question. Don't tell the caller that the answer can be found in your proposal.

Will You Say "I Love It"?

Your editor (or the copywriter, or the publicist) might also ask you about endorsements. Your proposal bragged about an endorsement or two, and now you need to produce them! Why do they need endorsements so long before the book is published? Endorsements aren't just used on the back of the book or in advertisements—they are sometimes used in catalog copy as well. (The catalog and book covers are usually produced 6 to 8 months before your book is published. If your book will be publicized with bound galleys 4 months before publication, your publisher will need cover quotes and other materials even months earlier.)

You need to spend time and energy rounding up endorsements for your book, often both professional and celebrity ones. But you will be amazed at how the words, "I'm under contract to Publisher X to write a book …" helps you open doors and get responses to requests for endorsements. You'll find that this is a great time to expand your personal and professional network. And never forget that most folks *love* to see their name in print!

You're Excited; They're Excited

Understand that publishing people will ask you all kinds of silly questions and for all kinds of silly stuff. Just smile and provide the answers and materials they need. The easier you make it for them, the more excited they will be about you and your book. Conversely, the less cooperative you are with them, the more their excitement will dim.

def•i•ni•tion

The word-of-mouth publicity created before a book is actually published is the **buzz**. You want a lot of buzz for your book, from the publicity department to the sales department. The more buzz, the better.

The more enthusiasm that builds around you and your book, the better your chances for strong sales. And you can help create the excitement and enthusiasm by supplying your publisher with as much information as possible to create a *buzz*, the impression that you and your book are destined for greatness.

But I Haven't Heard from My Editor in Months!

You're working diligently to meet your deadline. You've created a writing schedule, and you sit down to write every day, regardless of whether you feel creative. You take your contract deadline seriously. So why haven't you heard from your editor in a while? Has she forgotten about you?

No. No one will forget about you. But yes, there may be long stretches when you will not hear from anyone.

Another reality check from the world of publishing: your editor is responsible for many books at once, perhaps as few as a dozen or as many as 30. It depends on the size of the publishing house and how many editors are on staff. What's more, all the books the editor oversees are in different stages—acquisitions, contract negotiation, manuscript review, typesetting, publicity—so her attention is sometimes fragmented.

Speaking as longtime editors, we can assure you not to worry about the long absences. If an editor leaves you alone for a while, take it as a sign of trust. The editor trusts that you are a professional who is working away on your own, not needing constant encouragement and reinforcement from her. Editors adore writers who don't need constant attention.

What's Going on with My Book?

You are writing easily and are pleased with the progress you've made so far. Your check for the first half of the advance has arrived, and your editor has expressed his confidence in your ability to do the job. Let's leave you alone for a moment and check in to see what's happening at the publishing house.

You aren't alone. It may seem that way as you write deep into the night, with your computer screen glowing in the darkness. But you are not alone. Much is happening with your book.

♦ Editorial and marketing are finalizing the title of your book with any subtitles or taglines.

♦ Copywriters are producing copy for the catalog, which the sales reps will take with them to sell your book.

♦ Cover designers, art directors, and marketing folks are designing a cover for your book.

> **Experts Say**
>
> If you thought writing a book was a lonely pursuit, just wait until you sit through those long silent months of anticipation until your book arrives in finished form! "You need to involve yourself in lots of non-book-related things during this phase," one much-published author recommends. "Go hiking, build a house with Habitat for Humanity, anything to keep yourself from obsessing about what is going on with your book!"

What's in a Name?

You learned in Chapter 15 that the publisher has the final say over your book title. If the publisher does change your book's title, it won't be a casual decision. The title of your book will be discussed again and again. In every meeting on any marketing issue—from catalog copy to cover design and everything in between—the title will be reexamined.

> **Slush Pile** _____
>
> You might find yourself talking to someone from the publishing company who knows very little about your book. Perhaps it's the copywriter, a publicity person, or an editorial assistant. If this happens (and it probably will), don't be snippy. Understand that yours is just one of many books that person is handling. Be polite, and use this as an opportunity to educate, not attack.

When a group of people cluster around a table to see the sketches for your book's cover, the title will be questioned.

When a group of people sit together to examine the sales department issues for your book, the title will be questioned.

When your book is presented to the sales department (more about that in a future chapter), the title will be questioned.

Why does everyone care so much about what your book is eventually named? Because a good name can make a book, and a lousy name can kill it. When these same folks aren't obsessing over the title of your book, they are probably obsessing over the subtitle, if your book has one, which is equally critical to the success of your book.

Catalog Copy

Using your own book proposal as a basis, a copywriter is struggling away to describe your book in 100 words or less for the catalog the sales representatives use. On rare occasions, a copywriter may call the author to learn more about the book. The more he knows, the easier it is to choose the most important points that must be included in the 100-word description.

Hot Off the Press

Books are cataloged and sold by seasons. Winter season is typically for books that publish January through April, spring/summer season is for books that publish May through August, and fall season is for books in September through December. When a publisher schedules a publication month for your book, they will take into account any "seasonality" or if there's a time during the year that books on your topic are more popular. For example, January is big month for weight loss and fitness books, September is the big month for cookbooks and gift books, and July is usually the big month for back-to-school topics.

Judging a Book by Its Cover

Another busy person at the publishing company is the cover designer. This person's title might vary somewhat, from art director to cover coordinator. But somewhere, someone is working on designing a cover for your book.

The same group of people who met to decide whether to publish your book might also be getting together to discuss the cover ideas. Or it might be a group that includes more folks from sales and marketing and fewer from editorial. Regardless of the group's makeup, its task is a critical one: to decide how to best convey your book's message in such a way that it accomplishes these points:

◆ The cover is eye-catching and unique.

◆ The title can be read from a distance.

◆ The purpose of the book is immediately clear.

This is easier said than done. The proper solution for each book is different.

Will these cover folks include you in their discussion? Possibly. Another harsh fact (are there more?) is that, as with the title, the publisher has the contractual right to determine what the cover says and what it looks like. As the author, you might be included as a courtesy (this is called "consultation"), but it isn't guaranteed.

The Good, the Bad, and the Ugly

What if you don't like the title? If your editor sends you a copy of the cover in the works (not all do) or you read the catalog copy and you think it stinks, do not react immediately. Count to 10. Count to 20 if you still aren't cooled down. Never make a phone call to your publishing house in the heat of the moment.

The best way to convey your thoughts about the cover is on paper. Write a measured, professional letter in which you offer alternative suggestions. Don't just offer criticism in your letter. Make useful suggestions, too. Jennifer received a thoughtful e-mail from two of her authors not long ago with their thoughts on the cover. They made professional suggestions regarding the type size and colors on the cover and also pointed out that as a married couple they preferred their names read somewhat differently than shown—critical information they needed to pass along, and it was appreciated.

If you have an agent, let the agent know how you feel about the cover. With your agent to back you up, the publisher just might make some changes.

The Clock's Ticking

But enough about these other people—let's get back to you and your computer again. The time is ticking away, and the deadline looms closer …

Although this is a book about getting published, not about actually writing a book, we can't resist offering you a few suggestions. Here are nine ways to meet a deadline:

- Write every day, even if it's for just 15 minutes.

- Set small goals, and reward yourself when you meet them.

- Turn off the phone, e-mail, fax, television, and radio.

- Take yourself away for a weekend to write in solitude.

- If you find yourself stuck on writing, go do research for a little while instead; then come back to your writing.

- If you're stuck on Chapter 3, work on Chapter 5 instead.

- Write your ending first and then go back and fill in everything that comes before it.

- Call your mom and ask her to scold you into writing.

- Find a buddy writer, or join a group, and report regularly on your progress.

Remember the old writing adage: if you write just one page a day, in one year you will have a 365-page book. We hope your deadline leaves you that much time!

The Least You Need to Know

- Maintain your businesslike attitude, particularly about meeting manuscript deadlines.

- If you're going to miss a deadline, give your editor as much warning as possible. Don't wait until the last minute to ask for an extension.

- Long before your book is published, you need to provide material for the sales, marketing, and publicity departments.

- There'll be long periods of time when you don't hear from anyone at your publisher. Don't worry, they haven't forgotten about you.

- While you're writing the book, other people are also working on your book, including the cover designer and the catalog copywriter.

- Keep seeking endorsements for your book while you're writing.

Saying Good-Bye to Your Baby

In This Chapter

- ◆ Tips on typing and formatting your manuscript
- ◆ Send in polished prose (not a first draft)
- ◆ What to do about the art
- ◆ Information on acknowledging the proper people

You met your deadline, and with a pounding heart you prepare to send off your manuscript. Is there a right way and a wrong way to submit it?

To keep your editor happy (and don't you just love the phrase "your editor"?), you need to submit a clean and polished manuscript prepared according to the publishing house's rules. These rules are known as the manuscript guidelines.

Go with the Guidelines

Typical *manuscript guidelines* stipulate things such as the following:

- What type of word-processing software is acceptable, such as the most current version of Microsoft Word or WordPerfect

- What type of disk to send (floppy, ZIP, or CD/DVD) or how to submit by e-mail or ftp server (some large publishers have a dedicated site on which to transfer large files)

- How many printed hard copies of the manuscript to send

def•i•ni•tion

Manuscript guidelines (or author guidelines) pertain to the actual formatting, disk preparation, and hard copy requirements of the final manuscript. These guidelines vary among publishing houses and sometimes among editors within a house. Be sure you have a copy of the manuscript guidelines in hand before you start to prepare your manuscript.

Slush Pile

Andy Rooney, Danielle Steel, and a few die-hard newspaper columnists still use old manual typewriters. But don't think that you, as a first-time writer, can turn in a typewritten manuscript. Those days are behind us now. Plug in your computer and get typing!

Disks? Formats? Say what? If these terms are unfamiliar to you, you might be—dare we say it—computer illiterate. In this age of cyberspace and hard drives, a writer needs to know the basics of word processing, the Internet, and file formats. Traditionalists might object, but even the die-hards are submitting electronically these days. As in other parts of the business world, publishing has embraced technology, too.

Why not simply pound out your masterpiece on your trusted old Underwood manual typewriter and then pay someone to input it on a computer for you? You could. But by the time you pay a typist to not only input your manuscript but also make any corrections that come up later in the editing and production phases, heck, you could buy a pretty fancy computer—and hire someone to train you. Your publishing house most likely has an optical scanning service available to convert your manuscript, but you will probably be charged for the cost of preparation.

Submitting your manuscript on a disk might not be enough. Today, you will most likely be asked to communicate and even submit electronically, via e-mail or ftp. So you're going to need a modem and an e-mail account. Moreover, if you are e-mailing your chapters, you might be asked to follow guidelines similar to these:

- Create an individual file for each chapter of the book. Do not write your entire book in one file.

- Save the files as attachments to an e-mail. *Do not* cut and paste text into the e-mail message area.

- Save all files as Microsoft Word docs or compatible (per your publisher's instructions). To ensure that your editor can read your files, send a test file using only one **chapter**.

- If at all possible, avoid submitting incomplete files. If you must update a file after it has been submitted, talk to your editor and get instructions on the best way to do this.

- Be sure you're using an Internet provider that lets you send and receive multiple files. If you love your AOL account, you might want to investigate setting up another account just for your manuscript, as AOL will only let you send or receive one attachment per e-mail. Many writers have Hotmail or Yahoo! accounts for this very reason.

- To reduce the number of e-mail submissions and maximize the number of files submitted per e-mail, you might want to utilize compression software such as WinZip (or StuffIt if you're on a Macintosh).

Experts Say

You need to be comfortable sending and receiving files electronically when you enter the publishing world. If this will be a new skill for you, start practicing now.

Sound complicated? It might seem so at first, but look at e-mail submissions this way: they cut down on the cost of postage (and those trips to the post office) and allow for *nearly instant* confirmation that your files have been received. If you're still confused, consider investing in a simple book on Microsoft Windows, the Internet, or the word-processing program of your choice. If all else fails, ask a teenager to help you.

Hot Off the Press

Submitting your manuscript by e-mail? Don't submit and just assume your editor received the files. A project editor at Prima Publishing told us about the stressful time an author e-mailed his entire manuscript at the very last minute on the day it was due in a text format that was unreadable. Then the author left on a month-long trip traveling to an inaccessible part of the Middle East and was unreachable. "It caused quite a panic for a day or two," remembers the editor, "but luckily his assistant also submitted a disk a few days later. Whew!"

The Best Software

By definition, the best software for you to use is the software stipulated in the manuscript guidelines. But when you first started writing so many months (or years) ago, who knew what publisher you would end up with and what kind of software that publisher would require or recommend?

Your best bet, then, is to stick with the largest and most popular programs—Microsoft Word or WordPerfect. Most editors work on PCs, not on Macintoshes. As a general rule, the more current the version of your program, the better.

If you're submitting electronically, your publishing house might even have many editors edit the files electronically or "online." Programs such as Microsoft Word have features that allow editors to track their changes, make comments, and edit your manuscript so you can see very clearly any additions or deletions. It's worth it for you to become familiar with the revision features in your software. You will most likely need to use them.

Hot Off the Press

Working with a co-author or several contributors? It might go quite smoothly computer-wise, or it might not. In our case, it was a bit of a hassle in the early years. Jennifer, who wrote in an old version of Word for Windows, couldn't read her co-author Sheree's files written in WordPerfect. We tried saving and then e-mailing files in a variety of different file formats, but no luck. So we resorted to long faxes flying back and forth. It seems so old-fashioned now, and our equipment and our skills have improved greatly over the years. If you are not writing alone, one author needs to take the lead in preparing the manuscript. Work this out before you get too far into the project to avoid misunderstandings and future complications.

Proper Formatting

Back in the days before computers, *formatting* was pretty straightforward. Your editor would ask you to submit your manuscript neatly typewritten (with a new ribbon!), on standard, white, $8\frac{1}{2} \times 11$-inch high-quality bond paper. Margins were to measure 1 inch all around, and text was to be double-spaced with $\frac{1}{2}$-inch indentations.

It was quite simple, actually. The tricky stuff such as italics, bold, *headings*, and the like, were left to the typesetter.

def•i•ni•tion

Formatting refers to the set of instructions that determines the way the printed words appear on the page, including things such as margins, indents, type size, and fonts. A **heading** (often called a head) is the title introducing a chapter or subdivision of the text. Typically, a manuscript has a hierarchy of different-size headings throughout, which you need to designate as Head 1, 2, 3, or Head A, B, and C. Your author guidelines will specify how your publisher wants heads handled.

Those days (and the typesetters) are gone at many, if not most, publishing houses. In the age of computerized publishing, the rules have changed considerably, for both the publisher and the writer. Now, formatting requirements are designed to facilitate the production process. More than one author has grumbled about the extra work, but it is a fact of life these days.

As you've learned, most writers are asked to submit computer disks as well as hard copy (a printed manuscript). How the writer is asked to format the text on those disks varies somewhat from publisher to publisher. It depends entirely on the publisher's computer sophistication and editorial conventions. However, some fairly standard formatting requirements exist:

♦ One-inch margins around the page

♦ Standard 12-point type in a typewriter font, such as Courier or Times New Roman

♦ Single line spaces between paragraphs, rather than indents

♦ Double-spaced copy

♦ Unjustified text

♦ No double hard returns

♦ One computer file per chapter, named according to the house's naming convention

♦ Hard copy printed on a desk jet or laser-quality printer, on good, 8½ × 11-inch white paper

♦ No double spaces after periods

Slush Pile

If your personal equipment isn't up to current standards, spend time and money at a FedEx Kinkos or other business where you can rent computer time.

> **Slush Pile**
>
> Don't make the mistake of turning in a disk with one enormous file on it (unless your editor has preapproved this). Your editor will not be happy. At one unnamed publishing company, faced with a 340-page manuscript all written in one file (instead of saved one chapter per file), the editor had to hire a freelancer to electronically break up the file chapter by chapter. If you submit your manuscript this way, your editor could send it back to you and make *you* redo it.

Most publishing houses have prepared very detailed formatting guidelines for writers under contract. These guidelines often specify particular coding for various design elements such as headings. Many publishers send these guidelines out when they return the signed contract. Don't wait for that—as you know from Chapter 15, you might have finished the book before the signed contract comes! If you have any questions at all, just ask your editor to send the guidelines early.

Don't assume these guidelines are just suggestions and you really don't have to follow the page setup guidelines or formatting instructions. Also, don't assume your publisher will just fix the problems themselves and not bother you with it. You might get lucky, and you might not. It's terrible to have worked so hard to meet a deadline only to have your editor send your entire manuscript back to you to be put into the proper format. It could also jeopardize the schedule for your entire project. The work has to be done—and if it's your responsibility, it's going to fall to you.

> **Slush Pile**
>
> Don't forget to number the pages on your manuscript before sending it in. We've heard horror stories of large manuscripts accidentally dropped, with pages flying everywhere, only to find that—yikes!—the pages weren't numbered. Don't let this happen to your editor!

You should also understand that not following the publisher's guidelines could affect the page count (if they ask for 1-inch margins, for instance, and you use 1.25 instead), which could make your book run too long or too short.

If you don't understand something in the publisher's guidelines, do speak up. Speak up sooner, rather than later. Editors and production people are happy to explain and can easily clear up any confusion. Remember, there are no stupid questions in life.

Why So Many Copies?

Most publishing contracts specify that you submit your book on disk, along with at least two hard copies of the entire manuscript. This might seem excessive to you (especially at 5 cents or more a page for copying), but it is still required. Having more than one copy of the manuscript is critical for the production process. Here's why:

As soon as your manuscript arrives at the publisher, your editor opens it with great expectations. Typically, she hands your computer disk right off to an editorial assistant. The editorial assistant makes an extra copy of the disk for the design and production departments.

The editor keeps one hard copy of your manuscript for herself to read; the other copy of the manuscript goes to the editorial assistant. This extra copy is copied and copied and copied in-house. Copies of your manuscript end up in the hands of any other editor in line to read your book—everyone from other acquisitions editors who are curious about it to developmental editors, production editors, publicists, and other folks you haven't heard of yet. (You'll learn who all these folks are in Chapter 18.)

Without two copies, each ready to initiate the editorial and production processes, delays could occur. And you wouldn't want that. So cough up the 5 cents a page and be done with it.

Garbage In, Garbage Out

GIGO is tech-talk for the phrase "garbage in, garbage out," an expression as applicable to publishing as it is to computers. The cleaner the manuscript you send to your publisher, the cleaner the book that comes out from your publisher.

Writers often complain about the finished product, as if that product were completely out of their hands. Particularly loathsome to writers are unnecessary tinkering by copy editors, typos, and formatting bloopers.

Yet as the writer, you have more control over this process than you might think. If you turn in a manuscript riddled with grammatical errors, typos, and formatting inconsistencies, you're asking for trouble.

So polish your prose. Check your grammar and your spelling. Follow your publisher's formatting guidelines to the letter. You'll be glad you did (and you'll impress your editor, to boot!). If you've forgotten everything you learned in English class, take a look at *The Complete Idiot's Guide to Grammar and Style*, now in its second edition, for a refresher course.

File Management Matters

You'll turn in those chapters, each tucked neatly into an individual file, cleverly named. Sometimes too cleverly named …. Choose clear file names like "Chap. 1" and so forth. Stay away from using the actual name of the chapter—"Chapter One, How It All Began." Clearly named files are critical because when the developmental editing or copy editing phase begins, many versions of your files will be flying back and forth through cyberspace, and it is easy to become confused. We like to do it this way:

> Chap1
>
> Chap1-revise
>
> Chap1-revise2
>
> Chap1-final

You'll develop a system that works for you, or your publisher might have a system they want you to use. Just remember to keep it as simple and clear as possible so you (or your editor) can tell at a glance which version of the chapter this is.

Experts Say

The Chicago Manual of Style is the book publishing bible and every writer's best friend. It's a veritable treasure trove of information that addresses all the spelling, grammar, and language usage issues you're likely to encounter in a lifetime of writing. "Using *The Chicago Manual of Style* as your guide marks you as a professional and impresses your editor," says book doctor John Waters. The book is available in the reference section of the bookstore, or you can even search it online.

What About the Pictures?

Many book projects include *interior art*, a term that in book publishing refers to the photographs, illustrations, maps, and cartoons that might appear on the pages of the book. If your book does have interior art, you need to find out exactly what your responsibilities are concerning it.

Some publishers—particularly the larger ones—provide all the art, and they like it that way. If this is the case, you, as the author, might be encouraged to contribute ideas for possible art. Or you might well be discouraged from contributing art ideas. Check your book contract to see what your publisher expects from you.

What if you're responsible for providing art? You'll have to provide it in the proper way. Here again, this varies from publisher to publisher. Most often, it depends on the production department's technical sophistication.

Here are a few possible scenarios:

- If you're providing black-and-white photographs, you might be asked to provide simple 8 × 10-inch black-and-white glossies. Or you might be asked to provide color slides or electronic versions that you've scanned and delivered electronically in GIF or JPEG files at the publisher's required resolution.

- If you're providing maps, you might be asked to provide simple sketches that the publisher's art department can use to render final art. Or you might be asked to deliver *camera-ready*, professional-quality maps.

- If you're providing actual illustrations (this is unlikely), you might be asked to deliver the originals or the camera-ready versions of those originals.

def•i•ni•tion

Camera-ready art refers to the finished artwork that is ready to be photographed or scanned, without alteration, for reproduction. Sometimes it's called mechanicals.

Slush Pile

Including art or photographs in a book can increase its production cost—and, thus, its price—considerably. So despite your opinion, if the publisher decides not to include art in the book, try to understand and be gracious. This is a business decision, not an emotional one.

Permissions

Regardless of the form, remember that you must also obtain written permission to reprint any art that's not your own or that's not in the *public domain*.

Art is not the only thing that requires permission or a signed release form from the copyright holder. Many new writers make the mistake of not paying enough attention to the fact that they probably need permissions or releases when dealing with the following:

◆ Artwork, photographs, or screen shots from websites

◆ Interview subjects whose comments and names you plan to include in the book

◆ Quotes taken from other published works such as books, magazines, or websites

◆ Song lyrics

◆ Contributions from other writers, such as in a story collection or when you have asked a writer to make a substantial written contribution to your book

def•i•ni•tion

Written works or artwork that is no longer protected by copyright law is in the **public domain** and can be used without permission or cost by anyone. Artwork that is free to be used by anyone without obtaining permission is called clip art.

Ask your editor early in the game if the publishing house has a standard release form you can use. If you aren't clear on how or when to seek permission, your editor might be able to hook you up for a conversation with someone in the legal department so you have a better understanding.

Identify early in your project what material you will need, including releases, permissions, and who you'll need to contact. Keep good records, and organize your paperwork. Your editor will be expecting all this documentation with your final submission.

Plagiarism

Plagiarism is a very real issue for publishing houses today. There are many misconceptions about what kind of material is *fair use*, how much you can use before permission must be obtained, and how it must be cited.

def•i•ni•tion

Fair use could be the most misunderstood concept in writing today. Many authors think two sentences is fine, while others think there's a 500-word rule. The truth is, fair use can vary greatly depending on the size, type, and content of the original work. The legal definition has more to do with *how* the content is used—not so much *how much* of it is used. If you're excerpting material from other sources, be sure to check with your editor and get the publisher's guidelines for use.

> **Slush Pile** _____
>
> We've known several editors who have had projects fall through because authors submitted a manuscript full of uncited or improperly used material. "We don't think most of them deliberately set out to plagiarize work. We just think most of them don't truly understand what they are doing is wrong," one editor told us. "We had a fully written manuscript almost published when an editor did a routine check of material. The authors had done their research using websites and cut and pasted material from various sites into their book with no rewrites and no cites!" The authors' response about the plagiarized material? They said, "It was on the Internet. You can't copyright material on the Internet. It's free." Needless to say, their book wasn't published.

Publishers do spot checks on manuscripts, and some even go through legal vetting. But contrary to popular belief, rewriting isn't enough. Be sure you talk with your editor in advance of using material from other sources. Publishers are often the most up-to-date sources of information on what's happening in copyright law, as their cases are often defining the standard.

Show Them the Money

Few new writers understand that if a fee is required to include material (such as a poem or song lyric), it is your responsibility as the author to pay it. Check your contract, and you will find that in almost all cases the author is responsible. Keep this in mind when you're writing your manuscript so you don't have to go back and cut things you literally can't afford, like that great Rolling Stones lyric you think sets the tone for your whole book. When you find out how many hundreds of dollars just a few lines can cost, you might quickly change your mind.

"I'd Like to Thank My First-Grade Teacher ..."

Ah, the acknowledgments section. Here is your chance to tell the world where you learned to write, who has influenced you in your life, and to whom you will feel eternally grateful.

Many writers turn in the acknowledgments section of their manuscript last. And because it's sometimes quite lengthy, it might seem to the editor that the author spent the most time writing this section of the book.

As a reader, aren't you annoyed by the endless log-rolling and name-dropping that goes on in the books you've bought? Don't put your own readers through the very experience that annoys you!

Again, we would like to impress upon you that the most businesslike and professional approach to the acknowledgments section is to keep it short, perhaps just a few paragraphs. Understand that if you turn in a long one, you just might be asked to cut it.

Bye-Bye, Book!

Good job. You've prepared your manuscript in strict accordance with the publisher's guidelines. Your manuscript is now ready to begin the labyrinthine journey known as the editorial and production process. It's ready to become a book. Read on to learn exactly how this happens.

The Least You Need to Know

- Computer illiteracy is not acceptable in today's publishing world. You must learn how to use a computer if you don't already know how.

- No one accepts manuscripts on paper only; all publishers require a disk or e-mail version as well.

- Save each chapter in an individual file, never write a book as one long file, and be sure to manage your files during the editing phase.

- Ask your publisher early on for manuscript guidelines.

- Remember that getting signed permissions and paying any required fees are the responsibilities of the author.

- Number the pages, make several copies, hold your breath, and send your manuscript on its way!

Chapter 18

Welcome to the Home Team!

In This Chapter

- ◆ Book production, step by step
- ◆ Who's who in the publishing business
- ◆ Tips for responding to editorial queries and changes
- ◆ Production deadlines to be aware of

Much is often made of the solitary nature of the writer's life. Some writers—loners and dreamers at heart—like it that way.

Well, writing a book may be a solo act, but making a book is a collaborative one. Making a book requires that the author put aside her artistic, sensitive, prideful self and join forces with the cast of folks needed to produce a bound book. Maybe for the first time since you started writing your book, you've joined a team.

The process of producing a book is by no means simple. You, the writer, have provided the text of the book. But a book is much more than simply text. It's a product that must be polished, designed, manufactured, marketed, promoted, sold, and shipped into retail outlets all over the country, and, finally, sold to readers.

Production in a Nutshell

The steps to producing a book include the following:

- ◆ Developmental edit
- ◆ Copy edit
- ◆ Interior design
- ◆ Front, spine, and back cover copy and design
- ◆ Indexing
- ◆ Final page proofs and proofreading
- ◆ *Bluelines*
- ◆ *F&Gs*

def•i•ni•tion

The term **bluelines,** sometimes called blues, refers to the cheap proof—the test run off the press that's usually blue (hence the name)—the printer sends to the publisher to check before proceeding with the actual printing. The **F&Gs** are the sheets of a book that have been "folded and gathered" in preparation for printing. In the rush to market, many publishers do not bother to review F&Gs, having already reviewed the bluelines. A notable exception to this is heavily illustrated books.

Join the Team

You are now part of a team of talented and resourceful publishing professionals whose contribution—whether it's the copy edit or the cover illustration—is as important to them as your words are to you. Let's meet this team and learn how you can make yourself a welcome addition to it.

We'll introduce you to these publishing professionals in the order you're most likely to meet them—or hear of them, as the case may be.

The Acquisitions Editor

The first person to read your final manuscript is usually your old friend, the acquisitions editor. By definition, this person is already a big fan of yours, having had the wisdom and foresight to offer you a book contract in the first place.

The acquisitions editor works for a publisher, an editor in chief, or a publishing director who may oversee an entire imprint or topic of publishing for a house.

The publisher also approves any final financial decisions the acquisitions editor makes. While you won't work directly with a publisher, he or she is aware of the decisions being made on your book.

But I Thought You Liked It!

At this point in the process, however, your biggest fan may become your worst critic, all in the name of making the best book possible. She'll take a big-picture look at your manuscript, performing what's called a content edit. She'll review your manuscript for the following:

- Content
- Style
- Voice
- Structure
- Pacing and more

Slush Pile

Just because you think you're done, you might not be. Jennifer went through a blue period in her career as an author when every one of her completed projects came back with a request for more material. Be cheerful, and supply the publisher what they need.

Especially for Fiction

If the book is fiction or creative nonfiction, the acquisitions editor will also be looking to see how you've handled these elements:

- Setting
- Plot
- Characterization
- Dialogue
- Point(s) of view
- Narrative
- Themes and more

When your editor has completed her review, typically she'll write up her comments, proposed changes, and questions and then forward them on to you. As we'll discuss in a later chapter, it's your job to incorporate all your changes with grace, professionalism, and speed—especially if you want to get your hands on that acceptance check. (The acceptance check doesn't come until these changes are made to your acquisitions editor's satisfaction.)

The Developmental Editor

If your acquisitions editor believes substantial changes must be made to your manuscript before approving it for publication, she may assign your project to a developmental editor. In some houses, the acquisitions editor and developmental editor are the same person. Developmental editors work on actual content, helping you rework and reorganize your manuscript to the publishing house's expectations.

If you are for any reason unable or unwilling to make the changes requested, the developmental editor may serve as a book doctor, rewriting your book as she and the acquisitions editor see fit. The fee for this developmental editing either is paid by the publisher outright at no cost to you or is paid by the publisher and then charged back to you against your royalties.

The Production or Project Editor

When you and your acquisitions editor have ironed out all the big-picture issues, you and your manuscript are handed off to the production editor, who runs your manuscript through the next lap in this publishing relay.

Just as your acquisitions editor has seen you safely through the acquisitions process (from query letter to signed contract to acceptance of the final manuscript), your production editor sees you safely through the production process (from copy edit to final proofs to bluelines to printed book).

Note: In some publishing houses, the production editor also assumes responsibility for the content editing, either doing the edit herself or sending it out to a freelance developmental editor.

The Copy Editor

The way some writers rant and rave about copy editors, you'd think they were insensitive, intolerant, inflexible … well, you get the picture.

Wrong! Copy editors can be a writer's best friend. Sure, they're a little picky, but then, they're paid to be picky. Who else catches all your inadvertent misspellings, grammatical errors, questionable punctuation, and inconsistent capitalization? Not to mention all those other things you didn't even know those meticulous copy editors check, including these elements:

- ◆ Pagination
- ◆ Illustrations
- ◆ Front and back matter
- ◆ Contradictions and ambiguities
- ◆ Parochialisms and anachronisms

- ◆ Abbreviations and contractions
- ◆ Accuracy of names, dates, and places
- ◆ Cross-references
- ◆ Coding for headings, illustrations, and the like

Who (and where) your copy editor is varies according to the publishing house. At some houses, the production editor does the copy editing herself. At other houses, the production editor sends the manuscript to the copy editing department, where an in-house copy editor does the job. At still others, the production editor sends your manuscript out to a freelance copy editor.

No matter where she comes from, the copy editor deserves your respect, and maybe even your undying love.

The Art Director

The art director is the person responsible for the way your book looks, both inside and out. In large houses, the art director heads up a design department that creates the interior and cover designs for each title. In smaller houses, the art director may create the designs herself or send them out to freelance designers.

Interior Design

Interior design varies greatly in its complexity, depending on the type of book you have written. Novels, made up primarily of *text*, typically require very simple interior designs. Nonfiction books can run the gamut, from simple text to highly illustrated, to books like the one you hold in your hands. This nonfiction book, *The Complete Idiot's Guide to Getting Published, Fourth Edition*, incorporates a number of design elements such as *sidebars*, bullets, and numbered lists. If the design of your book dictates that text be arranged in a certain way (like this one does), you may be asked to write the text accordingly (like we were).

def•i•ni•tion

Words on a page are called **text**. Text that is set aside in a box or that runs down the side in a smaller size type is a **sidebar**. Sidebars are like little asides in a conversation.

Cover Design

You may not be able to tell a book by its cover, but you can sell a book by one! The cover is a book's major sales tool. Now maybe you can see why it's important for the publisher to state flatly in the contract that the cover text and design is its decision, not yours. Moreover, the cover is usually the most expensive piece of the production process—it typically costs thousands of dollars for even the most basic cover and can cost thousands more if the cover includes an illustration or photograph. For a how-to book, the art director may choose a straightforward type of solution with no illustration. For books such as novels, the illustration is paramount.

The art director presents his designs for your book's interior and front and back covers to a panel that includes your editor, the marketing director, and the publisher.

The Copywriter

The copywriter writes the copy that appears on the cover of your book (front and back) as well as the inside flaps on a hardcover book. The cover copy must work with the cover design to entice the bookstore browser to pick up your book and buy it, right then and there. In effect, this is sales copy.

At some houses, the acquisitions editors write the copy for the books they acquire; at other houses, in-house copywriters in the marketing department write the copy. No matter who writes it, this sort of copy is an art form.

Will this be the same copywriter who wrote the description of your book for the catalog? It might be. But it might also be someone who is new to the project, so be kind and patient if that person calls you for information.

The Proofreader

The proofreader is the last person to read the formatted book pages before they're shipped off to the printer for manufacturing. The proofreader's job is to catch glaring mistakes, such as typos, pagination problems, and so forth. Think of proofreading as a last-ditch quality-control effort.

Here again, who does the proofreading depends on the house. At larger houses, in-house proofreaders in the proofreading department perform this function; in smaller houses, the proofreading may be done by editorial assistants or may be sent out to freelancers.

Indexer

Not every book has an indexer, and not every house has in-house indexers, but these folks do work here toward the end. Many indexers today work electronically, while others work on index cards. Indexing is a fine and traditional art in itself, and the finished index adds greatly to the usefulness of a book.

The Manufacturing Manager

The manufacturing manager is your publishing house's liaison with the printers. He's typically in charge of buying the paper on which to print the books and decides which printing company to use. In this age of escalating paper prices, many manufacturing managers are buying cheaper paper to keep costs down. As an author, you should know that paper is the most expensive component of the book—something like 70 percent. Complain to your editor if you like, but there may be nothing your editor can do about it, to his frustration as much as to yours!

Over to You Now

Okay, now you've met the major players in the editorial and production processes at most publishing houses. Now let's go step by step through the interactions you'll have with some of these people as your book is produced.

As we've tried to make clear in the last several pages, much of what goes on at your publishing house is out of your control and is in the hands of your team members. And the order as we've described it might vary slightly from house to house. But when the ball does bounce back into your court, you want to be sure you do your part to keep the process going smoothly.

Responding to Your Editor's Comments

Your part first comes into play when your acquisitions editor reads your final manuscript and delivers her content editing comments. No matter how pristine your manuscript, you can expect revision suggestions that include the following:

- ◆ Cuts (where you run too long)
- ◆ Additions (where you leave too much unsaid)

◆ Clarifications (where you might confuse the reader)

◆ Rearrangements (where your structure falters)

◆ Rethinking of sections (where you veer off track)

Especially for Fiction

If you're writing fiction, you can also expect comments concerning these factors:

◆ Characters who work and characters who don't

◆ Holes in the plot or plot contradictions

◆ Milking certain scenes and eliminating others

◆ Building suspense or stepping up the pace

◆ Dramatizing your beginning

◆ Sustaining interest in your middle

◆ Nailing your ending

What's Best for the Book

Take these comments in the spirit in which they are given. Your editor's only interest is in making your good book even better. No one is trying to hurt your feelings. The book's success (for both you and your editor) depends on it being the best book it can possibly be.

Sometimes editors are better at seeing what's wrong than they are at seeing how to fix it. Take a hard look at the problems your editor has identified, and if you don't like her solutions, come up with your own. Feel free to discuss these issues with your editor, but don't drive her crazy over every detail. (You learn more on maintaining this all-important relationship with your editor in Chapter 19.)

Get the job done, make the changes your editor needs, and get the manuscript back to her within the deadline she's given you. If you are slow in this step, you jeopardize the production schedule and your book may not be published on time. This is not a good thing.

Hot Off the Press _____

The publishing industry is replete with writers who have sabotaged their own book projects—and ultimately their careers—by objecting too strenuously to editorial comments. A case in point: a writer sold a book proposal to a major publisher about marriage and the devastating effects of adultery on the bonds of matrimony. When the manuscript came in, however, the editor objected to large sections in which the writer examined the feelings of the third party (the other man or woman). The editor insisted that the section be cut; it was inappropriate in a book about marriage. The writer insisted that it remain. The impasse was never resolved, and the manuscript was declared unacceptable. Deal over.

Copy Editing Changes and Queries

When you've made the content changes as requested by your acquisitions editor, your manuscript is handed off to the production editor. He reviews the manuscript and chooses a copy editor based upon that review. The copy editor makes her edits, which most likely include _author queries_.

It's your job to answer these queries as completely and swiftly as possible. If the copy editor seems a little overzealous, keep in mind that, by definition, copy editors are suspicious of everybody's copy. Don't take it personally—they are merely doing their job.

Of course, there are times when copy editors really do go overboard. If you feel this is the case, first get the opinions of other publishing

def•i•ni•tion _____

Author queries are questions the copy editor needs you, the writer, to answer before the text proceeds to the layout stage. These questions can relate to meaning, accuracy, and research, among other things.

pros as a double-check. If they, too, agree that the edit is excessive, talk to your acquisitions editor first. He may want to handle it himself. Be polite—no ranting and raving. If your editor agrees with you, he might tell the copy editor to tone it down, or he may reassign the job to someone else.

Slush Pile _____

"But I gave them a perfect book," co-author Jennifer once heard an unhappy author lament. Wrong. There is no such thing as a perfect book, and that attitude won't make you any friends at your publisher. There's always room for improvement, even if it's only a buff and polish.

More Deadlines to Meet

After the copy editing process is completed, your manuscript is ready to go to layout. In the typesetting days of old (before computers), authors received galleys to review. Galleys were long proofs pulled off the machine before the copy was divided into pages. Ask your editor if you can see a sample design for the interior layout for your book. Many houses use standard designs, but some books have custom designs.

def•i•ni•tion

Manuscripts are no longer sent off to typesetters, but rather to **compositors**. The compositor then formats the book on a computer and gets it ready to go to the printer.

But galleys are mostly history now. What you are more likely to receive are page proofs, straight from the layout person's (also called the *compositor*) laser printer. These page proofs are reviewed by a number of people, including the proofreader, the acquisitions editor, the production editor, the developmental editor, the art director, the manufacturing manager, sometimes the publisher, and then, last but not least, you, the writer.

Page Proofs

As the author, you'll usually review what's known as the first pass, the first set of page proofs from the layout person. Do not go overboard on corrections or additions here; your opportunity to make big changes was during the copy editing phase. This stage is really just to catch layout errors and typos. Don't panic if you do see a few typos. Chances are a proofreader is looking at it at the same time you are.

Changes at this stage are very expensive. And if you make too many, you have to pay for them. Check your contract for details; each publisher draws the line at a different place. Even if you don't get charged, you'll possibly delay publication.

Usually there are two more passes of page proofs, but the author seldom sees these. One ensures that the first-pass changes have been made, and then there's one more: the final pass just before the book is shipped to the printer.

Stop the Presses!

As the printer prepares to print your book (a process known as "make ready"), he first makes a proof. This proof, as we learned earlier, is called the bluelines. Publishing pros just call them "the blues."

Will you get to see the bluelines? Probably not. Blues are meant to be reviewed post-haste by the production editor only hours before the presses actually start to roll. Although some writers may insist on reviewing the bluelines, very few are allowed to do so. Without the clout of a best-selling track record behind you, you won't see the bluelines.

Even if you could, who'd want to? Leave the last-minute quality control to the pros and get started on your next book. There's no better feeling in the world for a writer than to have one book at the printer and another one in the computer.

Hot Off the Press

Desktop publishing has revolutionized the editorial and production processes for much of the industry. The managing editor of a computer game book publisher described how quickly their books appear. It's crucial for the game guides to appear in the stores when the games do. "We do everything electronically," he told us. "Our writers deliver their manuscript via e-mail, chapter by chapter as they write it. The project editor reviews them and sends them on to the copy editor, again by e-mail. The same goes for design and layout. We often even send the finished book to the printer electronically—all to save time and get our books out to the marketplace as quickly as possible."

The Least You Need to Know

- The editorial and production processes require teamwork; this means cooperation between the publishing staff and you, the author.

- Try not to take editorial criticism personally; the editor's goal is to help you write the best book possible.

- Make all requested changes, and answer all editorial queries promptly so you don't delay production.

- The later it is in the production process, the less likely you will be allowed to make changes to your book.

Proper Care and Feeding of Your Editor

In This Chapter

- ◆ Be good to your editor!
- ◆ A day in the editing life
- ◆ Getting through to your editor when you need to
- ◆ 'Fessing up when you're in trouble
- ◆ Keeping everybody on your side

Your manuscript has now left the safety of your nurturing arms and has headed off to the big city. Its fate is now in the hands of strangers, many of whom will remain strangers.

The notable exception to this is your editor. She is your link to this strange new world, so it's in your best interest to make this person your new friend.

Make a Friend for Life

Writers and editors as friends? It works for John Grisham.

When Grisham signed with Doubleday for his second novel—and first big hit—*The Firm*, he made sure to befriend his new editor, David Gernert. It's an association that has gone well beyond the usual editor/writer relationship.

Gernert edited (heavily, according to Grisham) the next several Grisham best-sellers. They both profited from the arrangement. Grisham went to the top of the best-seller lists, and Gernert went to the top of Doubleday as editor in chief.

When Grisham's agent, Jay Garon, died in 1995, Grisham asked Gernert to become his agent. Gernert, who left his job at Doubleday, acts not only as Grisham's agent, but also as his personal editor. And the best-sellers just keep on coming.

Your Book's Best Advocate—and Yours, Too!

David Gernert is literally John Grisham's advocate. And your editor, having acquired your project for the publishing house, is your book's advocate. And you want your editor to become your advocate, too.

The trick is to fuel your editor's enthusiasm for you and your book as your manuscript makes its way through the editorial and production processes. Be sure to maintain your editor's enthusiasm after the book is published, too, all the way through the marketing and promotion. At every point, your editor is crucial to the success of your book.

Hot Off the Press

The most celebrated editor of all time was the legendary Maxwell E. Perkins of Scribner's. Editor and friend to such luminaries as Thomas Wolfe, Perkins was renowned for his ability to draw the best work out of his authors. "Do not ever defer to my judgment," he admonished F. Scott Fitzgerald in one of his remarkable letters. It's worth noting that, despite Perkins's warning, Fitzgerald took his editor's comments and criticism seriously—to his and his work's great credit.

However, while your editor's excitement was initially high when the book was signed, this may fade over time. This apparent loss of enthusiasm and/or interest in your project is more a function of workload than anything else.

Remember, at any given time, your editor is juggling three lists:

◆ The list of books currently being acquired

◆ The list of books currently being produced

◆ The list of books currently being promoted

Depending on the house, this can add up to anywhere between 20 and 100 books. That's a lot of books to track. When it comes to your editor's interest, there's quite a bit of competition for your book.

It's your job to sustain this interest and to accomplish this with grace and professionalism. This means you'll need to learn as much as you can about editors and how they operate. Let's observe an editor in the field, so to speak, and find out how she spends her time.

Hot Off the Press

Most acquisitions editors toil in relative obscurity. But a handful have become industry superstars and have earned the biggest reward of all: their own imprint. When this happens, an editor's name is right up there on the book's spine with the publisher. And so you have Nan A. Talese Books/Doubleday and Regan Books/HarperCollins. That means these editors run their own mini-publishing companies inside a larger house. Both editors have had multiple best-sellers from high-profile names, and Judith Regan even had her own television show for a while. So there you have another reason to be nice to your editor: she might have her own imprint someday.

Editor for a Day

Your editor's day typically begins early. Although the workday may officially begin at 9 A.M., many early bird editors are already at their desks by 8 A.M.—and many can be found at their desks long after 5 P.M.

As you've learned before, there's little time in the editor's day to do the "real" work of reading and evaluating manuscripts and proposals. You'll recall that most of this work is done on the editor's own time, either at home or on the train, subway, or carpool. Many an editor has fallen asleep at night next to a stack of manuscripts.

8 A.M.

At your editor's office, the early birds are getting as much done as they can before the daily meetings start up:

Reading and responding to e-mail. One editor we know gets 200 e-mails a day, from authors as well as agents, other editors, and all manner of in-house staffers. Editors feel as overwhelmed by e-mail as do folks in other parts of the business world.

Going through snail mail. With any luck, your editor has an editorial assistant who sorts through the mail first. Still, many editors prefer to perform this formidable task themselves. For many years, Jennifer sat in her office at Prima and read every query or proposal that arrived addressed to her (even the ones that spelled her name wrong). Formidable? Yes. Each day the mail may bring a dozen queries, a dozen requested manuscripts and proposals, and just as many unrequested ones! That's not to mention contracts from agents, catalogs from other publishers, trade publications and newsletters, interoffice correspondence, faxes, and maybe even the occasional postcard from a long-time author.

Making overseas and transcontinental phone calls. Many editors conduct a great deal of business with foreign publishers. They evaluate projects, make deals for translations, and work together on other projects. The best time to call Europe is early in the day. Likewise, West Coast editors are calling back east as early as they can.

Writing rejection letters. Yes, some editors do write their own rejection letters. This is a time-consuming job, but many editors consider it a professional courtesy crucial to maintaining good writer-editor or agent-editor relations. Let it never be said that editors don't care about writer's feelings!

9 A.M.

By 9 A.M., the meetings start. Ask any editor how she spends her day, and she will likely say (with some irritation), "In meetings!"

The first meeting on the schedule is the production meeting. Here, your editor meets with the production editors to discuss the problems and issues regarding books currently in production. At today's meeting, your editor learns that a conflict concerning the copy edit of one title has arisen. The writer is unhappy with the copy edit and is dragging his heels on responding to the author queries. The production editor asks for your editor's help in resolving the issue. They agree to meet later in the day to call the writer together and work things out.

10 A.M.

By this time, the production meeting has ended and the cover meeting has begun. At a cover meeting, the art director, editors, marketing execs, and often the publisher get together to brainstorm ideas for new covers and to review covers already in the design process. At today's meeting, they discuss ideas for four new covers and review the art for front covers on four books in production.

One cover for a new cookbook gives them particular trouble. Cookbooks are expensive books to produce, especially when the front cover boasts a beautiful photograph of a savory dish. Cover photos featuring recipes from the cookbook require a photo shoot, a top photographer, a food stylist, the cooperation of the cookbook author, and, of course, the food. It's an expensive production from start to finish.

Even then, the results are not guaranteed. Maybe the final photos are not what anyone—including your editor—had hoped they would be. The art director is defensive, the marketing executive is fighting for another photo shoot, and the publisher is unhappy at the prospect of doubling the cover costs with another shoot. Your editor knows the cookbook author (a best-selling author currently being wooed by other publishers) will not like the photo, either. "If we run with this cover, we could be giving the agent the ammunition she needs to convince the author to switch houses," your editor argues. The publisher agrees and approves a new photo shoot.

Noon

By the time these and other issues have been resolved, it's after 12 P.M. Your editor, late for a luncheon with a top agent, runs down the street to the appointed restaurant, cell phone in hand. Once there, she sits down for a quick bite (no three-martini lunch, this) with the agent. In between bites, the agent pitches a few of his clients' top projects.

As the editor pays for lunch, the agent tells her that he will be in touch with her on the projects that most piqued her interest.

1:30 P.M.

Your editor rushes into her office to check her messages before the next meeting begins. As quickly as possible, she returns the most urgent phone calls. One is to an agent about a final contract point, one is to an author about a rewrite in progress, and one is to a rights manager trying to close a deal with a book club.

By the time she hangs up the phone, 45 minutes have gone by. She has only 15 minutes to collect her thoughts (and her information) for the most trying meeting of the day: the acquisitions meeting with the pub board. This is the meeting in which editors try to sell their colleagues and bosses on projects they'd like to sign for publication.

The degree of formality at these meetings may vary from house to house, but the pressure does not. Your editor, and the projects she pitches, fall under close scrutiny during these meetings. As you read in Chapter 14, each editor at the meeting presents one or more titles. This round-robin approach continues until all the books have been discussed or the time is up. Not surprisingly, acquisitions meetings often run late.

At today's meeting, your editor is able to present two projects. The first, a follow-up book by an author whose first book did very well, is an easy sell. The other, an offbeat project by a first-time author the editor loves, is not. Despite her passion for the project, she fails to convince her peers and will have to turn down the writer.

5 P.M.

Your editor finally returns to her office. Again, she listens to her voicemail messages and returns the most urgent calls. She checks her e-mail and her snail mail for afternoon FedEx packages. She sorts through her in-box, pulling out the catalog copy for a couple of new books left there by the copywriter, which must be reviewed and returned before she goes home. Ditto for the proofs of two covers for books due to ship to the printer the next day.

> **Experts Say**
>
> "There's a fine line between too much contact and too little," one weary editor admits. "The first note to strike is one of professionalism. If you treat your editor like a pro, odds are she'll return the favor."

Depending on how late she works, she may also make the less urgent calls on her list and write more rejection letters. She writes a very encouraging and complimentary rejection letter to the writer whose project she was unable to sell at her acquisitions meeting earlier in the day. She recommends another editor at another house to the writer.

6 P.M.

She packs up the manuscripts she hopes to review at home that evening and leaves the office.

11:30 P.M.

Your tired editor falls asleep, a stack of proposals in her lap.

Tomorrow brings more of the same. It's a tough job, but your editor loves doing it. It's her love for her work that keeps her coming back, despite the relatively low pay and heavy workload.

Why Doesn't My Editor Ever Call Me?

Unless you slept through the last couple of pages, you now know why. She's busy—busier than you imagined. But don't panic that she hasn't called lately. Generally, no news is good news.

Still, you want to believe your editor has not forgotten you and your book. If you need to discuss an issue, call and talk to her about it. Given the time she spends in meetings, you may often be reduced to leaving messages on her voicemail. Voicemail can be frustrating, but don't allow your frustrations to influence the message you leave. Be brief and succinct. Be sure to let her know the best time to return your call so you two don't wind up playing phone tag. An even better way to get together on the phone is to schedule a time via an e-mail exchange or just use e-mail to send regular updates.

If you don't hear back from your editor in a reasonable amount of time, you can do a number of things:

◆ If your editor has an assistant, try getting through to him. Often he may be able to resolve the situation himself. Befriend the assistant. Not only can he help you now, but he may be able to help you later—when he's an acquisitions editor himself!

◆ Try contacting your editor via e-mail. Most editors have e-mail now, and many are finding it an increasingly efficient way to communicate.

◆ If an issue has come up during the editorial or production process, try to resolve it with the production editor first. Only as a last resort should you antagonize your production editor by running around him to your acquisitions editor.

Slush Pile

Have an attitude? Don't. One writer we know turned in a manuscript twice as long as the contract specified and then refused to speak to her editor about it by phone. The writer demanded that, from now on, the staff communicate with her only by e-mail. The book was eventually published, but by then she'd made enemies all over the building. Did she sell them another book? No.

◆ The same thing goes for going over your editor's head to her boss. Before you do anything like this, talk to your agent. Let your agent talk to your editor or her boss. This is one of the biggest advantages of having an agent: you get to stay pals with the editor while your agent looks like a meanie. If you don't have an agent, do the best you can to work it out with your editor. If you do go over her head (and we advise against it), proceed at your own peril.

> **Hot Off the Press** _____
>
> If you feel you need to go over your editor's head, find out who her boss is and politely raise the issue at that level. One busy editor we know at a large house was surprised when an unhappy author sent an e-mail to the CEO of the publishing company's parent corporation complaining that his book hadn't received enough marketing attention. "I got a call from the CEO's assistant in London asking about the e-mail she'd received and if I could shed some light on the situation," she said. "Of course, the CEO understood the situation from our perspective and the author didn't get what he'd hoped. If he'd actually gone to my real boss—my publisher—he might have had his concern heard with a more sympathetic ear."

When to Confess You're in Trouble

Tell your editor sooner, as opposed to later. If for any reason you find yourself unable to meet your deadline, complete your rewrites, or turn around your author queries, speak up. Let your editor know as soon as possible.

The sooner she knows, the sooner she'll be able to do damage control. Damage control? Yes, your lateness will cause damage. Your editor will need to rework production schedules and perhaps postpone the publication of your book.

Writers hate to deliver bad news to editors. But the longer you wait, the fewer your editor's damage control options. You have to tell her straight away, while she can still do something to save your book! As long as you speak up soon, odds are that your editor will understand. Remember that books are published in seasons, and if your book misses the manuscript deadline, it might need to be pushed out to another season. This is important info to have as early as possible, as it might mean your book will have to be represented by the sales force. If there's a chance your book will slip, your publisher needs to know sooner rather than later.

Play Nice

As you've seen, editors are hardworking, underpaid people who love books and writers. They are also often job-hoppers, jumping from one publishing house to another. In

New York, where much of the book publishing industry operates, switching houses is as easy as crossing the street.

This revolving-door pattern is one many writers come to hate. It's what's known as the "orphan syndrome": you develop a good relationship with one editor, only to lose that editor to another house. Your new editor—often a hastily promoted assistant— may lack the experience your departed editor had. Worse, she may lack enthusiasm for your project. Then you find that you and your book are orphans, with no strong sponsor.

What to do? Befriend the new editor as you had the former editor. Take the time to educate her about your book. Don't assume any knowledge has been passed on from your former editor. No matter who your editor is, you need her. As your primary advocate at the publishing house, your editor is your single most important contact there. It's a relationship you must both guard and nurture.

Writers who do manage to develop strong and happy working relationships with their editors are loath to let them go. Many follow them (contracts permitting) from house to house. Of course, if you become a best-selling author, you can always do what John Grisham did—hire your favorite editor to be your editor/agent!

The Least You Need to Know

- ◆ Your editor is your primary advocate at the publishing house. Befriend her ASAP.

- ◆ Your second most important contact is your editor's assistant. Befriend him as well.

- ◆ Respect your editor's time; she's busier than you imagine.

- ◆ Give your editor time to read your manuscript. Remember that she does most of her reading at home.

- ◆ When you have bad news, deliver it early so your editor can look for solutions.

- ◆ Editors come and go, so try to make as many friends as you can among the in-house staff.

Chapter 20

So How Does My Book Get into the Stores?

In This Chapter

- An overview of the sales process
- Sales conferences: do I get to go?
- Why won't Barnes & Noble take a display?
- At the printer and warehouse
- Should I go to the BEA?

When your book comes off the printing press, where does it go? The finished books are sent directly to your publisher's warehouse and from there (many, you hope) go directly to bookstores around the country.

How did that happen? When did those bookstores learn about your book? How did they know to order it? And how did they decide how many to order?

Good questions, all. What follows is a brief lesson in the sales process as practiced by the book publishing industry. The more you know about it, the less frustrated you will be later. Writers have a vested interest in how the sales process works, so here's your chance to get educated.

A Short Course in the Sales Process

As you know, the book publishing business was once a quaint pursuit, and the sales process is still more than a little quaint. The two critical elements in this process are the publisher's catalog and the publisher's sales representatives.

The Dynamic Duo: Catalogs and Sales Reps

You've read about the sales catalog in earlier chapters, so you know how important it is that your book be well described in the catalog description. But you haven't heard much about sales representatives yet. Here's how the two critical elements—catalog and rep—come together.

> **Experts Say**
>
> Sales reps are so important that when Lewis Buzbee was putting together his proposal for a book about the pleasures of bookstores, he gathered and included letters of support both from publishers' reps as well as booksellers. How did he manage to do that? He had a bit of an in: Lewis himself is the former sales rep for Chronicle Books.

Several times a year, the sales representatives make appointments with the bookstore accounts for which they're responsible. Some sales reps have large geographic territories (all the Pacific Northwest, say, or all the Midwestern states), and some sales reps have large-volume national accounts (for example, all the Barnes & Noble stores, or all the Borders stores).

Most large publishing houses have their own full-time sales force. Many medium and small publishing houses use commissioned reps—sales reps who handle the sales for many publishers at once and receive commissions on the sales they create.

Are You Free on Tuesday?

The sales rep makes an appointment with a book buyer. That's the person who's responsible for deciding which of all the new books published the bookstore will carry and in what quantities. In small, independent bookstores, the book buyer is often also the owner or the manager who buys books for the store in every category. These folks not only make buying decisions, but they also work on the bookstore floor and are in close contact with their customers' needs. With the large national chains, however, the book buyer is a staff position based at headquarters, far from the selling floor. These national book buyers also may specialize by topic area such as health and fitness or business and personal finance. Reps meet with individual buyers depending on what topics their books cover.

The actual sales call might be either a leisurely affair over lunch or coffee (with smaller stores) or just a hurried appointment in a national buyer's cubicle.

Let Me Show You ...

During the sales call, the publisher's sales rep presents the titles that will be published in the next few months (or in the next season). With the catalog between them, the sales rep and the buyer move through page by page. The rep gives a short (very short) presentation on each book using a tip sheet or sales sheet. The tip sheet includes the editor's vision, book contents, market statistics, and other data that isn't included in the catalog. The presentation includes these points:

 ◆ A description of the book and its contents

 ◆ The publisher's plans to promote, market, and publicize the book

 ◆ The author's credentials, other books he has written, and sales by the account

Sound familiar? Except for the publisher's publicity and marketing plans, these are essentially the same things you needed to give the publisher to show that the world needed your book. Now it's your publisher's turn (through the rep) to convince the bookstores that the world needs your book.

You can see how important the material you provided is. The sales rep has just a few minutes to convince the book buyer to buy your book, and he needs the best and most compelling information possible.

You can also see, we hope, once again how important it is not to exaggerate or lie in your proposal (particularly about your credentials or your past book sales), because that information gets used over and over and over again throughout the process. If you didn't tell the truth, it will eventually be discovered. Booksellers can instantly access their accounts' previous sales on a book, and editors and booksellers have access to services such as BookScan that reveal the overall sales numbers of books in the marketplace. It will kill your book's chances for success if the rep discovers incorrect information in the middle of a sales call.

The Numbers Game

If the book buyer likes your book, how many will she order? Small stores buy in quantities ranging from just 1 copy to 10 or 20 or more for a potential best-seller. Large chains follow pretty much this same formula per store, but the total order for the entire chain might be several thousand.

Just-in-Time Inventory

Bookstores used to order what they thought they could sell in the first 30 days. With the rise of "just-in-time" inventory management, most stores now order only what they think they can sell in the first 10 days. When those copies sell, bookstores either turn to wholesale distributors (rather than the publisher) for fast reorders or ask the publisher to begin sending them the amount they need automatically each month. The theory is that less of the bookstore's money is tied up in inventory that way—and fewer copies of your book are sitting in either your publisher's or the bookseller's warehouse. This allows publishers to better control their print quantities, inventories, and—better for you—their returns.

Comparative Sales Can Make or Break You

Now that computers grace every office, book buyers rely on them to help with buying decisions. Imagine the rep has just presented a cookbook on vegetarian pasta. The book buyer turns to his computer and brings up the sales figures for other cookbooks on vegetarian pasta. If the sales look good, the buyer might order this new title, too. But if the sales look slow, chances are he might buy very few copies or—worse— completely pass on it.

Can that really be true? All the hard work you and your publisher put into writing and publishing your book, and the book buyer won't even put it on the shelf because of the slow sales of a similar book? Sad, but all too true. This is a business, and the book buyer just made what he thinks is a sound business decision, based on his knowledge of his customers' needs.

Imagine another sales pitch, this one by an author who's been published before. "This is his second novel?" the buyer notes. "Let me see how well his first book sold for us." The book buyer punches in the *ISBN* from the author's first book, and the buy for the author's second book is based in large part on the success of the first. Also frightening, but also true.

def•i•ni•tion

All published books have an **ISBN,** or an **International Standard Book Number.** These numbers are assigned by an industry publisher, R. R. Bowker. The first series of numbers always identifies the publishing house. Currently ISBNs are 10 digits long, but the system is changing to 13 digits. You can find the ISBN on a book's copyright page. Check out the ISBN on this book, and you'll see that Alpha Books is identified by 1-59257.

Prepping the Rep

The amount of time the book buyer listens to the sales rep talk about your book is frighteningly brief—sometimes less than a minute per title. Does the sales rep base this critical sales pitch only on what he learned from reading the catalog? Not exactly. The rep also heard about your book at the sales conference he attended. Let's move back to that time and go to a sales conference.

Experts Say

Just a handful of accounts (Barnes & Noble, Borders, Ingram, Wal-Mart, Target, and a few others) make up most of a book's advance orders. So if one of these passes on your title, it can affect the initial print run. If several of them pass, the publisher may reconsider publishing the book at all. On the other hand, if they really like your book, it can be an almost instant success.

Death of a Sales Conference

The traditional sales conference is a face-to-face meeting between the sales staff (who are based all around the country in their sales territory) and the editors, publicity, and marketing folk. The purpose of the sales conference is to introduce the new books for that publishing season and educate the sales reps on how to best sell them.

These meetings, sometimes held over the course of several days for the larger publishing houses, unfold like this:

◆ Each editor gives a 3- to 5-minute presentation on the books he's acquired (with longer presentations for the major titles).

◆ A large color slide of the front cover for the book is shown, and maybe some inside art as well, if it's a heavily illustrated book.

◆ The sales reps ask questions during the presentation.

◆ The sales reps break up into smaller groups with the sales and marketing managers to work out how to best present each book.

◆ The editors are alerted to any potential problems with individual titles the sales reps anticipate.

How They've Changed!

In past years, the larger sales conferences were more like big parties than business meetings, often in resort areas such as Florida or even Puerto Rico. The conferences were seen as an opportunity to reward the tired sales staff with a little vacation treat before the next season began. Jennifer remembers fondly her trips to the Ritz-Carlton on Amelia Island in those halcyon days. But as the publishing industry changed, so have the sales conferences.

Slush Pile

Sales reps are very nice people, but do not attempt to call them. They (and your editor) will not be amused if you track them down and chat them up about sales for your book. There have been many instances in which overzealous authors have soured the publisher's sales reps on pushing their book.

Some publishing companies have even cut the face-to-face aspect of these conferences. They use video-taped presentations of the books, with each editor talking about the titles as though sitting up at the dais in a conference room.

Some large publishers such as Random House have even tested the idea of using the occasional huge conference call in place of a live sales conference to keep costs down. Hundreds of folks around the country—sales reps, editors, marketing folk, and so on—all sitting and listening in to the same phone call to hear the book presentations.

Random House also supplies their sales reps with audio recordings the editors make describing their books. This way they can develop greater knowledge of each individual title and be able to craft their own fresh-sounding way to pitch it to their customers.

Do Authors Go?

Occasionally, authors are asked to attend the sales presentation. Celebrity books and other types of books driven by the author's personality are the likeliest candidates for this. When this happens and the author has charisma, it does make a difference. Having met the author, and having heard the author's own take on his book, the sales reps are often more enthusiastic about selling the book.

Should you offer to attend the sales conference? If you're a dynamite public speaker and are comfortable addressing large audiences, sure. It never hurts to ask. But don't take it personally if you're given a polite "no, thanks." Author presentations are rare these days.

Getting Reps Revved Up

Short of attending in person, is there anything you can do to try to jazz up the sales reps? Over the years, many authors have tried many things. Cookbook authors have endeared themselves by sending along sweet things based on recipes in their books. Natural health authors have sent along herbal supplements. T-shirts, CDs, and all sorts of little freebies are generally welcome, but they should tie in with your book somehow. Ask your editor how he feels about the idea before you rush out to the store to buy gifts.

Dumps and Other Promotional Ideas

While the sales rep is working to convince the book buyer to order your book, he is also trying to convince her to take a number of copies. One of the best ways to do this is to package several copies of the book together in a display pack and offer it at a higher discount: "Order 12, get an extra copy," or "Order 8 copies and get this attractive *counter display.*"

The days of *dumps* and displays are fading, however. The large chains seldom buy them because space in their stores is at a premium, and the publishers don't get enough orders to justify producing them. But savvy publishers continue to offer multiple-copy *pre-packs* to encourage larger orders.

def•i•ni•tion

Several copies of the book placed in a cardboard holder can be called either a **counter display,** a **pre-pack,** or a counter pack. Larger displays that stand on the floor and display eight or more copies are called **dumps.**

Charging for Store Exposure

Booksellers are just as anxious to make money as publishers are. One of the more ingenious ways for them to make money is to charge publishers for special placement or displays. This is a part of the book business every writer needs to understand. We all want to see our books on the tables in the front of the store, and many a disappointed writer has called his publisher to complain when they didn't see their books displayed there. The bottom line is that prominent display costs money.

Let's say Valentine's Day is approaching, and bookstore chain X is planning to build special Valentine's Day-themed displays in all 500 stores. But they won't just wander around the stores pulling romance novels, sex books, and books with red or pink covers to use in the display.

These stores sell positioning. For a fee, a publisher can buy a place in the holiday display. Sometimes the display is on the *endcap*, the small area on the end of each aisle; sometimes it's on a table. Keep in mind that almost all the special display space you see in a bookstore is paid placement by the publisher. In many cases, publishers can't even purchase the space unless the bookstore has already decided they'd like an extra large order.

Remember those free bookstore gift catalogs we urged you to collect for research? The publishers of the books featured in those catalogs paid for them to be there. The cost to be included in these catalogs can run into several thousand dollars per title.

def•i•ni•tion

The **endcap** is the shelf at the end of an aisle, a prime place for bookstore browsers to see your book. Publishers can sometimes pay booksellers for the chance to have a display of their books on the endcap.

It Can't Hurt to Ask

Ask your editor about all these things. You, as the author, have no control over whether your publisher decides to offer a counter display or pay for an endcap display for your book. Depending on the subject of your book, it might not be appropriate at all. But it never hurts to ask your editor if there are any special plans for displays or in-store promotions.

Printing and Shipping Your Baby (and Warehousing the Rest)

After leaving the account with orders in hand (or in the laptop, as the case may be), the sales rep transmits these orders to the main office. When all the accounts have been seen and all the advance orders for your book are in, these numbers are then used to set the size of your book's first print run, or *first printing*.

When the printer has printed and bound all your books (this takes 4 to 6 weeks, on average), it's ready to begin filling orders. Large bookstore orders are sometimes shipped directly from the printer to the store's main warehouse, bypassing the publisher's warehouse and distribution system. Other orders may be filled from the publisher's warehouse.

When all advance orders have been shipped, the rest of your books are stored in the publisher's warehouse. There they wait, hoping to

def•i•ni•tion

Just before a book is shipped to the printers, the publisher takes a close look at the advance orders received from bookstores and uses this information to decide the book's **first printing,** or the number of books to be printed the first time out.

be sent out to fill other orders and reorders. Depending on the size of your book's print run, the publisher may have anywhere from 500 to several thousand copies of your book in the warehouse. Smaller, more frequent printings are now the rule. The publisher hopes that demand for your book will soon deplete the stock on hand and that the book will go into a second, a third, and a fourth printing—and beyond!

Why such small numbers of extra copies? Because the publisher's best chance to make money is by not overprinting. Many a profit has been squandered on an unnecessarily large second printing.

If any of your books are returned unsold by the bookseller, those copies probably will rejoin the others in the warehouse. Returns affect the inventory levels and are always taken into account when a new print run is under consideration.

Book Shows

No description of the book sales process would be complete without at least mentioning the annual booksellers' shows and conventions. Many come in all sizes and shapes and may cover more than just books (such as the Christian Booksellers Association shows in winter and summer that include music and gifts).

While the smaller shows can be of interest, the biggest of them all is Book Expo America, or BEA. Held once a year in late May or early June, this is the trade show for the publishing industry. The location varies around the country from year to year, but it's such a big show that it usually ends up in a big convention town such as Chicago, New York, or L.A. Publishers take large booths and display glossy blow-ups of the covers of their top titles. Their booths are stocked with catalogs for the fall list, and many publishers have freebies to pass out to booksellers: posters, advance reading copies, pins, jelly beans, T-shirts—you name it. Some of the larger publishers hold parties to fete their big clients and their big authors.

Yearly, publishers debate the value versus the cost of this show, which was designed to cater directly to independent booksellers buying books for the year but has increasingly become simply an industry gathering place. Agents actively sell rights for titles, editors set up meetings, and publishers prowl the floor looking at what the competition's offering.

Do Authors Go?

Yes, some authors do go to the Book Expo. Should you go? It depends on *why* you want to go. Unless you're a big celebrity author, no one will make a fuss over you. It can be quite a humbling experience to be an unknown author at this big event. Long lines form for free, autographed books from well-known authors. Not-so-long lines form for authors whose books are little known. Your publisher may not be willing to invest the money or the time in having you there.

One thing to ask about though is whether your book will be featured at your publisher's booth. If your book is just a few months away from being published and if it's a key title on the list, your publisher might decorate its booth with large posters of the book cover or pass out galley copies to book buyers and media folk to generate buzz. Understand that the books featured at BEA are from the fall list; the books are scheduled to be published in the autumn after BEA is held. Many an author whose book has just been published prior to BEA has been crushed to learn that his book won't be featured or that his publishing house may not even have a booth. But this isn't the kiss of death by any means. You can ask your editor what the presence will be, but don't be discouraged if your book isn't a key title. Being featured at BEA may help a few books, but the vast majority do just fine without it.

If you want to go to the Book Expo on your own as a visitor to learn more about the book business, go ahead. This is a great opportunity to pick up catalogs from many other publishers and learn about new books coming out. (Your publisher may be able to get you a free convention badge; just ask.) You can check out the information for this year's show at www.bookexpoamerica.com. This site should also fill you in on the cost to register as a guest.

Smaller, regional booksellers' conventions also are held around the country. Ask your editor if there is a regional show in your area. These shows are more likely to feature local authors.

The Least You Need to Know

- Bookstores order books up to 6 months before the book is actually available.

- The size a book order depends on the popularity of the topic, the popularity of the author, and the publisher's publicity plans.

- With computer sales information, the order process is now formulaic and takes into account the actual sales history of other books on the topic, as well as the author's previous book sales.

- Celebrity authors might be invited to a sales conference or a bookseller's convention, but most authors are not.

Maximum Publicity for Maximum Sales

In This Chapter

- ◆ What's publicity, and what can it do for your book sales?
- ◆ What to expect from the publicity department
- ◆ How two big promoters became mega-best-selling authors
- ◆ Tips on generating your own publicity
- ◆ The beauty of radio
- ◆ Ways to hone your radio talk skills

"Publicity? But I landed a big-time publisher," you say. "Why should I have to learn about publicity?" Your publisher has a whole department that does publicity. So isn't that its job?

Yes, it is the publisher's job. But it's also your job. You should learn about publicity, and you should start learning the minute you sign the contract with the publisher. Publicity is a critical element in the success of your book. As the author, you should become publicity-savvy, just as knowledgeable about this part of publishing as you've become about all the other steps thus far.

Remember the study we mentioned in Chapter 19 that the National Writer's Union did? Although writers groused about the high turnover for editors at big houses, the number one gripe that aired was in the area of promotion. Many authors felt their publishers hadn't lived up to the promises made in the sales catalog and that promotional efforts were quickly abandoned if the book didn't take off immediately. So learn what you can, because it will be important later. On the other hand, big publishers work hard to stretch already-thin budgets across many books and authors. They have to balance expensive advertising, press tours, and marketing materials, doing less with more.

It's never too soon to begin thinking about publicity for your book. By starting early, you can make media contacts now you can call on in the future. You can send out copies of your proposal or manuscript-in-progress to writers and celebrities in the hopes that they will give you an endorsement. You can even watch more television and listen to more radio so you have a better sense of which shows would be best for your book. Get started acting and thinking like a book publicist right away.

Publicity: Now and Then

The role of the author has changed dramatically over the years. In times past, we hear, an author could turn in a completed manuscript, dust off her writerly hands, and allow the publisher to take it from there. Authors didn't sully themselves with commerce. The in-house publicity staff would handle all the details about the book's publicity, sending sweet and gentle notes to the author to let her know the details on the many upcoming reviews, book signings, and publicity appearances.

def•i•ni•tion

More publishers are looking for authors who have a **platform**, a ready-made existing audience for the book. Your platform might include lectures, a radio or television show, or a widely syndicated column. These aren't the planks that hold up your platform? Better start building a bigger platform now! Become an expert somewhere, if only in your local newspaper.

Today, the publisher expects the author to take a very active role in publicizing the book, possibly even taking the lead (depending on how large the publisher's publicity staff is). "Does this author have a *platform?*" is a question asked in most editorial meetings today. When evaluating the feasibility of your nonfiction project, the publisher places a great deal of weight on how hard you plan to work on the book's behalf, with speeches, newspaper editorials, local appearances, magazine columns, and the like. The publisher took all this into consideration on that fateful day in the editorial meeting when your book received the go-ahead.

If you don't have an obvious platform, talk to your editor or marketing manager anyway. You may have contacts that are useful. One publisher we know rarely pays for author tours or appearances but can work to schedule signings and media appearances if the author is traveling to a city for another event. If you speak at seminars or conferences, travel for business, or are going to visit your great aunt in San Francisco, let your publisher know—they may be able to capitalize on your schedule.

Just What Is Publicity, Anyway?

According to the dictionary, *publicity* is defined as "the process of drawing attention to a person or thing." You should know, however, that in the world of publishing, publicity refers more correctly to "the process of drawing attention to a person or thing for free." Publicity is not an ad in *People* magazine; publicity is an article in *USA Today.* Publicity is not a direct mail piece sent to a million homes; publicity is your voice on the radio station broadcast to a million homes.

def•i•ni•tion

Books become known to the reading public through **publicity:** reviews, articles, and mentions of the book and its contents in the media.

Print and television advertising is seldom done in the book business. Why? It has to do with the economics of advertising, the huge cost of the ad compared with the retail price of what's being advertised. General Motors buys lots of ads to sell cars, but remember how much a car costs. If just 10 or 20 cars sell, that pays for the ad. But if a publisher bought the same ad for your book, imagine how many books he'd have to sell at $22.95 to come close to breaking even. So don't tell your publisher that your book would be a best-seller if only the publishing house would advertise on the *Today Show*.

The exception is targeted advertising (placing an ad for a massage book in a massage magazine) or paying for the book to be featured in the catalogs published and distributed by large bookstore chains.

Experts Say

"We write up a press release and send it along with a review copy to our sources at all the major media," explains a publicist at William Morrow. "To be quite frank, our efforts are often dictated by the size of the book's first printing. If a book's shipping in numbers of, say, 25,000 copies and above, it'll receive greater attention and a longer publicity effort than one with smaller numbers."

Publicity is the stronger way to sell a book. Articles and interviews make you appear to be an expert and give an independent endorsement to your book.

What the Publicity Department Can Do

As dazzling as the idea of glamorous television appearances and a late-night interview with CNN's Anderson Cooper might be, it seldom happens with most books. Here is a clear-eyed view of what you, as a first-time author, can reasonably expect from the publicity department.

The actual legwork to publicize your new book begins in the publicist's office some 3 or so months before your book is scheduled to be released. Publicists might send out bound galleys or *review copies* to reviewers, work on setting up book signings and local tours, and try to be sure your book gets into the hands of the right magazine and newspaper people. The publicists also make follow-up calls to be sure the information arrived, to gauge interest, and to arrange for book interviews. Publicist Arielle Ford calls this part of the publicity process "smiling and dialing."

Although all authors dream of a nationwide book tour, it's becoming a rare thing indeed. To avoid disappointment later, ask your editor several months before your pub date if there are plans for a tour. You might as well find out now. If there *are* plans for a tour, you will need the advance warning to rearrange your schedule.

def•i•ni•tion

The publisher might send out free **review copies** of your book to anyone who might help promote the book. Books might get sent to book reviewers, celebrities, television and radio producers, columnists, and the like. Sometimes these folks' mail is so heavy with free books that they need help lugging the sack inside.

Novel Approaches

Publicizing fiction is a challenge. With fiction (particularly first-time fiction), a publicist can't do too much beyond sending out review copies to well-known authors in the hope of creating a stir, targeting literary review sources such as *The Bloomsbury Review*, and trying to arrange for profile pieces in an author's local newspaper. "We also try to arrange readings at well-known literary bookstores such as Elliot Bay Booksellers in Seattle or Tattered Cover in Denver," a fiction publicist explains.

Novels can also be promoted through magazine excerpts or serialization. This is arranged not by the publicity department, but rather by the rights department. If you retained first serial rights in your contract, it's your responsibility (or your agent's) to sell these rights. No matter who's selling them, this has to happen many months before the book actually is published.

A recent **trend has** developed toward newspaper and magazine lifestyle articles about young novelists. These articles seem to talk more about the loft apartments they live in, where they hang out with friends, or an intriguing story behind the writing of their book than about the work itself. If you think there might be a cool lifestyle (as opposed to literary) angle your publicist could use, by all means tell him about it.

Jeff Kleinman of FolioLit, the agent for Robert Hicks' best-selling *The Widow of the South*, feels that the fact Hicks' book was set in a real place helped publicity. "A producer could read the scene about young boys dying in the halls, then send a crew out to film those same halls to show their viewers. You could create a story about something real." The Hicks book was also the focus of lifestyle pieces that featured his own quirky home and his involvement in the successful attempt to preserve the mansion that serves as the centerpiece in his novel. Be creative about what in your life as a writer could translate well on a visual medium like television.

The Publicity Department's Full Plate

If you think the publisher's publicity department is going to work 24 hours a day to drive your book onto the best-seller list, guess again. The folks in publicity are responsible for doing what they can for as many as 10 or 15 books at a time. Understand that there's nothing for you as an author to gain by complaining about this situation.

Instead, you can use this opportunity to take your book's fate into your own hands. To avoid duplication of effort and some bad feelings all around, it's best to let the publicity department have a clear shot at your book for the first few months after it's released. When the people in the publicity department have let you know it's time for them to turn their attention to other books (and they will be honest with you, if you ask), that's the green light you need to roll up your sleeves and take it from there.

Slush Pile

Feel the need to call the publicity department for daily check-ups on what's going on with your book? Don't. Frustrated by what you view as a lack of effort and interest? Be careful how you communicate those feelings. A cranky author can turn off the staff—and once you're viewed as a problem, people in the publicity department may do even less for your book. Remember what your grandmother told you: you can catch more flies with honey ....

"We are thrilled to work with authors who have taken the time to learn the ropes about publicity and can take an active role in it," says a longtime industry publicist. Don't worry that the interest will have disappeared because the book has been out for a few months. If your book is well written, well researched, and well targeted, you can promote it for years to come. Read on to hear how two guys whose first book came out years ago are still on the road flogging it.

Chicken Soup for Everyone!

Mark Victor Hansen and Jack Canfield are the well-known authors of the best-selling series *Chicken Soup for the Soul*, with a mind-boggling 100 million copies in print. But were they always best-selling authors? Did their publisher (Health Communications) have a superhuman publicity department that did all the work for them? Not by a long shot. Let's see how Mark and Jack did it.

Ask the Experts

The two friends decided they wanted their first book, *Chicken Soup for the Soul*, to be a best-seller. But instead of sitting back and waiting for a publisher to make that happen, these two took active steps to achieve their goal.

Long before their book was even published, they set out on a mission. They interviewed best-selling authors, people like John Gray of *Men Are from Mars, Women Are from Venus* and M. Scott Peck of *The Road Less Traveled*. Mark and Jack asked each of these best-selling authors a very simple question: "How did you become a best-selling author?" Makes sense, doesn't it?

The Secret Formula

So what did they learn on their fact-finding mission? The key to a best-seller truly is publicity—and lots of it! M. Scott Peck told Hansen and Canfield that he gives one interview a day to any radio station, regardless of its size. His approach seems to have worked in a big way: *The Road Less Traveled* was on *The New York Times* best-seller list for 12 years—not 12 weeks or even 12 months, mind you, but *12 years!*

Hansen and Canfield have taken Peck's advice to heart. They not only give an interview a day, but they also let producers around the country know they are always available as last-minute guests to fill in for a cancellation (a little trick they learned from best-selling sex advice author Dr. Ruth). Although their books have been best-sellers for more than a decade, they have not slowed their daily publicity efforts and try to do at least one interview a day if not more. No media outlet is too small for them to appear.

It's worth noting that Hansen and Canfield pay for most of their publicity efforts themselves. They work well with their publisher's publicity department, of course, and keep the staff informed of everything they do. But they firmly believe it's the author's responsibility to create demand for a book.

The Complete Idiot's Guide to Publicity

So how can you put what the authors of *Chicken Soup for the Soul* learned into action? Here are ideas and suggestions to get you started planning your publicity campaign.

Hot Off the Press _____

Start now to gather things for your press kit. Make a file in which you keep a bio, a professional picture of yourself, videotapes of your appearances or audio tapes of your speeches, and newspaper and magazine clippings of articles about you or about the topic of your book. The earlier you start to build this file, the more you will have to choose from when the time comes to assemble your press kit.

Press Release Basics

A press release is a one-page announcement sent to various members of the media. Like the query letters you now know how to write, a press release serves to catch the interest of the person reading it. We've included a sample press release on the CD. Follow the style shown there to learn where to place your dates, phone numbers, and other basic contact information.

Press releases start out with a catchy headline. Often these same headlines will be used in the newspaper or magazine articles that result, so choose carefully! Here are a few sample press release headlines:

◆ Authors Reveal Stunning Reasons for Juvenile Crime

◆ Rock Musicians Share Their Vegetarian Recipes in *Food Without Faces*

◆ Secrets to Surviving Your Husband's Midlife Crisis

Each of these was crafted to convince a jaded press person (who has seen and heard it all) to keep reading and to learn more about you and your book. A press release needs to deliver the basics of who, what, when, why, and where. It also needs to have a clear purpose: are you trying to interest the media in writing a feature article, announcing a press conference, or just hoping for reviews? To learn more about writing an effective press release, we recommend Marcia Yudkin's book, *Six Steps to Free Publicity*.

Useful Contacts, Bookstores, Newspapers, and Magazines

Draw up a list of media contacts you have now (and ask your friends who they know), and work hard to expand this list by joining organizations or attending events where you might meet members of the media.

Talk to your local bookstores about the fact that you have a book coming out, and ask for advice on how to promote it in their stores. Make it a point to attend events in many bookstores to learn what kind of event draws a crowd and what draws only the author's family members. An event in a bookstore described as a "book signing" is a flat-sounding event and only draws a crowd for a celeb who has many die-hard fans content to just stand in line for a chance to gaze upon them briefly while waiting for a signature. We know one author who is usually so worried that no one will show up that he sends e-mails and flyers to all his friends and family. His signings are usually well attended, but he doesn't sell many books.

> **Hot Off the Press**
>
> The cub reporter you befriend today may be the editor of the business section by the time your book is published!

Read papers and magazines, and take note of who writes articles on topics that relate to your book. Jot down not just the book reviewer, but also the names of reporters whom you can try to interest in writing a feature-length piece about you and your book. One author sent a note to a woman at *USA Today* years ago to let her know how much he enjoyed one of her articles; now she is in regular contact with him as an expert in that field.

Promotional Items

When your publisher has the finished artwork for your front cover, have a printed postcard made with the book's cover, publication, and ordering information. They make great thank-you cards or note cards and help keep the name of your book in front of everyone's eyes. (On a similar note, co-author Jennifer and her co-authors on *Christmas Miracles* had ink stamps made that said "I Believe in Christmas Miracles" and then used them on the outside of all their correspondence.) Other great, inexpensive promotional items can include bookmarks, sticky notes, and bookplates.

With these promo items, you can circulate the image of your book long before it appears on bookstore shelves. Of course, be sure to send out a whole bunch when your book is published to remind people to buy it.

One tiny tip—many of these types of promotional items aren't that expensive, and so publishers can almost always be convinced to pay the tab for you as a small way to keep an author happy. Don't be afraid to ask. If they say no, you can pick up the tab yourself.

"And Our Next Guest Is ..."

Among the best ways authors can help publicize their book when they're available in bookstores is to arrange radio interviews. Radio is a tremendous medium for books; of all the different types of media, it sparks the quickest response. How does it work?

> ### Hot Off the Press
>
> Steve Harrison of Bradley Communications has published his *Radio-TV Interview Report* for years and seen countless success stories of huge publicity bookings. He decided to take it all one step further and get top radio and TV producers together in a room with the authors and experts who want to pitch them. Now in its third year, the National Publicity Summit in New York has become the place to go to get launched. Details are available by calling 610-259-1070.

Radio Sells

If you see an ad for something on television, you file that impression away in your mind and perhaps act on it in the future. But countless advertising studies have shown that the information we hear on the radio sparks an immediate response. If you hear something on the radio about a book that interests you, you think to yourself, *Hey, I'm going to stop off at the bookstore on the way home tonight and pick that up!* Radio is a powerful way to sell books.

All those folks trapped in their cars on the roadways have nothing else to do but listen to you explain to them how much better their lives will be and how much more money (or love, or sex, or jobs) they will have if they will only rush out right now and buy a copy of your book. Make it your goal to become an expert radio talk show guest, and your book sales will shoot through the roof.

> **Experts Say**
>
> "Authors as authors and books as books concern us not at all. Authors as experts who can talk knowledgeably about topical issues, that is what we want on the radio," says Joel Roberts, morning talk show host turned media trainer. No producer for radio or television is really booking you to talk about your book, why you wrote it, and what's inside. She's trying to put together a show that will interest her audience, a lively and topical show that will grab and hold their attention.

Selling Yourself to Radio

But how can you get yourself booked as a guest on the radio? There are two ways to become a guest on radio shows. The first is to call up and try to get someone interested in you. The second is to let someone get interested and call you!

All the information you need to research radio stations across the country (from the size of the station to the phone numbers and addresses of the hosts and producers) is available in a really big and heavy book called *Bacon's Media*. Try to find this reference book at your library—the cost to buy one is well over $100. Also, check out www.bacons.com to see if there's any less costly way to get the info, and also take a look at BurrellesLuce.com, which offers a similar service. These companies run occasional "free trials," and you might be able to get the information you need without paying the professional price tag. Using the information in *Bacon's*, you can draw up a list of stations you would like to target and can begin your campaign to sell yourself as a guest.

Which Stations, Which Shows?

How do you decide which stations in which markets? Ask friends and relatives across the country for advice about which radio stations in their area are the most popular and which ones have live talk shows. Make it a point when you travel to listen to the local radio stations, station-hopping along the band until you've identified a few that seem appropriate. Ask other authors you might know which stations have worked for them.

Be on the lookout for the largest stations in the area, those with the greatest broadcast area. Radio shows with *syndicated* programs (programs that play on more than one station) are gems you should always dig for.

def•i•ni•tion

Radio shows that play on more than one station are **syndicated** across the country. Giving one interview to a syndicated host helps you reach several media markets and millions of people at once.

Smiling and Dialing

When you've identified the likely stations, you're ready to begin your campaign. Call the station first to confirm that the information listed in *Bacon's* is still current; stations can change their format at any time. It is very important that you have the correct name for the producer, as it is the producer's responsibility to put together an interesting show.

Spend time and effort in creating your "pitch," your 30-second speech about why this particular producer should book you as a guest. Don't start your pitch by saying, "I wrote a book on …," but instead say confidently, "I'm an expert on … and your listeners will be interested in the topic." If you don't come across well in those 30 seconds on the phone, the producer won't have high hopes for how you'll handle yourself once you get on the air. When you're confident that your pitch is compelling, pick up the phone and call! Follow up a successful pitch with a copy of your book and that press kit you've put together.

> **Experts Say**
>
> "With the web, radio listeners can now just fire up their computers and order the book they just heard about," one author told us. "Which means that after every big radio interview nowadays, I check my sales figures on Amazon.com and can literally see the books selling from the earlier interview. It's a secret thrill!"

Longtime radio and television producer turned media trainer Michelle Anton (for five years she produced the number two-rated show in the country, the *Dr. Laura Show*) believes that to get booked on big shows, you need to work hard to be sure you look and sound different from the other experts already out there. "There is hardly anything new on the planet, and chances are good that the producer will have heard similar pitches from other experts and may have already had those experts on the show. Visit the show website and check into past guests. If they have had someone recently in your field, figure out how to change your angle to be dramatically different."

Michelle warns authors that you need to work hard before you pick up the phone to pitch a producer. "Create a real sense of value in your message for the producer of the radio show. What problem are you solving for their audience? Be sure you can convey that in seconds."

Get Them to Come to You

Is there an easier way to get booked? Do the producers ever call authors, instead of authors calling them? Yes. Each month, *Radio-TV Interview Report* is sent to radio and

Slush Pile _____

On most radio programs, the producer is responsible for coming up with a lively show that sounds good on the air. Producers are always on the lookout for good guests. If you can present yourself and your topic in a way that sounds like it will make a good show, it won't be long before you hear the words "You're on the air."

television producers around the country to alert them to possible guests. Instead of calling producers around the country, you can simply buy yourself an ad in this magazine and let producers know about you and your expertise.

Not sure how to advertise yourself in a jazzy way to make producers call? Don't worry, the magazine staff folks can help you position yourself and your topic to appeal to producers. For more information on _Radio-TV Interview Report_ rates and scheduling, call Bradley Communications at 610-259-1070, extension 408.

A Cross-Country Whirlwind Radio Tour

One way to hit a great many stations and markets in one short period of time is to arrange a satellite tour. Satellite radio tours are prearranged interviews with a large number of stations, all done in one single morning. You can sit at home in your bathrobe and give the same short interview over and over and over again to stations from coast to coast.

This type of interview is expensive (several thousand dollars) and needs to be professionally arranged; it is not something you can do on your own. Planned Television Arts in New York (212-593-5820) is the best-known firm for satellite tours.

Should You Be Media-Trained?

Not everyone makes a natural radio guest. But learning how to get your point across quickly, how to deal with questions, and how to work the title of your book into every other sentence are all skills that can be acquired. You can do it yourself by listening carefully to radio shows and analyzing what works, or you can have someone teach you. Practice talking in short sentences that will stick in people's minds. Media trainers specialize in helping you with your communications skills and your ability to field questions and think on your feet.

If you're serious about being effective on the radio, media training can be money well spent. Training increases your confidence and lessens your fears, and it increases your ability to sell your book on the air. You can find the names of media trainers in the Yellow Pages or even by asking radio producers for recommendations.

Experts Say _____

When first-time author Heather King hit the road to promote her book *Parched* about her life as "a down-and-dirty barfly," she quickly learned a valuable lesson: she had to be prepared to talk to folks live on the air who don't know the first thing about what you wrote. Over and over she had to deal with interviewers who hadn't actually read her book. She tells other authors, "It's a good idea to have some stock stories and anecdotes on hand ... and make sure you always carry a copy of your book."

Three Key Points

To get your point across on the air, you must always have two or three key points at your fingertips. Write them down on index cards and have them handy while you're being interviewed. And don't forget that great politicians' trick: no matter what the question is, you can always turn it to your advantage by saying, "I'm so glad you asked that, it reminds me of something I point out in my book ...." Then you're off and running with your own agenda!

Touring the Libraries

A quieter way to get the word out on your book is to arrange a tour of your regional library system. In the same way you thought up an "event" for your local bookstore rather than a dull book signing, think of a lecture topic or presentation that would interest library patrons. Co-author Jennifer spent a Saturday morning not long ago driving to libraries in the Seattle area, giving talks to writers gathered there. Libraries are happy to host novelists—sometimes more eager than bookstores, in fact. Call and ask for the head librarian and ask whether that location has author events. If they don't, ask which libraries do!

Libraries also sometimes organize or host writers' conferences or other author events. Be sure your local library knows about you and your book so you'll be asked to participate as a speaker.

Reality Check

Editors love authors who see the reality of the situation and are willing to contribute to their own promotional platform—that is, bring in a publicist or PR firm to help promote them, or their speaking circuit, seminars, etc. and the book along the way.

However, we've also had bad experiences with this approach. PR firms and publicists sell the author on what they can do (book them on big, big shows and pitch them to big, big magazines), and all too often, authors sign up to pay for the full PR treatment. In the meantime, though, your editor has seen the actual advance sales numbers from their accounts and knows the industry isn't responding in an encouraging way.

When the book comes out, the publicity folks pitch your book and … nothing happens, or perhaps just a few small hits that don't really get much of a sales response. The sad truth is that you can't make a best-seller happen by sheer force of will and money alone.

Maybe the lesson here is that as an author, you can do everything right and the publisher can do everything right and the book just doesn't pop. No one has a magic formula, but you can increase your chances of success by doing extra publicity on your own.

Publicity Pays Off

Now you know: publicity can sell books, and lots of publicity can sometimes sell lots of books. You've learned that you may have to do much of the publicity for your book yourself, and that it really isn't such a hard thing to do after all. If you believe in your book and can craft a message that appeals to producers, you'll be on the air in no time. In Chapter 22, we explore two other avenues for book publicity: television and the Internet.

The Least You Need to Know

- Publicity sells books better than anything else.

- Your publisher will do some publicity, but a more sustained effort is your responsibility as the author.

- Publicity techniques can be learned, and persistence is the key.

- Radio producers decide which guests will be booked on a show. Your press kits should be targeted to them instead of the host.

- It is possible to advertise your availability as a radio and television guest.

- The longer you publicize your book, the longer it sells.

Chapter 22

Television and Online Publicity

In This Chapter

- ◆ Ways to get on television
- ◆ Pack your bags: satellite TV tours
- ◆ Tips on getting on the big shows
- ◆ Dress the part
- ◆ What really works online

You've learned all about radio interviews, but how do you get yourself on TV to talk about your book? The short answer is: you don't. You don't get yourself on television to talk about your book; you get yourself on television because you have something to say of interest to television viewers.

Bright Lights, Big City

Remember the advice from Joel Roberts, the radio guy in Chapter 21? He said, "We don't care about authors as authors and books as books." What he meant was that a producer's main concern (both on the radio and on television) is putting together an interesting show viewers will enjoy. If viewers enjoy the show, more viewers will watch, so the channel can charge more for advertising, and the producer gets to keep his job. Got it?

"So," the interviewer begins, "why did you write this book?" And the viewer reaches for the remote control. An author sitting in a chair being interviewed about his book makes for flat TV. But someone sitting in a chair being interviewed about dramatic current events, or sharing information that viewers could use, or sharing a heartfelt story that moves the audience—that makes for good television. The fact that the person in the chair wrote a book is secondary.

So how do you get yourself booked on television to talk about your book? By convincing the television producer that what you have to say is of interest to her viewers and will make a lively show.

Gonna Make You a Star!

The process of getting booked on a television show is basically the same as for a radio show:

1. Find the show you want

2. Learn the producer's name

3. Send information to the producer

4. Follow up with a phone call to make your pitch

The standards for press materials for TV are quite a bit higher, however. Your press materials have to be more extensive. Instead of just the pitch letter and sample book that sufficed for a radio producer, your press kit for television should contain these items:

- ◆ A press release
- ◆ Suggested interview questions
- ◆ An author bio sheet
- ◆ A professional-quality author photo
- ◆ Suggestions for shows based on your book
- ◆ A copy of your book

Hot Off the Press _____

Family connections coach Beth Craig started getting booked on local television shows in her area even before she finished her book proposal. Seem premature? It wasn't. With the impressive tapes of Beth seated next to the TV hosts chatting about how women could be less stressed at holiday time and learn to give the gift of themselves to their families, Beth's publicist, Robin Lockwood, was able to approach national TV shows on Beth's behalf.

Sending along a list of sample questions in your press kit is a great way for you to help the producer see how lively and thought-provoking your segment can be. If the producer ends up using those questions in the interview, you will be totally prepared and sound impressive.

Also send a list of sample show ideas. This is your chance to help the producer envision just how he could build a show around you. Help make his job easy by describing as best you can a segment that features you and your book. But remember, your show ideas must be timely, informative, provocative, and/or amusing—not just you sitting around being interviewed about your book.

Slush Pile _____

Don't go to the trouble of getting booked on television without also taking steps to be prepared once you step in front of the camera. Practice, practice, and then practice again. Write down your key points and then memorize them. Develop short "sound bites," or talking points, with the information you want viewers to remember.

Perhaps you've written a book about dating. You can suggest to the producer that you'll find several single people and counsel them on the air about the perils of being single and then the cameras can follow them out on an actual date. That's much more interesting to watch than just you and an interviewer.

Pay attention to the news. Can you somehow tie a current event into your book? Authors of relationship books can comment on celebrity couples, authors of health books can tie into recent health studies, and authors of parenting books can comment on juvenile crime sprees. You get the idea. From now on, you must watch the news with an eye toward your own publicity.

We've included a sample television pitch letter in the CD so you can better learn how to craft these materials.

Getting on Regional Shows

Sure, you know which local television shows you'd like to be on in your area, but how can you find the regional shows across the country? And is it worth your time to try to get booked on regional shows?

The very same reference books and websites like www.bacons.com that list radio stations across the nation also list television shows. And don't forget to ask your friends and family across the country what they watch in their area.

def•i•ni•tion

A producer might ask you for a **video clip**, a tape of an appearance you've made on another television show.

Does regional television make a difference? "Regional TV is valuable," says Robin Lockwood, a California-based book publicist. "You reach a smaller market, but if you do enough regional TV, it can really add up. A great example of a strong regional show is *Good Day Atlanta*. They do lots of authors on that show." It also gives you a *video clip* you can use to pitch a larger show.

When you've targeted the television show—and the producer—you want to reach, pop your press kit in the mail. Then wait. A good rule of thumb is to give your press kit a one-week head start before you make a follow-up call. Call the show and ask for the producer. Tell him you are following up on a press kit you sent—did he receive it? And does he have any questions? Practice your 30-second phone pitch; the producer won't give you much time, so try to hook him quickly.

Satellite Television Tours

As with satellite radio tours, it's also possible to sit in one place and do television interview after television interview. You're simply the talking head shown on the screen, while the host asks questions (the same questions the last host asked). These satellite television tours must be professionally arranged. Again, the best known firm is Planned Television Arts in New York.

With a satellite television tour, you spend a few hours in a studio doing television interviews across the country, one station at a time. "In 2½ hours, you can do 22 interviews," says Rick Frishman of Planned Television Arts. Most of the shows you're hitting are the local noon-hour broadcasts on affiliate stations for NBC, ABC, CBS, and Fox.

How much is a satellite television tour? To do the whole country costs in the $12,000 to $15,000 range. It's an expensive undertaking, but it can hit many markets all at once. And it's reasonable compared with the cost of actually going on tour, which could be $1,500 to $2,000 per city in travel costs alone.

> ### Experts Say
>
> Satellite television tours didn't even exist until a few short years ago. "We started doing them in 1989," says Rick Frishman of Planned Television Arts. "To succeed in publicity, you've always got to think of new ways to reach people faster, cheaper, smarter. Think of a satellite television tour as the ultimate armchair publicity tour."

Oprah and Friends

These small stations are all well and good, but what author isn't dazzled by the prospect of the big time: a nationally syndicated afternoon talk show like *The View* or *Live! With Regis and Kelly?* And all authors, regardless of what kind of book they've written, harbor hopes of appearing on *Oprah* before her show goes off the air for good.

There are two kinds of shows—*live* shows and *taped* shows. Live shows are really and truly shot in front of an audience and aired immediately. When you appear on a taped show, you have to ask the producers when the episode will air.

def•i•ni•tion

Shows that are aired as they are being filmed are **live**. Shows that are filmed and then shown some time later are **taped**. Barbara Walter's show on ABC, *The View*, is live. *Oprah* is taped.

Am I the Main Attraction?

Does an appearance on *Oprah* guarantee a best-seller? No. Although the show has certainly built many best-sellers, countless other authors have appeared on *Oprah* and have seen little effect on book sales. What makes the difference? On *Oprah*, as on any other television talk show, the theme of the show itself makes a difference.

Jennifer Openshaw was the only guest during an entire segment of *Oprah*, and her financial book *What's Your Net Worth?* was mentioned and shown on camera several times. Did it put her on the best-seller list? There was certainly a spike in sales, but Jennifer's financial book didn't seem to grab the audience in the same way a more emotional self-help book might have. "An appearance on *Oprah* clearly credentials you as an expert in your field and gives you a bump in sales," Openshaw told us, "but one appearance on any show isn't going to make you an overnight best-seller."

Will It Sell Books?

Be sure to ask the producer if you and your book's topic are the sole focus of the show. If so, and if the host holds up your book on the air and says, "This book is incredible. Everyone should buy a copy," that could make a dramatic difference in sales.

def•i•ni•tion

On television, featured guests are those who are central to the show. **Panel** members are those who make up a roster of experts on a topic.

But if you are on the stage as a part of a *panel* of experts (each with a different viewpoint), there'll probably be little impact on book sales. But what the heck, you got a free trip to New York (or Chicago or Los Angeles). And all the producers from all the shows are watching, so you might get a call from another show. At the very least, you will have a tape of your appearance you can now send to other television producers as proof of your knowledge and charisma.

Hands Off (for Now)

With the top national talk shows, let your publisher's publicity staff handle the bookings. If your book has been out for several months and nothing is forthcoming, ask as politely as you can if they mind if you take a crack at it. Remember, be diplomatic. Thank them for all the efforts the publicity department has made on behalf of your book. Then take it from there.

How do you pitch these big talk shows? The same way you pitch your local noon news: with a pitch letter, a press kit, and a follow-up phone call.

Outwitting Producers

Many years ago, literary agent Bill Adler Jr. wrote a book called *Outwitting Squirrels: 101 Cunning Stratagems to Reduce Dramatically the Egregious Misappropriation of Seed from Your Birdfeeder by Squirrels*. It was rejected by 20 publishers (yep, even agents get rejected). Finally, Chicago Review Press agreed to publish it in 1988. Since then, Adler's book has been the focus of countless newspaper, magazine, and television stories and now has more than 200,000 copies in print. How did he do it?

Persistence Pays Off

He never gave up. He sent press releases to every newspaper he could think of—and some of them wrote about *Outwitting Squirrels*. He pitched television stories over and over again—and sometimes *Outwitting Squirrels* was on TV. He sent ideas again and again to the national talk shows, and one day, Rosie called. Well, not exactly; one of the producers of the now-defunct *Rosie O'Donnell* show called.

Like millions of people who feed birds, Rosie had problems with squirrels. And Adler's book had answers (he suggests that, as a last resort, you can throw the book at them). Rosie liked *Outwitting Squirrels*, but doing a major talk show is more involved than simply showing up the day they want you. To get the most mileage out of his appearance, Adler brought along props: stuffed squirrels and sample birdfeeders, to be exact.

Do the Producer's Work for Him

"I've learned from other talk show appearances that producers love it when their guests can help put a show together," Adler says. "Anything you can do to make it easier for the show will make it easier for you to get on the show. Producers are typically juggling a dozen or more shows at a time, and they appreciate the help."

Was Adler's spot on *Rosie* successful? The week after the show aired, his book shot up to the number one position on book distributor Ingram's nature best-seller list.

About That Plaid Jacket ...

Going on television? Hey, great! Now, what are you going to wear? This seems like a silly question, but it really isn't.

Here's your chance to watch a great deal of television and call it "work." Turn on the set and watch closely. Study what the news anchors wear, how reporters are dressed in the field, and what the characters on your favorite sitcom are walking around in. Take notes.

Does the woman on the 11 P.M. news wear a bright white sweater? No, she knows it would create problems with the camera. And her co-anchor, is he wearing a loud plaid jacket and a paisley tie? Nope. He is decked out in a dark navy jacket and a light shirt, with a tie that has a medium-sized print on it.

Dress for (TV) Success

There is a real science to dressing for television. You need to consider not only the way your clothes look on screen—especially the colors and patterns—but also what your clothes say about you. Are you trying to position yourself as an expert on a scientific topic? Better dress like a scientific expert. Are you a romance novelist? Go ahead and let your outfit show it.

One great way to check how your clothes (and you, too) look on camera is to do a practice run with a video camera. Have a friend or family member tape you in a few different outfits and then look at them all with a critical eye. Choose the outfit that both looks the best and presents you in the proper mode.

Hot Off the Press

Jan Tilmon of KVIE has produced many television shows featuring best-selling authors. Covert Bailey, of the *Fit or Fat* television series, and Leo Buscaglia are among the successful folks featured on the PBS specials she's produced. From time to time, she's had to give wardrobe advice to her authors: "The first show we did with Covert, we didn't control the wardrobe," Tilmon recalls. "He showed up in an awful gray suit with cuffs. Here was this trim, energetic man wearing a stuffy-looking, poorly fitted suit. We put him in khakis, bright colored shirts, and fun ties that matched his wit and charm. He came to life on camera. It made all the difference in the world."

Different Looks for Different Books

Once during a two-week period, co-author Jennifer was featured on several different television shows, for several different books. So she had several different looks.

She appeared on the national show *American Journal* as a small-business expert with her book *101 Best Extra Income Opportunities for Women*. She wasn't there as a big-business expert in a dark blue suit, but as a small-business expert in a light turtleneck sweater and a camel-hair jacket. The effect was very friendly and approachable.

The next week, she appeared on a local television show for the *Christmas Miracles* book. Same outfit? No. She needed to look like the author of a Christmas book, not a business book. And although she does have an off-white suit embroidered with gold thread and decorated with sequins and bugle beads to wear to bookstore readings, she knew it wouldn't work for a minute on a television screen. So she appeared on camera in a bright blue, fuzzy sweater.

She made yet one more appearance that same month for an earlier edition of the very book you hold in your hands, this time as a publishing expert on *C-Span's Book TV*. Was she in the fuzzy sweater? You guessed right, she wasn't. The dark blue suit was the appropriate choice for the topic and the show.

What Really Works Online?

A nice thing about the Internet is that you don't have to worry about what you're wearing! Unlike other types of media such as newspapers, radio, and television, the idea behind web marketing is to "fish where the fish are." You can find highly specialized user groups that are most interested in your book. These are not mass audiences made up of people who may or may not be interested in you and your book; they're highly targeted groups of people.

Here are the steps to promoting yourself online:

♦ To properly promote your book on the web, you must first get a domain name that features your book's title, such as www.mybooktitle.com. You should be able to get this from your local Internet provider at a cost of around $75.

♦ Register your domain name with all the major search engines, such as Google, Yahoo!, Excite, and others. As of this writing, this is a free service. Companies such as Exploit will register you with all the obscure search engines as well. This way, you will be listed in all of them.

> **Experts Say** _____
>
> Joining newsgroup discussions related to your topic can be a great way to promote your book. But don't be a jerk about it. "The most subtle way is to make sure that your book's title is embedded in your online signature," says author and agent Bill Adler Jr. So if your book is called *My Story*, try to get author@mystory.com as your e-mail address.

♦ Join lists and participate in newsgroups related to your book's topic. Don't overdo it, but try to mention your book where you can. You want to create positive word of mouth about the fact your book exists, not annoy other members by talking endlessly about your book.

Should I Create a Website?

Creating a website can also promote—as well as sell—your book. As a matter of fact, websites can serve as a sort of 1-800 number for you. When you are promoting your book in an interview, you can tell folks that it's available from your website at www. mybooktitle.com. To actually sell books to the people who visit your website, both Barnes & Noble online and Amazon.com will partner with you as an affiliate. You can register with them to have them handle the sales from your site. Creating a website can be free—many e-mail services let their customers create free websites—or quite costly (if you hire an expert to do it for you).

But if your website is just a vanity site about your book, don't expect to be flooded with visitors. People who surf the web visit a new website and ask themselves, "What's in it for me?" If there isn't anything in it for them—excerpts, quizzes, interactive functions, links to related sites, or other jazzy tools—why would they stay? Ask yourself that question as you're planning your site. Try to achieve what web marketers call "stickiness."

> **Hot Off the Press**
>
> In addition to creating a website for your book, make every effort to link your website to other, similar topics. Contact other websites that would complement yours. With a health title, for instance, ask to be linked with the major websites for diseases and afflictions covered in your book. That will make it even easier for folks to find you online, even when they aren't looking for you!

Read All About Me!

Another great aspect of the web is that more journalists are poking around there. Why? They're looking for story ideas, for experts, and for ways to legitimize trends. Curtis Hougland, director of new media for Middleberg and Associates in New York, shared this success story with us:

> We had a client, AncientSites.com, who wanted more than anything to be featured in *The Wall Street Journal*. That was their number one goal, and a daunting one at that! Their site was for history buffs, and we concentrated on getting them the best online PR we could. One of the stories we got was on *Wired News*. And just one week after the *Wired News* story appeared, a writer from *The Wall Street Journal* called us. She'd seen the story, and in no time at all, there was a two-column story on AncientSites in *The Journal!*

So keep trying online; you never know who is out there.

Don't overlook another great way to get folks to read about you and your book online—by creating your own e-mail newsletter! Try to capture the names and e-mail addresses of friends, fans, and visitors to your website and send out a regular e-mail newsletter in which you can tastefully promote both yourself and your books to your readers. E-mail newsletters can generate tremendous book sales almost instantly. Best-selling financial author David Bach has successfully increased sales this way, as did Mark Victor Hansen not long after *The One Minute Millionaire* was published. Hansen sent e-mail messages to his thousands of fans on his newsletter list asking them to help him become the number one book on Amazon.com that day. By including a link to Amazon.com so readers could respond instantly, his book shot up quickly to that very spot!

Online Coaching

Is yours a self-help book? Then take a page out of AOL's playbook and put together a coaching program offering your services to those who discover you online. In addition to promoting your book, you could also be adding to your income as an expert consultant.

AOL has launched its AOL Coaches program to entice publishers to participate financially (natch) to position their authors as higher-profile experts. Here is what AOL Coaches promises to those who participate: interactive workshops, book excerpts, author interviews, podcasts, blogs, mobile messaging, newsletters, and interactive quizzes. Gee, aren't those all things you could be doing yourself on your own website and sending out press releases to promote? You bet.

Future Shock

Over the past few years, amazingly creative ways to promote books and authors have sprung up online. Some come from the authors, some from the publishers, and some from businesses such as AOL who want to monetize the community they have at their fingertips. Get out there and be creative yourself.

Don't be frightened or intimidated by the online world. It can be an affordable way to publicize your book on your own. If you don't have the knowledge or the skills, seek out a web expert who does. Why ignore a great publicity venue right at your fingertips?

The Least You Need to Know

◆ Book TV publicity directly with the show's producer by sending a press kit and a pitch letter and then following up with a phone call.

◆ TV shows aren't looking for authors, per se, but rather for timely, topical, and interesting guests. So send them a list of great show ideas based on you.

◆ An appearance on *Oprah* does not an automatic best-seller make.

◆ You can hit many TV markets in one day with a satellite television tour. It's an expensive option, but it's cheaper than touring many cities one at a time.

◆ Get a domain name that includes the title of your book, such as www.mybooktitle. com, and create an e-mail newsletter to build a following for your book and its topic.

◆ Many publicity opportunities exist online; it can be a powerful way to create word of mouth for your book.

Chapter 23

Real-Life Publicity and Marketing Ideas

In This Chapter

- ◆ Tips on creating media interest in your book
- ◆ Secrets of the great book promoters
- ◆ Ways to make your bookstore event a success
- ◆ Can you really afford a best-seller?

Radio publicity, television publicity, online promotion—what does this all really mean for you and your book? It seems so unreal. Could you and your book really end up on national television?

Sure. From major *media markets* like New York to small markets like Lubbock, Texas, the media need programming 24 hours a day. Hundreds of newspapers are published around the country every single day of the week. Just think of how many stories need to be generated to fill up that space. And they can't all be about Paris Hilton and *American Idol.* Many of those stories could be about you and the book you wrote. Your book could be getting *placement* in the news every day of the week!

def•i•ni•tion

A **media market** is a geographic area covered by a particular station or newspaper. Some markets, such as New York, are large media markets; others, such as Omaha, are small. A **placement** is a story or a mention of the author or the book that has been placed in the media due to PR efforts.

Yes, P. T. Barnum would be proud. No, not because of his famous quote, "There's a sucker born every minute." Barnum was the original publicity hound, creating media events out of thin air to draw attention to his circus. You also need to learn to create events. You need to learn how to get the media to come looking for you!

Creating Media Events

Some of what you read in the newspaper or hear about on radio and television is the result of publicity efforts. It's either a staged media event, a press release, a *press conference*, or a story idea suggested by a public relations professional on behalf of a client.

def•i•ni•tion

A **press conference** is a meeting to share something newsworthy with members of the media.

A media event is an artificially created event staged solely for the benefit of the radio microphones, television cameras, and reporters' notepads. After the media event is over, these members of the press return to the studio or newsroom and write about what just happened.

You can learn to create media events to promote yourself and your book. A successful media event is one that draws a great deal of press attendance. Events that create a draw usually have one (or more) of the following characteristics:

- ◆ Timeliness
- ◆ Visually interesting activities or backgrounds
- ◆ Controversial content
- ◆ Humorous subjects or backgrounds

The Timely Event

Is there a way to tie your book and its topic into what's happening in the news right this minute? You learned to think about how to do this when crafting a press release in Chapter 21. Let's imagine you've written a book on sexual addiction and a major political figure has just been caught in the act. This is a perfect moment for you to create a media event by calling a press conference. Alert the media (via a press release) to the fact that, at the press conference, you will reveal the number one reason politicians are likely to cheat on their spouses—a topic radio producers will think is just perfect for *drive-time* talk radio! Will anyone show up to your press conference? You betcha!

As an exercise, sit down with the morning newspaper and circle the major national news stories. Study them, and see if you can tie your book or your book's topic into them in any way. If you're at a loss with the national news, flip to your local news section and see if there is anything happening locally you can tie into. If there is, redo your press release to build up that angle and start calling producers and reporters.

You should also spend time trying to think of seasonal angles for your book. Every year at Christmas Jennifer gets booked on major television shows. Sure, producers want her for her Christmas books, but also for her gift books *Wear More Cashmere* and *The Martini Diet.* She sends out press releases touting her picks for the best "affordable luxury gifts" of the year and also offers to appear on talk shows to give tips on how not to gain weight at holiday cocktail parties. Works every time.

> **def•i•ni•tion**
>
> Radio shows that play between 6 A.M. and 9 A.M. are morning **drive-time** shows. They're ideal for book promotions. Listenership is high during these hours, and many stations feature live hosts who do interviews.

> **Experts Say**
>
> Is there any kind of book that can't be promoted? Probably not. Even something as wacky as books about duct tape have received press coverage. Witness the story that appeared a few years ago in *The Wall Street Journal* about *The Duct Tape Book* and *Duct Tape—Real Stories.* According to the story, these two books have sold a combined 400,000 copies!

A Visually Interesting Event

We live in a visual world, and the press will come if you can supply a good visual image. You know the type—those large newspaper pictures of a cute child frolicking on the banks of a lake on a sunny day.

While managing a bookstore many years ago, co-author Jennifer created a media event on a sunny day by alerting TV stations to the fact that employees would be standing on a street corner blowing giant bubbles with wands. She was promoting a bubble book that came packaged with a plastic bubble wand. She was also promoting the bookstore. Did the television crews come? Yes. Those giant bubbles floating through the air made a wonderful visual image to show on the evening news.

Can you dress in a funny suit to promote your book? Can you ride a bicycle in public with a billboard attached to it? Can you have a large poster or photo on a tripod next to you as you speak? Anything that will make a cute picture stands a chance of drawing media coverage. Keep this in mind when you're creating an event. Always include a visual element to ensure that photos will run.

A Controversial Event

Is the topic of your book controversial? Can you create an event in which hundreds of angry people waving signs appear in front of a courthouse or a state capitol building? Then do it, because controversy sells. So does a surprise announcement or an amazing revelation. But if you plan to stage this kind of event, be sure you're prepared to verbally defend yourself and your beliefs.

A Humorous Event

Can you create an amusing event around your book? Perhaps design a silly contest or create an attention-getting award you will bestow on some public figure. These kinds of events are ideal for radio, particularly the kind of silliness that goes on during the morning radio shows. Producers of these shows are always on the lookout for something funny (or someone they can make fun of) and something that's outrageous. Be warned, though: wear a thick skin, because this sort of event could backfire. When Jennifer does radio and TV appearances as the author of *The Martini Diet*, she knows full well that the hosts will make all kinds of jokes and doesn't take offense. Because hey, it sells books!

Slush Pile _____

You've heard it before: practice before you go on the air! Practice before you stand at the podium facing a sea of television cameras. Practice before you call a newspaper reporter on the phone to discuss a story idea. If you don't practice and get it wrong the first time, there may not be a second time. To get over your stage fright, join a local Toastmasters speaking group and work on your skills. Check out www.toastmasters.org to find a chapter near you.

What Good Did That Do?

You staged an event and the media came. But when you turned on the TV that night, you heard the newsman say everything but the name of your book. And the lengthy newspaper article didn't even mention your book. So what good did that do?

Quite a bit. Even if your book didn't get any exposure, you did. You now have more experience in dealing with the media. You now have a newspaper article you can send out, or a video or audio tape of you on the air. Keep trying. You will soon learn how to be sure your book gets as much coverage as you do.

Experts Say

"Being on *The Rosie O'Donnell Show* was a hoot; it was one of the most enjoyable afternoons I had," says author and agent Bill Adler Jr. "When I suggested to Rosie that the best way to outwit squirrels is to get down on your hands and knees, crawl around your backyard, and look at birdfeeders from a squirrel's perspective, Rosie did just that on stage. The audience howled." And Adler's book sales soared! (See Chapter 22 for more of Adler's story.)

The Christmas Cash Box

In the past decade, one man has come to dominate the best-seller list at Christmastime: Richard Paul Evans, with his book *The Christmas Box*. With many millions of copies of *The Christmas Box* and his follow-up books in print, Evans is a master at publicity and promotion.

Was he always this way? No. Evans's story is now the stuff of publishing legend. He self-published the book and then sold it to Simon & Schuster for $4.2 million. But his background was not in writing and publishing; it was in advertising and campaigns. He took the same skills he'd honed while engineering political campaigns and applied the principles to book publicity. And it worked.

For the Christmas 1997 season, Evans created an unusual campaign. Drawing on his background, he produced a free 2-hour radio program on the story behind *The Christmas Box*. This tape was sent, along with a copy of the book, to 896 radio stations around the country. Many of the stations ran the broadcast around Thanksgiving. In essence, it was a 2-hour-long commercial for Evans's book—a brilliant publicity campaign.

> **Experts Say**
>
> Even *The New York Times* business section thinks Richard Paul Evans is good at what he does. In a lengthy article the paper noted, "Like any savvy pol [politician], he maintains a computer database with the names and addresses of 4,000 fans who have corresponded with him. His address is published in *The Christmas Box* and all of his other best-selling novels, and postcards are sent to his fans, alerting them to new titles." Good idea—an inexpensive way to stay in touch.

Could you do something like that for your book? Not right away. Evans's free programming was used because the stations were already aware of who he was and what his book was about. They'd seen his name on the best-seller list year after year after year ....

But take heed of what Evans did: he made a producer's job easy. Whether it meant showing up with a stuffed squirrel as Bill Adler Jr. did (see Chapter 22) or sending along a free 2-hour radio program as Evans did, both authors succeeded because they smoothed the process, making it easy for producers to create a show around them.

Effective Bookstore Events

Okay, so maybe you're not quite ready for primetime TV. But what about an appearance at your local bookstore? That sounds easy enough. It's simpler than getting on TV, but to have an effective in-store event still takes quite a bit of planning.

Many bookstores—particularly the large national chains—have a staff member whose primary function is to coordinate in-store activities. These folks are called *community relations coordinators*, or *events coordinators*. The book business is quite competitive nowadays, and every bookstore tries hard to become a community center of sorts, the type of place where you head on a Friday night just to see what's happening. Music, poetry readings, author signings, appearances by children's book characters—all kinds of activities go on at bookstores.

Few experiences in life are as disappointing as an author appearance that flops. To sit at a desk surrounded by a stack of books, looking hopefully at people as they walk past without stopping ... it's pretty awful. Many authors have been there. Read on to learn how to create a successful bookstore appearance.

def•i•ni•tion

Many bookstores have an **events coordinator** on staff. This person's primary function is to arrange author appearances and other kinds of bookstore events. Sometimes he or she is called a **community relations coordinator**.

An Event Is Better Than a Signing

An author book signing is a pretty dull event, especially if the author is unknown. So anything you can do to turn a bookstore appearance into an event helps create excitement and a crowd. Steve Allen (or a Steve Allen look-alike) telling jokes and playing the piano before signing books is an event. Giving an informative talk on your topic is an event. Don't sit behind a table and expect strangers to approach you. They won't. Give them a reason to come over and see what's happening for themselves.

> **Hot Off the Press**
>
> Invite everyone you know. A crowd builds a crowd. If a bookstore customer sees a crowd of people in a corner, curiosity will draw them over, too. For the author, it is always better to look out and see friendly and familiar faces. Just to play it safe, ask everyone you invite to bring a friend.

Don't Rely on the Bookstore for Publicity

Ask the bookstore what its standard procedure is for publicity and then do more. Don't make the retailer angry, but don't assume the bookstore will do it all for you. This is a perfect time to approach a reporter for a feature article on you and your book. Bookstore appearances that are preceded by a newspaper story (and mentioned in the story) are always more successful than those that haven't received any coverage. Be creative about where you try to get publicity; try to get the message out to whatever group you believe will be interested in your book. Appearing on local television shows a few days before the event is also a way to build attendance. Ask the producer to flash the information about your event on the screen while you're talking.

Ask for a Display

Even if your appearance is a disappointment, you might make some gains if your book is on display. Many stores have a special area where they display the books whose authors are coming. Many stores also make large posters for your book or display a poster you make. If your book is on display for a week or two, that's a victory in itself.

If all else fails, bring food. Yes, a plate of cookies can sometimes make a difference. Anyone who comes by for a bite will feel obligated to stop and listen to you for a moment, anyway.

Hot Off the Press

Every author has a tale of a disastrous bookstore signing. If no one comes, use this as an opportunity to learn how to do the next one better. While giving in-store readings from her book, *Christmas Miracles,* Jennifer spent several hours one weekend afternoon at two different San Francisco bookstores sitting alone on a chair reading Christmas stories into a microphone. Embarrassing, but true. Even an ex-boyfriend who happened by unexpectedly wouldn't stay and listen! So if it happens to you, don't feel alone. You are now a bona fide member of a very, very large club.

Can You Really Afford a Best-Seller?

After all the information we've shared about publicity and how to get it, why would we ask you if you really can afford a best-seller? It may seem like an odd question, but it's worth thinking about.

Many of the authors we've mentioned in this book—everyone from the authors of the *Chicken Soup for the Soul* series, to Richard Paul Evans and *The Christmas Box*, from David Chilton of *The Wealthy Barber* and M. Scott Peck of *The Road Less Traveled*—have one thing in common. They are driven to succeed. Becoming a best-selling author is a job that requires work 24 hours a day, 7 days a week.

Do you have that drive? Can you afford it emotionally, physically, or even financially?

Are you willing to spend less time with your family? Many best-selling authors tour constantly, living in hotel rooms across the country and sleeping on overnight flights. More than one marriage has been strained as a result of this lifestyle.

Do you have the stamina to be on the go all day long, from early morning interviews through to late-night talk shows? It can be a physically demanding job.

Some authors pay for constant promotion of their books. Richard Paul Evans runs (and pays for) an elaborate publicity network that employs four people. Jack Canfield and Mark Victor Hansen pay for much of their own publicity. It is a costly undertaking, one few publishers are willing to fund forever. (Of course, if your book makes it big and makes big bucks, you'll recoup your investment.)

Before you take the plunge and dedicate yourself to building a best-seller, stop and consider the effect your decision will have on others in your life. This is a major lifestyle change, and once undertaken, it's hard to turn back.

Hot Off the Press

"I heard that Steve Allen was coming to town for a special Valentine's Day piano performance," says Terry Foley, former community relations coordinator for a Borders bookstore in northern California. "And I got on the phone and pleaded with his publisher to let him come for a book signing" to promote his latest mystery. In addition to his other talents, Steve Allen wrote many best-sellers. To make certain there was a crowd, Foley alerted the retirement communities near his store. There was a standing-room-only crowd of 350 rapt fans who listened to Allen's snappy banter and piano playing for several hours. It was one of Allen's last appearances before he died. The moral of this story? Think about who your audience is, and then make every effort to let them know about your event.

The Least You Need to Know

◆ The media is in constant need for new and interesting stories. Learn how to exploit this for your book's benefit.

◆ Creating media events that receive coverage can be a powerful way to spread the word about your book.

◆ To catch the media's eye, your event should be timely, controversial, visual, and/or humorous.

◆ Anything you can do to make a producer's job easier increases your chances of getting a good spot on TV.

◆ Bookstore events need promotion and publicity to really work.

◆ Having a best-selling book can extract a heavy toll emotionally, physically, and financially.

Part 5

My Brilliant Career: Continuing Your Career as an Author

Your book is on the bookstore shelves, but for how long? The more you understand what happens in the stores and what it means to you, the better you can make decisions about your future.

And is the life of an author really for you? How do you decide if your book is a success? Do you want to do it again? In Part 5, we help you make the decision on where to go from here, and we give you ideas on other ways you can make money with your writing talents.

Chapter 24

After the Party Is Over

In This Chapter

- ◆ The shelf life of a book
- ◆ Returns to sender
- ◆ Another chance as a paperback, new edition, or sequel
- ◆ Evaluating your success
- ◆ Getting better all the time
- ◆ Moving on to the next phase

Meanwhile, back at the bookstore … What's happening with your book? Both you and your publisher are working as hard as you can to let the world know that your book exists. What happens to books after the box is unpacked and the book is placed on the shelf?

There was a time when books sat on bookstore shelves for years, growing ever dustier. Once or twice a year, a bespectacled bookseller would comb the shelves for the oldest-looking books and return them to the publisher. The average life span of a published book was long. But today, it's a different story.

You may remember from the beginning of this book that the retail book business is 100 percent returnable. Books that are ordered from the publisher, placed on the bookstore shelf, and then remain unsold may be returned to the publisher for full credit.

Sold Once ... and Then Again

One of the more peculiar aspects of publishing is that books essentially have to be sold twice. The first time, the sales rep sells it to the bookstore. Then the bookstore has to sell it to the customer. Until that second sale occurs, you haven't really sold a single book.

> **Experts Say**
>
> It strikes fear in the hearts of publishers and authors: several times a year the large chains thin their stock and send back large returns. The chains analyze which titles have been moving and which ones haven't and the "haven't" books get boxed up and returned for credit. Yet another reason to constantly promote your book so there's always steady movement on it.

> **def•i•ni•tion**
>
> In the long run, how many books were shipped out to bookstores doesn't matter. What matters is the number of books that **sell through**. Books that sell through are books that bookstore customers bought.

Will a customer be able to find your book when she goes into a bookstore looking for it? If your publicity creates demand, will there be supply to meet that demand? If someone goes into a bookstore looking for your title, both you and your publisher hope she can easily find a copy on the shelf. And if she can't find the book (and a bookstore employee can't find it, either), she can order it just as easily.

And remember when we learned about how bookstores buy and reorder books? In today's bookstore, you hope your book is moving off the shelf. That is, if the bookstore has ordered multiple copies and week after week those multiple copies remain on the shelf, that means excess inventory is stacking up in their distribution center as a result of the automatic ordering they have set up with the publisher. This inventory eventually comes back—as returns. If one day there are three copies of the book on the shelf and four days later there are none, don't despair! That means the book is *selling through* or moving from the publisher through to the customer. The book store will restock, and books will be on the shelf again in a few days.

Online book buying habits have changed this somewhat. Publishers have always feared lost sales due to a book not being in stock at the bookstore at the moment a customer wants it. They fear these can never be regained. But more book customers are becoming accustomed to the idea that, hey, if it isn't on the shelf, why not order it at the bookstore? It would take the same amount of time as buying it online anyway …

Your Book's Inventory: It's Gotta Move

In this fast-paced world in which we all now dwell, the shelf life of a new book has shortened considerably. Some industry experts believe the window of opportunity for a new book is as short as 6 weeks. The clock begins ticking the minute a book is placed on the store shelf. You as the author hope it's placed on the shelf faced out with the cover showing, but all too often books are put on the shelf sideways with only the *spine out*.

def•i•ni•tion

Books placed on the shelf with the cover facing out catch a customer's eye better than books that are **spine out,** or placed sideways on the shelf so only the slim edge of the book shows. But don't worry if your book can only be displayed spine out. Publishers and design teams spend a great deal of time designing the spine to make it as eye-catching as possible.

With a heavy reliance on computers, many bookstores know exactly when an individual book arrived in their warehouse and when (and where) it was placed on the bookstore shelf. Unless the computer notes that it has sold, the book will someday be hunted down for return.

Why? As far as the bookstores are concerned, an unsold book is money sitting there on the shelf. And money tied up in a book that isn't moving could be freed up and then spent on buying another newer, hotter book—one that might sell quicker!

Experts Say

Small, independent bookstores seldom return unsold books as aggressively as their larger cousins. "It is a dying habit, but we will give a new hardcover book 6 months or more before pulling it," says Ann Magruder of Beers Books in Sacramento. "We'd much rather sell it than return it."

Extending Shelf Life

What keeps your book on the shelf? Steady sales. Publicity. Customer requests. Bookstore appearances. It has happened before (and will happen again) that an expensive publicity and marketing campaign has gone for naught because the book had already been returned by bookstores.

Do you, the author, have any control or input in this process? Not really. You might be able to convince bookstores in your area that you're an aggressive marketer who will send an endless stream of customers in looking for your book. But with the rest of the country, you just have to cross your fingers. This is where your own commitment to continually publicizing your book nationwide can make a big difference. Every interview on a small radio station somewhere in the country could be sending someone in to their local store asking for your book. Day in and day out, these kinds of requests do help.

Returns to Sender

Returns not only make your book disappear from the shelf, but they also make dollars disappear from your royalty account. When books are returned to the publisher, that is noted in the publisher's inventory system. When the publisher's royalty department factors in that information, your account could sink slowly into the west.

Remember, if you have received an advance, you're already in the hole. Your book must sell enough to earn back the advance and move into the black before you make any more money. Books returned unsold can easily drag you back into the red ink, delaying the long-awaited day you earn back your advance and begin to accrue more royalties. That's another reason to cross your fingers and say your prayers (and send out another press release or two).

For many years, publishers have accused bookstores, both large and small, of returning books in lieu of paying bills. That may be the case. Streamlined ordering practices can lessen that problem, but this has also lessened the size of publisher's print runs.

End of the Line

One day you get a letter in the mail from your publisher. Your book is being taken *out of print* (or "OP"). What does that mean? And what will happen to the rest of your books?

def•i•ni•tion

A book that's currently available from a publisher is *in print*. A book that's no longer available from a publisher is **out of print**.

Coming Out Again?

If your book was published first in hardcover, you might have something else to look forward to: a paperback edition, either in a trade paperback size or as a mass market paperback. The decision to publish in paperback is based on sales.

The path from hardcover to paperback used to be quite routine but is now reconsidered with every book. Do the sales figures justify bringing it out again? They might, if the total figure is somewhere north of 10,000 copies and the information in your book is still current. A book on a topic that was timely in hardcover might not be a candidate for a paperback, though, if interest in that topic has flagged. But if your book meets these criteria, get ready for another round of cover design, copywriting, and publicity. If not, let's consider what else might lie ahead.

A Rose by Any Other Name ...

As Peggy Lee would sing, "Is that all there is?" If your book dies a slow death on the shelf, or even if it succeeds and sells for many years, is that all there is? You worked so hard for many months (and, in some cases, many years) to produce this book! Is it time to move on to the next thing?

Not necessarily. With a novel, yes, you'll have to take what you've learned from this first experience and get busy with another book. But with nonfiction books, a few other options are left:

◆ A revised and expanded second edition

◆ A renamed and repackaged book

◆ Electronic publishing

◆ Series and sequels

Revised and Expanded!

If your nonfiction book sold in respectable numbers the first time around—respectable being solely determined by your publisher—you can certainly discuss with your publisher the opportunity to revise, update, and expand the material for a new edition, provided, of course, that it's a topic that still has an audience. Almost any nonfiction book can go through this phase—health books, travel books, reference books, and even cookbooks can be revised and expanded. If the second edition succeeds, you can look forward to a third, fourth, fifth, or sixth edition, and so on.

It never hurts to go into a book project with an eye on developing long-term income, and annual editions or a frequently revised book is a great way to go.

Renamed and Repackaged

So your book didn't sell well. The book has gone out of print. Check your contract to see what the publisher's process is for reverting the rights back to you. You might also be able to buy the remaining copies of the book for a fraction of the original price. If you do want a supply of your books, you have to buy them quickly. The publisher offers any unsold stock to a remaindering company, who, in turn, sells it to booksellers for a small price for their bargain tables.

Is it over? Again, if the topic is still timely, it doesn't have to be. But you need to completely change your book. To dust it off and make it salable to another publisher, your book needs to undergo quite a face-lift as well as a name change. Your book could be reborn with a better title, a tighter editorial focus, or a different format.

If you do decide to work to improve your book and resell it, you need to be up-front about it. Tell your agent, and tell any publisher that expresses an interest, that you once published a similar book under a different title. They'll probably find out later, anyway, and that could spell trouble.

> **Experts Say**
>
> Sometimes a publisher changes the name of a book between the hardcover and paperback editions. This is done to give the paperback book a fresh start and a better, more tightly focused title. A good example is a book on women in the corporate world called *New Success Secrets for Women* in hardcover that was changed to *What Women Don't Learn in Business School* in paperback. The second title gives browsers a better idea of what the book is about.

After the rights have officially reverted, you could also bring it out again in an edition you publish yourself. Ellen Reid, the "Book Shepard" (check out www.bookshep.com), works with clients to shepherd them gently through the process of self-publishing and has seen more than one book given a second life. "You can change the name to give it a tighter focus the second time around," she suggests. "Or you can redo the body of the book to broaden the focus." If you decide to go this route, revisit the first three chapters of this book to remind yourself how to find a healthy niche audience. Spend time thinking about how your book can be repositioned for a new and healthy life.

Sell a Small Booklet?

Best-selling author Jim Collins (his book *Good to Great* spent more than 4 solid years on the best-seller list) wanted to put out information targeted to nonprofits so they, too, could learn how to apply the success principles he'd uncovered. He didn't want to muddy the market for his next book, though, and decided on a radical approach. He self-published a 35-page booklet called *Good to Great and the Social Sectors*. An article in *Newsweek* helped get the word out, and his self-published booklet quickly ranked among Amazon.com's fastest-selling books.

Is this a technique you could use? If your first book has found its audience and you aren't yet ready for another big book effort, why not a smaller, self-published book for a specific audience?

Taking It to the Superhighway

We've discussed electronic publishing in several different parts of this book, and we bring it up yet again because it's something to consider for the future of your book. If the rights to the book have reverted to you, you can take what you've written and do several things with it:

◆ Turn it into an e-book, or break it up into a series of "special reports" that you market through your own website.

◆ Sign up with one of the print on demand services such as Xlibris (xlibris.com) so your book is always available somewhere, somehow.

Although electronic publishing possibilities are thrilling, that still leaves you, the author, with a basic problem: how to create sales for your book. It's up to you to create demand, a critical part of the print on demand equation. Here's how author Joe Vitale thinks it can work: "After 10 years of being published by mainstream publishers and never making enough to pay the rent, I came out with my first e-book and tasted blood. In 24 hours I sold 600 e-books of *Hypnotic Writing* for $29 each. The secret is a dedicated website with powerhouse sales copy on it, a strong guarantee, bonuses to encourage action now, a tested price, secure ordering, and oh yeah, a good book focused on a specific theme for a specific audience helps." You can learn more about what Joe does and how he did it at his website, www.mrfire.com.

Series and Sequels

Are the sales of your book strong enough to warrant more of the same? Has your editor hinted that she would like to see you do another similar book? Welcome to the world of series and *sequels*, where, if one book sells, another just like it should do fine, too!

def•i•ni•tion

A second book that features many of the same characters as the first is a **sequel**.

Deciding whether to pursue either a sequel to a book or to build it into a series is strictly the publisher's call. If you aren't sure whether your publisher is interested in a series or a sequel, ask your editor. She will be honest about the chances that might happen.

Evaluating Your Success

How do you know if your book is a success? How many books sold are enough? Or worse yet, how many are too few? Evaluating your book's success strictly by the numbers is relatively easy. Evaluating your book's success in other ways is a little harder.

Show Me the Money

How many books need to sell to make it a success? That question needs to be considered in relationship to the size of your book's first print run.

- If your book had a modest first printing of 7,500 and sold at least 5,000 copies, you did fine.

- If your book had a first printing of 10,000 and sold 5,000, you didn't do as well.

- If the publisher printed aggressively (more than 25,000 for a first-time author) and you didn't sell through more than 50 percent, you didn't do as well.

Remember, the size of the print run was determined by the advance orders. The advance orders were determined by how well the bookstores thought your book would sell. So if a book with a small print run (a book with modest sales expectations) sold well, that's a heck of a victory. But if a book with a large print run (big sales expectations) didn't do well, that's a disappointment. Does that make sense?

Personal Best

But was the book a personal success for you, the author? You wrote a book; you published a book. That sets you apart from most other people on the planet. Instead of just talking about how someday you plan to write a book, you did it.

Let's return to the reasons to write. In Chapter 1, you looked at a list of reasons:

- ◆ I'm compelled to write.
- ◆ I want the personal satisfaction of being published.
- ◆ I hope to advance my cause.
- ◆ I want to share my knowledge.
- ◆ I'd like to advance my career.
- ◆ I'd like to achieve fame.
- ◆ I'd like to earn a fortune.
- ◆ All of the above.

Which reason (or reasons) was yours? Did your book help you achieve it? Even a book with modest sales can easily achieve many of the reasons on the list.

Are you compelled to write? You wrote. Did you seek the personal satisfaction of being published? You have it. Did you want to advance your cause or share your knowledge? Everyone who bought a copy of your book, read about you in the newspaper, or heard you talk on the radio is now aware of both your cause and your knowledge.

Has your career been advanced? You now have the prestige and distinction of being published. And regardless of how well your book has done in bookstores, you have the opportunity to speak around the country and sell books to clients and your professional audience. If you want, you could keep your book in print forever in a self-published edition.

Experts Say _____

Many folks on the professional speaking circuit make money with "back of the room" sales. If a roomful of people has already paid to come and hear you speak on a topic, those people are primed to buy what you've got to sell. These people won't look to see which New York publisher is behind your book; they just want to take a little of you home with them. A speaking career is a great way to promote and prolong the life of your book. Buy copies in bulk from your publisher; when those run out and the rights have reverted, publish it yourself. This can make a big difference in your bottom line.

But Really, Show Me the Money!

Did you achieve fame or fortune? Ah, here's the tricky one. As you learned in the first chapter, it *is* possible to achieve fame without fortune, and vice versa.

Fame may still be achieved. If you continue to promote and sell your book on your own long enough, you can achieve a measure of fame.

Fortune is not always elusive, either. The mere fact that you published a book may someday spawn other opportunities. Other opportunities may have occurred to you during this long, long ride as well. Or maybe fortune will come with the next book.

But This Book Was Perfect!

"The publisher screwed up." Ask most authors why their books didn't sell, and that's the reason you'll hear: the publisher screwed up, not me.

Slush Pile _____

When trying to sell another book, don't ever point the finger of failure for your previous book at your publisher—at least, not when talking to an agent or an editor. Your complaints will fall on deaf ears, and your listeners will consider you a whiner.

The book didn't get to the stores in time. The cover (or the title) was awful. They didn't do any publicity. They never cared about my book. The staff was incompetent. My editor left. The sales reps didn't sell it. The stores returned it too soon.

Perhaps. But indulging in that sort of thinking won't further your career as a writer. A better way to spend your time post-book is to do some follow-up work:

- Continue to work on your writing.
- Sharpen your ability to create a book that large numbers of people will buy.

And remember, if you feel this way about your first publishing experience, keep it to yourself. Grouse to your friends and family all you want, but button your lip when talking to industry folks. Agents and editors know full well from years of experience that someone who complains about their first publisher will sooner or later complain about their second publisher. They take it as a sure sign to steer clear.

Work on My Writing?

Yes, work on your writing. Continue to take classes, attend conferences, and seek out other writers. Build your own community of writers around you. A group of published authors in northern California meets twice a month as "The Rich and Famous Writers' Club" to share ideas, contacts, and inspiration with each other. Every writer benefits when he continues to practice and polish his craft.

You have been published. Now take that accolade and build on it. Write more. Get better.

> **Experts Say**
>
> Why continue to go to writers' conferences after you've already been published? Other unpublished writers will look at you with awe. It can be a nice little ego boost. You also will make new contacts with agents and editors, sharpen your skills, and come away reinvigorated.

What Book Will Large Numbers of People Buy?

Hopefully, they'll buy your next one. Again, take what you've learned with this first book and build on it. If that's your goal, work on developing novels and nonfiction books that have the potential to affect large numbers of readers.

Chapter 3 might not have interested you when you began reading this book. After all, you already knew what you wanted to write. Is it time to go back and reread that chapter? It gives you a clear-eyed view of how book professionals try to develop book ideas with big potential. Read that chapter, and try out a few of the exercises. It will help you begin to think like a publisher.

Co-author Jennifer's favorite writing success story holds great encouragement for anyone whose first published book didn't quite set the world on fire. Some 10 years ago she discovered a wonderful food writer named Marlena de Blasi. Marlena wrote a delightful cookbook called *Regional Foods of Northern Italy*, which Jennifer published at Prima.

Despite its beauty and charm, the book was not a terrific success. Marlena did find terrific writing success though, but it wasn't as a cookbook writer, which was how she originally perceived herself. She wrote the lyrical story of her midlife romance with an Italian man who swept her off her feet and convinced her to move on a whim to Venice, leaving her familiar American world behind. Marlena's book, *A Thousand Days in Venice*, became a literary travel best-seller in the vein of *A Year in Provence* and *Under the Tuscan Sun*. And a scant 2 years later she wrote a sequel, *A Thousand Days in Tuscany*.

Moving On to the Next Phase

What's your next move, anyway? Will you try to write another book, or will you try to return to your life as it was before you embarked on all of this?

If you're returning to your previous life, be proud of what you've achieved. You now have a lasting symbol of a great and unusual accomplishment: a published book.

The Least You Need to Know

- The life span of a new book on a bookstore shelf can be short, but steady sales, constant publicity, and customer demand combine to keep a book on the shelves for a long time.

- Between special orders placed with distributors and the rise of online book-selling, while your book is in print it is almost always in stock and available somewhere.

- If the sales were satisfactory, a hardcover book will come out in paperback, and a paperback might someday come out again as a revised and updated second edition.

- Sometimes a book is renamed during the transition from hardcover to paperback to give it a better chance for better sales.

- To be considered a sales success, a book must sell through a majority of its print run.

- Even if your book has not been a sales success, you might have achieved your reasons for writing.

Appendix A

Glossary

acquisitions editor   An editor responsible for bringing in new books to publish.

advance   The money a publisher pays to an author to write a book. Usually one half is paid upon signing a contract, and the remainder is paid upon delivery of an acceptable manuscript. This is an advance against future royalties earned, and the book must sell enough to earn back the advance before more royalty money will be paid out. Advance can also mean the number of copies sold by the sales reps for the first 2 months of the book's publication.

agent   A literary agent represents an author to the publisher and secures a publishing contract in exchange for an agreed-upon percentage, usually 15 percent.

assistants   The young, unsung folks who answer the phones, sort the mail, and otherwise keep publishing offices going (also known as editorial assistants).

auction   A sale, usually conducted by an agent, that gives several publishers the opportunity to bid on the rights to publish a book. The book goes to the highest bidder.

audience   That part of the population that will be interested in buying a specific book (also "readers").

author   The writer of a book or books; the term usually implies a published writer.

author guidelines   The set of guidelines a publishing house usually provides an author that details the way the submission should come in, formatting, and often the process and people involved.

author queries   A part of the editing process in which the editor and/or copy editor ask the author to further explain meaning, answer questions about accuracy or intent, or rewrite small sections.

backlist   The list of books the publisher has available for sale that are older than twelve months.

best-seller   A term used quite loosely in the publishing world. Strictly speaking, the term refers to a book that has appeared on a best-seller list somewhere. In reality, publishers and their publicity staffs attach the term to almost any book they haven't lost money on.

blog   A web log, an online based diary or postings on a particular topic.

bluelines   The cheap test proof of a book, usually in blue ink, the printer sends to the publisher for approval before printing the entire job.

boilerplate contract   A publisher's standard contract, before the author or agent requests modifications.

book doctor   An outside editor who can be hired (increasingly by the author or agent) to rewrite or suggest major edits on a manuscript. *See also* proposal doctor.

Book Expo   The annual publishing industry trade show. It used to be called the ABA (American Booksellers' Association), but now it is the BEA, short for Book Expo America.

book packager   Packagers (also called producers) create books for publishers, providing them with finished manuscripts to finished books—or anything in between.

book proposal   A packet of information about the writer's book idea. A proposal typically contains a solid description of the book's content, the potential market for the book, competition, and the author's credentials. It also contains a table of contents, an extensive book outline, and at least one sample chapter.

bound galley   Often a paperback version of the book (sometimes unproofread) marketing may have produced four months before the book's publication date to enable reviewers to read the work and review for publication.

buyer The bookstore employee who meets with publishers' sales representatives to decide how many copies of a book to order.

buzz The word-of-mouth excitement created in the publishing community before a book is released.

camera-ready art The finished artwork that's ready to be photographed, without alteration, for reproduction.

chain The large chain stores that sell books. Borders and Barnes & Noble are chain bookstores.

chapter book A category of children's books that have longer stories and are written for the intermediate reader.

chick lit A style of novel that appeals to women in their 20s and 30s and revolves around a young woman main character.

clip art Artwork specifically designed to be used by anyone without needing to obtain any permission.

commercial publisher A publishing company that assumes the full cost of producing, printing, and distributing a literary work and pays the author a percentage of the proceeds.

commission The percentage of the advance and subsequent royalties an agent receives as his fee after selling your work to a publisher. This can run anywhere from 10 to 25 percent (the larger percentages are for subrights).

community coordinator *See* events coordinator.

compositor A person who designs and typesets manuscripts and prepares formatted disks or final files that are sent to the printer. Also called a layout tech.

copyright "The right of authors to control the reproduction and use of their creative expressions that have been fixed in tangible form," according to *The Associated Press Style Book and Briefing on Media Law*.

counter display Several copies of a book in a cardboard holder for display in a bookstore. It is also called a counter pack or dump.

deadline The due date for the completed manuscript as specified in the publishing contract.

demographics Population statistics, age groups, buying habits, personal income levels, and other categories that can be used to estimate a book's potential success.

distributor   A business that calls on bookstores and takes orders for the publishers it represents.

dump   Publishing industry slang for a counter display. Dumps are usually the larger cardboard displays that stand on the floor.

e-book   A book that's not available in printed form, only in an electronic file. E-books can be downloaded (and sometimes printed out) and read on a PDA, electronic reader, or computer.

easy readers   A category of children's books with short, simple sentences designed for beginning readers.

editorial board   The group of people who collectively make the decision to publish a book. Acquisitions editors present book proposals to the editorial board for its approval. This is also sometimes called a pub board.

electronic publishing   Paperless publishing as e-books.

electronic rights   Refers to a variety of digital rights.

endcap   The shelves at the end of an aisle in the bookstore. Publishers pay booksellers for the chance to display their books on the endcap.

English cozy   A type of mystery book set in England that often features a quaint English atmosphere.

events coordinator   A bookstore employee who is responsible for arranging author signings, author appearances, and in-store events. This position may also be called a community coordinator.

exclusive submission   When only one agent or editor is considering your proposal.

F&Gs   Sheets of paper that have been "folded and gathered" in preparation for printing. This is another test step the publisher can review and approve before seeing finished, bound books.

face out   Books that are placed on the shelf with the cover facing out toward the customer.

featured guest   A guest who is central to a television or radio show's segment. If a number of experts are used on the same show, the guest is a panel member rather than the focus of the show.

fiction   Works of the imagination.

first printing   The number of books printed in the initial print run.

first serial   An excerpt that appears in a newspaper or magazine before the book's publication and actual release.

floor   The minimum bid in an auction.

foreign rights   The right to publish a book in another country or language.

formatting   The way the printed words appear on the page, including things such as margins, indentations, type size, and type font.

front matter   The first several pages of a book that typically contain the half-title page, the title page, copyright information, the dedication, acknowledgments, table of contents, introduction, and a prelude or foreword. Front matter pages are numbered i, ii, iii, iv, and so forth.

frontlist   The publisher's current list of books just published, typically any book fewer than twelve months old.

galley (or **loose galleys**)   *See* page proofs. *See also* bound galley.

genre fiction   A term applied to Western, romance, sci-fi, horror, thriller, and fantasy novels.

ghostwriter   A professional writer who writes a book without getting author credit for it.

head   The title introducing a chapter or subdivision of the text.

hen lit   Women's fiction aimed at the 35 and up crowd.

illustrated books   A category of children's books with lots of pictures and few words.

in print   Books currently available from the publisher. If a publisher decides to discontinue publishing a title, the book goes out of print and rights are reverted to the author.

independent booksellers   Locally owned and operated bookstores, not affiliated with a large chain such as Borders or Barnes & Noble.

instant book   A book that appears on bookstore shelves just weeks after the event about which the book is written.

intellectual property   According to *Random House Legal Dictionary*, this consists of "copyrights, patents, and other rights in creations of the mind; also, the creations themselves, such as a literary work, painting, or computer program."

ISBN (International Standard Book Number)   Each book has a unique number that identifies it.

list   A publisher's list of forthcoming titles; the books it plans to publish in the coming season or year. *See also* frontlist.

live show   A television or radio show broadcast at the same moment it is happening.

manuscript guidelines (or **author guidelines**)   A publisher's rules regarding the proper way to prepare a manuscript for submission.

mass market paperback   A 4×7-inch softcover book often found in book racks in airports, drugstores, and supermarkets as well as in bookstores. It's sometimes called a pocket book.

masthead   The section of a magazine that lists the editors and publishers.

mechanicals   Finished laid-out pages ready to be sent to the printer.

media market   A geographic area covered by a particular radio station, TV channel, or newspaper. Some markets, such as New York, are large media markets; others are small.

memoir   An account of the events in the author's own life.

midlist   Books that are acquired for modest advances, given modest print runs, and have a relatively short shelf life.

morning drive-time shows   Radio shows that broadcast between the hours of 6 A.M. and 9 A.M., while commuters are headed to work.

multiple queries   When more than one agent or editor is approached at once about a book idea. *See also* exclusive submission.

nonfiction   A work that contains true information or observations.

option clause   A clause typically found in publishing contracts that requires the author to give the publisher the first chance to buy his or her next book. Also called a next work clause.

out of print   *See* in print.

overview   A Hollywood term now leaking into the book world. The overview is a one-sentence description of a book and its audience.

P and L   A profit and loss statement an editor prepares in advance of acquiring a book.

page count   The number of book pages. Sometimes the minimum (or maximum) number of pages in a completed manuscript is stipulated in the book contract.

page proofs   A stage at which the printer sends sample pages to the publisher/ editor/author for one final check before the entire press run is done.

panel member   *See* featured guest.

parody   A comic imitation of a well-known literary work.

payment on publication   A term meaning the writer is not paid until the work actually appears in print. This is the policy of many magazine publishers and some book publishers.

pdf file   An electronic file that contains camera-ready images of book pages that cannot be manipulated. These are traditionally the final files sent to the printer.

permission   The legal right to use someone else's material in a book. The writer must get a permission form signed by the copyright holder.

placements   Stories or mentions of the author or book in the media resulting from the efforts of publicity; also placement, the location of a book in the bookstore, and/ or the placement of a book into a promotional position in the store.

platform   The author's proven ability to promote and sell his or her book through public speaking, a television or radio show, or a newspaper column.

podcast   A broadcast that can be downloaded and played on an MP3 player.

pre-pack   Several copies of a book offered at a special discount and packaged together in a cardboard display. *See also* dump.

press conference   A meeting to which members of the press are invited to hear something newsworthy.

press release   A 1-page announcement to the press about the new release of a book or an author's planned event.

print on demand   Short-run printing from an electronic file.

print run   The number of books printed each time a book goes to press.

promotion   Free publicity methods and/or paid advertising for a book or its author to create public awareness and stimulate sales. Can also be any paid placement in a bookstore paid for by the publisher to showcase a book, or a marketing/sales discount program to give bookstores incentive to buy more product from publishers, sometimes offering discounts back to the reader ("buy one get one free" or "buy one, get the second at 50 percent off").

proposal doctor   Experienced editors and writers who help others whip their proposals into shape.

public domain   Creative works, such as writings and artwork, that are no longer protected by copyright laws. Works in the public domain may be used by anyone without asking permission or paying royalties or fees.

publicity   Attention directed to a book or its author. Publicity is usually free and includes book reviews, feature articles, television and radio appearances or interviews, and online mentions.

query letter   The initial contact between a writer and an agent or editor. This short letter is meant to spark interest in the writer's project.

readers   The method by which university presses evaluate projects. Readers, or "referees," are experts in that field and are paid to read and pass judgment on the scholarship of a proposed work.

reading fees   A fee requested by an agent to pay for the time he spends reading a writer's project to decide whether it's worth representing.

rejection letter   A formal "no, thanks" letter from an agent or an editor passing on a project.

remaindered   Books that have been sold by the publisher to a discounter for a fraction of their worth. These books end up on the bargain tables at bookstores.

retail price   The price a retail store charges its customers for a book. Unlike other types of products, most books have the retail price printed on the cover.

review copies   Free copies of a book sent out to media people in the hopes that they will review the book or mention it in an article.

royalty   The percentage the publisher pays the author for each book sold.

SASE   Shorthand for a self-addressed, stamped envelope.

seasons   Publishers put together their lists of books and their catalogs according to two or three seasons, usually fall, winter, and spring/summer.

second serial   Excerpts from a book that are published after the book is published and available.

self-published   A book the author himself has paid to have edited, produced, printed, and distributed.

sell-through   Books that have actually been purchased by customers at the bookstore and are not going to be returned unsold to the publisher.

sequel   A second book that features many of the same characters as the first book.

series   Books linked by a brand-name identity or linked in theme, purpose, or content. You're reading a series book right now.

sidebar   Text that is set apart in a box, margin, or shaded area, or set in smaller type to distinguish it from the rest of the text on the page.

slush pile   The to-be-read stack of unsolicited manuscripts. They're usually read by an assistant instead of an editor.

small publisher   A general term that is applied to publishing houses with revenues of less than $10 million a year. Such publishers are also sometimes called small presses.

spine out   A book that's placed on a bookstore shelf with only the spine showing.

submission   The process by which a writer or agent submits a book proposal or manuscript to a publisher. If the author isn't using an agent, it is called an unagented submission.

subrights   A wide variety of rights, including book clubs, electronic, video or movie, dramatic, and merchandising.

syndicated   Used to refer to a column or show packaged and sold to more than one radio or television station, or published in more than one newspaper.

synopsis   A 10-page summary of a novel, written in third-person present tense. It spells out the plot of the novel in an effective and readable way. A synopsis is included in a proposal to an agent or editor.

taped show   A television or radio show that is not broadcast immediately but recorded and played at a later date.

text   Words on a page. This distinguishes them from artwork.

trade paperback   Any paperback book of any size other than the 4×7-inch mass market size books.

video clip   A video of an author's television appearance.

word count   The number of words on a page or in a book. This is often used in a book contract to stipulate the minimum or maximum number of words a manuscript should contain.

work for hire An arrangement in which a writer is paid one time for his or her work. Under a work-for-hire agreement, the writer does not own the copyright and receives no royalties.

writers' conference An organized gathering of writers, which editors and agents also attend.

YA (Young Adult) YA books are those targeted at the 10- to 16-year-old market. The YA market is dominated by mass market paperback series publishing.

Great Books for Writers

Beard, Julie. *The Complete Idiot's Guide to Getting Your Romance Published.* Indianapolis: Alpha Books, 2000.

The Chicago Manual of Style: The Essential Guide for Writers, Editors, and Publishers. Chicago: University of Chicago Press, 1993.

Children's Writer's and Illustrator's Market. Cincinnati: Writer's Digest Books (updated annually).

Eckstut, Arielle, and David Henry Sterry. *Putting Your Passion Into Print: Get Your Book Published Successfully!* New York: Workman Publishing Company, 2005.

Gross, Gerald. *Editors on Editing: What Writers Need to Know About What Editors Do.* New York: Grove/Atlantic Monthly Press, 1993.

Harrow, Susan. *Selling Yourself Without Selling Your Soul.* New York: HarperResource, 2002.

Jassin, Lloyd, and Steve C. Schecter. *The Copyright Permission and Libel Handbook: A Step-by-Step Guide for Writers, Editors, and Publishers.* New York: Wiley, 1998.

Kirsch, Jonathan. *Kirsch's Guide to the Book Contract: For Authors, Publishers, Editors and Agents*. Venice, California: Acrobat Books, 1998.

Kremer, John. *1,001 Ways to Market Your Books*. Fairfield, Iowa: Open Horizons, 1998.

Lamott, Anne. *Bird by Bird: Some Instructions on Writing and Life*. New York: Anchor/Doubleday, 1995.

Larsen, Michael. *How to Write a Book Proposal*. Cincinnati: Writer's Digest Books, 2004.

Laufenberg, Cynthia, and the editors of *Writer's Market. Formatting and Submitting Your Manuscript*. Cincinnati: Writer's Digest Books, 2004.

Levine, Mark. *Negotiating a Book Contract: A Guide for Authors, Agents, and Lawyers*. Wakefield, Rhode Island: Moyer Bell, 1988.

Levinson, Jay Conrad, Rick Frishman, and Michael Larsen. *Guerrilla Marketing for Writers: 100 Weapons for Selling Your Work*. Cincinnati: Writer's Digest Books, 2000.

Literary Marketplace. New York: R.R. Bowker (updated annually).

Lott, Lynn, and Nancy Pickard. *Seven Steps on the Writer's Path*. New York: Ballantine Books, 2003.

Lukeman, Noah. *The Plot Thickens: 8 Ways to Bring Fiction to Life*. New York: St. Martin's Press, 2002.

Maass, Donald. *Writing the Breakout Novel Workbook: Hands-On Help for Making Your Novel Stand Out and Succeed*. Cincinnati: Writer's Digest Books, 2004.

Maisel, Eric. *The Art of the Book Proposal*. New York: Tarcher, 2004.

Page, Susan. *The Shortest Distance Between You and a Published Book*. New York: Broadway, 1997.

Phillips, Brigitte M., Susan D. Klassen, and Doris Hall, editors. *The American Directory of Writer's Guidelines.* Sanger, California: Quill Driver Books/Word Dancer Press, 2004.

Poet's Market. Cincinnati: Writer's Digest Books (updated annually).

Poynter, Dan. *The Self-Publishing Manual: How to Write, Print, and Sell Your Own Book.* Santa Barbara, California: Para Publishing, 1989.

Rabiner, Susan, and Alfred Fortunato. *Thinking Like Your Editor: How to Write Serious Nonfiction—and Get It Published.* New York: W.W. Norton & Company, 2002.

Sander, Jennifer Basye. *The Complete Idiot's Guide to Self-publishing.* Indianapolis: Alpha Books, 2005.

Sexton, Adam. *Master Class in Fiction Writing: Techniques from Austen, Hemingway, and Other Greats.* New York: McGraw-Hill, 2006.

Shoup, Barbara, and Margaret Love Denman. *Novel Ideas: Contemporary Authors Share the Creative Process.* Indianapolis: Alpha Books, 2001.

Sloane, Sarah Jane. *The I Ching for Writers: Finding the Page Inside You.* Novato, California: New World Library, 2005.

Strunk, William Jr., and E. B. White. *The Elements of Style.* New York: Macmillan, 1979.

Underdown, Harold, and Lynne Rominger. *The Complete Idiot's Guide to Publishing Children's Books, Second Edition.* Indianapolis: Alpha Books, 2004.

Walsh, Bill. *The Elephants of Style: A Trunkload of Tips on the Big Issues and Gray Areas of Contemporary American English.* New York: McGraw-Hill, 2004.

———. *Lapsing Into a Comma: A Curmudgeon's Guide to the Many Things That Can Go Wrong in Print—and How to Avoid Them.* New York: McGraw-Hill, 2000.

Williams, Thomas A. *Poet Power: The Complete Guide to Getting Your Poetry Published.* Boulder, Colorado: Sentient Publications, 2002.

Writer's Market. Cincinnati: Writer's Digest Books (updated annually).

Yudkin, Marcia. *Six Steps to Free Publicity: And Dozens of Other Ways to Win Free Media Attention for You and Your Business.* New York: Plume, 1994.

Zinsser, William. *On Writing Well: The Classic Guide to Writing Nonfiction: 25th Anniversary Edition.* New York: HarperResource, 2001.

Zuckerman, Albert J. *Writing the Blockbuster Novel.* Cincinnati: Writer's Digest Books, 1993.

Appendix C

More Good Resources

Professional Associations

Agents' association:

The Association of Author's Representatives
PO Box 237201, Ansonia Station
New York, NY 10003
www.aar-online.org

Book packagers' association:

American Book Producers Association
160 Fifth Avenue
New York, NY 10010-7000
212-645-2368
www.abpaonline.org

Freelance editors' association:

Editorial Freelance Association
71 West 23rd Street, Suite 1910
New York, NY 10010-4181
212-929-5400 or 1-866-929-5400
www.the-efa.org

Self-publishers' group:

Publishers Marketing Association
627 Aviation Way
Manhattan Beach, CA 90266
310-372-2732
www.pma-online.org

Writers' organizations:

**American Society of Journalists
and Authors, Inc.**
1501 Broadway, Suite 302
New York, NY 10036
212-997-0947
staff@asja.org
www.asja.org

The Authors Guild
330 West 42nd Street
New York, NY 10036
212-563-5904
www.authorsguild.org

National Writers Union
113 University Place, 6th Floor
New York, NY 10003
212-254-0279
www.nwu.org

**North American Travel Journalists
Association**
310-836-8712
www.natja.org

Romance Writers of America
13700 Veterans Memorial Drive, #315
Houston, TX 77014
281-440-6885
www.rwanational.org

Sisters in Crime
PO Box 442124
Lawrence, KS 66044-8933
sistersincrime@juno.com
www.sistersincrime.org

**Society of Children's Book Writers
and Illustrators**
8271 Beverly Boulevard
Los Angeles, CA 90048
323-782-1010
www.scbwi.org

Publicity Agencies

Book publicists:

Planned Television Arts
Rick Frishman
1110 Second Avenue
New York, NY 10022
212-593-5820

Marika Flatt
www.prbythebook.com

Susan Harrow
Harrow Communications
4200 Park Boulevard, #333 W
Oakland, CA 94602-1213
1-888-839-4190
www.prsecrets.com

Annie Jennings
Annie Jennings PR
26 Wilshire Drive
Belle Mead, NJ 08502
annie@anniejenningspr.com
www.anniejenningspr.com

Sherri Rosen
Sherri Rosen Publicity
15 Park Row, Suite 25C
New York, NY 10038
212-587-0296
sherri@sherrirosen.com
www.sherrirosen.com

Book publicity information:

You're On the Air
A 90-minute videotape produced by
Book Marketing Works about how to
get on and perform well on television
and radio. $79.95 for the video and
two books. For information, call
1-800-562-4357 or visit www.
bookmarketingworks.com.

Media trainer:

Michelle Anton
Former *Oprah* producer, former producer of the *Dr. Laura Show*
323-353-3922

Jess Todtfeld, "The Pitch Doctor"
Success in Media
631-431-8251
jess@successinmedia.com
www.successinmedia.com

Seminars and Publications

Seminars:

**92nd Street Y—the Unterberg
Poetry Center Writing Program**
Sheree Bykofsky et al.
92nd Street YMCA

1395 Lexington Avenue
New York, NY 10128
212-415-5760
www.92y.org

Mega Book Marketing University
Mark Victor Hansen
949-759-9304
www.megabookmarketing.com

**SEAK—Medical Fiction Writing
for Physicians**
Sheree Bykofsky et al.
PO Box 729
Falmouth, MA 02541
508-457-1111
Fax: 508-540-8304
seakinc@aol.com

**Writing the Breakout Novel with
Donald Maass Free Expressions
Seminars' Writing Success Series**
2420 W. Brandon Boulevard, #198
Brandon, FL 33511
1-866-I-WRITE-2 (1-888-497-4832)
or 813-684-7988
Fax: 813-689-6952
lorin@free-expressions.com or
brenda@free-expressions.com

Short-run book printers:

Infinity Publishing
1094 New Dehaven Street, Suite 100
West Conshohocken, PA 19428
610-941-9999 or 1-877-BUYBOOK
(1-877-289-2665)
Fax: 610-941-9959
www.infinitypublishing.com

Morris Publishing
3212 East Highway 30
Kearney, NE 68847
1-800-650-7888
www.morrispublishing.com

Trade publications:

Publishers Weekly
245 West 17th Street
New York, NY 10011
1-800-278-2991
www.publishersweekly.com

Websites of Note

www.amazon.com
Online bookstore; good for competitive research.

www.barnesandnoble.com or
www.bn.com
Online bookstore; good for competitive research.

www.bksp.org
Resources for writers.

www.bookpublishing.com
General publishing information.

www.bookwire.com
Timely publishing news from Book-Wire.

www.publishersmarketplace.com
Info about agents, packagers, industry news, subscriptions to "Publishers Lunch" e-newsletter.

www.pw.org
Poets and writers, literary links, links to small presses, writers' conferences.

www.shawguides.com
Current info about writers' conferences.

www.shereebee.com
Information for writers.

www.writing-world.com
"A world of writing tips … for writers around the world."

www.writersdigest.com
Contact information for book publishers, information on conferences, and discussion forums.

Sample Proposal:
The Gross News

The Gross News: A Collection of Gross (but Clean) Stories from Around the World

Lovingly collected by
the Sander Family

A Big City Books Idea

The Idea

Let's get right to the point—the world around us is a gross place. Every day in every country events are happening that make ordinary folks wrinkle up their noses and say, "Ewwww!" Just in the past few weeks news stories have featured the Hong Kong woman who discovered a 2-inch leech living inside her nose, the efforts of NASA scientists to recycle human waste in space, and the efforts of Wyoming health inspectors to ban restaurant workers from wearing "facial jewelry." Seems more than one nose ring has turned up in the food there lately.

Yep, gross news is all around us. And we, the Sander Family, have been hard at work collecting it. Why? Two reasons—Julian and Jonathan. In an effort to interest our two young boys in the idea of reading the newspaper, we have long made it a habit to read stories out loud that might hold their interest. And it turns out, the kinds of stories they most enjoy are gross: gross science, gross habits, gross discoveries, gross anything, really. It also turns out that gross stories don't just interest young boys; they interest pretty much everyone. Peter and Jennifer Sander have been able to dazzle their grown-up (not to mention well-educated) friends with tales of farting whales caught on film, exploding toilets in public buildings, and the plucky surfer in Australia who sought help after a shark attack by driving to the lifeguard station … with the shark still attached to his leg. Who could resist a chance to spend a quiet afternoon (or a few relaxing minutes in the toilet) with a book that collected such compelling material?

In the tradition of *The Stupid Crook Book* (Andrews McMeel), *The Gross News* will be a small-sized paperback filled with story after story, each one reduced to a pithy page or two. Each of these stories is true, having been gathered from newspapers, magazines, and websites around the world. Although countless stories exist of gross deaths, our collection will steer away from anything that involves fatalities or acts of aggression. We truly do strive for a "clean" gross news collection.

The book and the stories themselves will be divided into several sections:

Introduction: In which the Sanders reveal their deep and abiding affection for gross news and invite readers to plunge in.

Part I: Gross Science News: Readers need to know what NASA is really up to as they prepare for long space flights, how male spiders move fast when they need to (they rip off a certain body part), and what kind of worms eat whale bones.

Chapters include the following:

- Creepy Crawlers
- Freaks of Nature
- From the Deep

Part II: Gross Everyday Life: In which stories of exploding toilets, bat infestations, really hairy people, and the discovery of appalling things in your food will delight dedicated readers.

Chapters include the following:

- There's a Fly in My Soup
- Bodily (Mal) Functions
- How Did That Get There?

Part III: Gross Crime: Because criminals are not only stupid, sometimes they are also really gross. Evidence: the woman who walked around a grocery store eating from a jar of pickled pigs feet and then left without paying. More evidence: the criminals who pinched wrapped meat out of a freezer, only to discover not steaks they could barbecue, but frozen cats and dogs.

Chapters include the following:

- Someone's Been Eating My Porridge …
- Body of Evidence

The Market

The market for collections of this sort is always strong, as demonstrated by the continuing popularity of the *Uncle John's Bathroom Reader* series. With more than a dozen volumes in print, the most recent, *Uncle John's Biggest Ever Bathroom Reader*, was published more than 3 years ago and is a strong #9,549 on Amazon.com. Other popular bathroom readers include *The Great American Bathroom Book* series of three volumes, and the much higher-brow approach, *Passing Time in the Loo*.

There does not appear to be a bathroom reader that, like *The Gross News*, focuses on this single topic.

Publicity and Promotion

The Sander family are master promoters, with countless national appearances in print and on the airwaves. From appearing on the *Today Show* to appearing in *USA Today*, Peter and Jennifer are popular guests who look forward to discussing *The Gross News*.

Even Julian and Jonathan (Pips, to his family and friends) have on-camera experience and look forward to the opportunity to promote their favorite topic—grossness.

The Gross News will be an easy book to publicize, as the back story of two sophisticated and cultivated people who accidentally became collectors of the gross-but-true will appeal to editors and producers everywhere.

Jennifer Sander is exploring the commercial television potential of *The Gross News*. She is an Emmy award–winning television producer with solid contacts in the entertainment world. The content of *The Gross News* could also be exploited in other media forms, both as a blog and the new iPod rage—podcasting.

The Gross News Editorial Team: Peter, Jennifer, Julian, and Jonathan Sander

Jennifer Basye Sander

Jennifer Basye Sander has been creating successful book products since 1983. That was the year she published her first book, *The Sacramento Women's Yellow Pages*, as a way of escaping a failing career in California politics. Since that time, she has worked in all aspects of the book publishing business, everything from book retailing to book publicity, from authoring *New York Times* best-selling books herself to acquiring them for a large trade publisher. A graduate of Mills College in Oakland, California, she has also attended professional publishing programs at Stanford University and the University of Chicago.

Jennifer creates books that sell. The books she has developed have achieved in excess of $40 million in retail sales. As the senior editor and chief book developer for Prima Publishing (a now-defunct division of Random House), she developed well over 70 new titles. Her most successful book ideas on staff were the *Cozy Series* of gift-sized cookbooks (more than 500,000 copies in print) and the *101 Home Based Businesses for Women* series (more than 400,000 copies in print). Since starting her own book development company, Big City Books Group, her best-selling creation is the *Miracle Books* series for William Morrow, a *New York Times* best-selling series with five titles and combined sales of more than 300,000. She is also the author, co-author, or ghost-writer of more than 20 books herself, including the recent gift-book hits *Wear More Cashmere* and *The Martini Diet*.

Jennifer and her books have been featured on CNBC, CNNfn, *The View* with Barbara Walters, *American Journal*, C-Span's *Book TV*, Fox News, *Living It Up with Ali and Jack*, *It's a Miracle*, and *Soap Talk* on ABC's Soap Opera Channel. Articles about Jennifer have appeared in *USA Today*, *Investors Business Daily*, the *New York Post*,

New York Newsday, *Chicago Sun-Times*, *Cosmopolitan* magazine, the *Boston Globe*, the *Los Angeles Times*, the *Sacramento Bee*, and many other magazines, newspapers, and television shows. For 3 years, she was a weekly online columnist writing about entrepreneurship for *USA Today* and *Fortune Small Business*. She speaks regularly on the topics of writing and publishing, small business, personal finance, and lifestyle topics like indulgence and affordable luxury.

Jennifer is also an active television producer, specializing in developing pledge programming content for public television. Her projects include *What's Your Net Worth?* with Jennifer Openshaw (2001) and *Breast Cancer Strength and Courage*, hosted by Michael Tucker and Jill Eickenberry (2003), which won an Emmy in May 2004. The breast cancer show was based on a book idea she developed and published at Prima. Television projects in the works include a 30-minute public television pledge show based on one of Jennifer's own books, *Wear More Cashmere*, and *Abundant Giving, Abundant Wealth*, a 60-minute public television pledge show with best-selling author Mark Victor Hansen.

Peter Sander

Peter is a full-time business and financial writer, the author of 12 books. An MBA graduate of Indiana University, Peter worked for 20 years as a marketing specialist for Hewlett Packard before turning his attention to the printed word. His most recent book, *Cities Ranked and Rated* (Wiley), debuted on the *Today Show* in March 2004 and was the subject of several articles in *USA Today* and other national newspapers. Peter's other books include *Value Investing for Dummies* (IDG Books), *Niche and Grow Rich* (Entrepreneur Press), and *The Pocket Idiot's Guide to Living on a Budget* (Alpha Books).

Julian Sander

Julian is a fourth-grader attending Franklin Elementary in Loomis, California, where every Friday he reads a *Gross News* selection to his classmates. In addition to his schoolwork, Julian is a member of his school's cross-country and track and field teams. Julian's hobbies include drawing, sculpting with clay, Legos, and listening to his iPod. This is his first book.

Jonathan Sander

A well-read kindergartener, Jonathan ("Pips" to his family and friends) is an expert on several video and computer game platforms. His hobbies include reading, watching *SpongeBob SquarePants*, and fighting with plastic swords.

What Kinds of Stories Will Be in *The Gross News?*

◆ A live snail spitting contest in France

◆ Man walks for help with shark attached to leg

◆ World's hairiest man has ear hair removed to hear

◆ Airline water found to be contaminated

◆ Woman discovers fingertip in salad

◆ Fat hamster saved from death by vacuum

◆ Whale explodes in Taiwanese city

◆ Whale flatulence captured on film

◆ Doctor says eating your boogers is good for you

◆ Thousands of exploding frogs in a German town

◆ British boy finds snake in his cereal box

◆ Monkey with nose so large he has to move it out of the way to eat

◆ Farmer swims in manure to save dog

◆ Small California suburb with mysterious smell

◆ New barcode system for cadavers used at university lab to prevent theft

◆ Teacher suspended after licking blood off student's wound

◆ Hong Kong woman discovers 2-inch leech living inside her nose

◆ And many, many more!

Index